M000024241

*tear here*

## 10 Steps to Planning a Creativ...

1. Give yourself plenty of time to plan. Original and imaginative touches often take more time to put together.

2. Set a realistic budget. There's no sense fantasizing about having a barge shoot off fireworks if it means you won't be able to afford to have any food at your reception.

3. Read, read, read! The more weddings you read about (on the Internet, in newspapers, in celebrity magazines), the more creative ideas you can collect...and borrow.

4. Keep files. Creative doesn't mean disorganized. In fact since your day will include a number of unique twists, you need to be even more orderly than other brides. Papers, contracts, names, and numbers should be close at hand throughout the planning process.

5. Rediscover your roots. Talk to family members, explore sites on the Internet, do a little research in the library (and check out Chapter 14 in this book) for creative ways to include ethnic traditions. A reading here or a favorite song or recipe there can be the perfect way to say, "This is who we are."

6. Be considerate of your family's wishes. Creative weddings often demand a certain flexibility on the parts of parents and future in-laws. Make sure that you talk to them in advance of committing yourself to any truly unusual ideas. If someone is going to be really inconvenienced by traveling to a distant locale to watch you tie the knot, or would feel utterly seasick out on a boat, rethink and reorganize! Compromise! A marriage is about the joining of two families, not just two people.

7. Use good sense and good taste when (and if) you bend rules of etiquette. Etiquette in the nineties is less about rigid rules and more about making guests feel comfortable. Yes, you should check out a few etiquette books but you should also trust your instincts.

8. Let your wedding represent who you are as a couple. Draw on your hobbies, interests, sports, favorite books, films, ethnic backgrounds, and more.

9. Be willing to take chances. Creative touches show your individuality. They can also make you feel a little insecure. Don't worry. Doing everything the same way as everyone else may be safer, but it just wouldn't be as much fun.

10. Relax. Creative weddings are not about being perfect or making all the right choices all the time. They're about two people coming together in front of family and friends to publicly announce their love and commitment to one another. There's no way anything could ever be wrong with that.

**alpha books**

# Countdown to the Creative Wedding

**Twelve Months Before the Wedding**

- ❏ Pick a date.
- ❏ Set a budget.
- ❏ Talk about the style of your wedding (How big? How formal?).
- ❏ Get together with both sets of parents to discuss the wedding and costs. If you are planning something out of the ordinary, such as an underwater wedding or a honeymoon wedding, put your cards on the table now and let everyone ask questions and adjust to the idea.
- ❏ Find a ceremony site and arrange for an officiant.
- ❏ Look for and book a creative reception site.
- ❏ Ask attendants to be in your wedding party. If your wedding requires anything unusual of your attendants (your ceremony site is a ski-in chapel atop a mountain, for example) be sure they're comfortable with it.

**Six to 12 Months Before the Wedding**

- ❏ Hire a photographer and/or videographer.
- ❏ Find a creative caterer who understands your ideas.
- ❏ Consider hiring a wedding consultant. If you have lots of creative ideas, she can really help you get them off the ground.
- ❏ Choose a baker and a cake style.
- ❏ Find a florist.
- ❏ Hire musicians.
- ❏ Shop for a wedding dress.
- ❏ Send a save-the-date card if you're having a long-weekend wedding.
- ❏ Compose and send a wedding newsletter if you're arranging a destination or long-weekend wedding.
- ❏ Reserve hotel rooms if you're expecting lots of out-of-town guests, or if you're planning a destination or long-weekend wedding.
- ❏ Make travel plans for a two-for-the-road wedding. (see Chapter 8) If you will be going abroad, make sure you have passports in order. Find out about visa requirements.
- ❏ Create a guest list.

**Four Months Before the Wedding**

- ❏ Order your wedding invitations.
- ❏ Find out about ordering wedding programs.
- ❏ Make honeymoon travel plans.
- ❏ Choose men's attire.
- ❏ Prepare a list of local attractions and maps for out-of-town guests at a weekend wedding.
- ❏ Select ceremony music.

**Three Months Before the Wedding**

- ❏ Plan the rehearsal dinner.

**One Month Before the Wedding**

- ❏ Send invitations.
- ❏ Choose gifts for attendants, favors for guests.

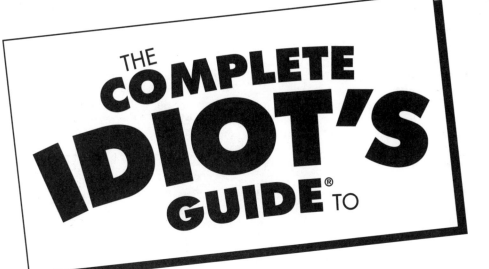

THE COMPLETE IDIOT'S GUIDE® TO

# Creative
# Weddings

*by Antonia van der Meer*

## alpha
## books

A Division of Macmillan General Reference
A Pearson Education Macmillan Company
1633 Broadway, New York, NY 10019

Macmillan General Reference books may be purchased for business or sales promotional use. For information please write: Special Markets Department, Macmillan Publishing USA, 1633 Broadway, New York, NY 10019.

International Standard Book Number: 0-02-863409-8
Library of Congress Catalog Card Number: 99-64698

01  00  99      8  7  6  5  4  3  2  1

Interpretation of the printing code: the rightmost number of the first series of numbers is the year of the book's printing; the rightmost number of the second series of numbers is the number of the book's printing. For example, a printing code of 99-1 shows that the first printing occurred in 1999.

*Printed in the United States of America*

# Alpha Development Team

### Publisher
*Kathy Nebenhaus*

### Editorial Director
*Gary M. Krebs*

### Associate Publisher
*Cindy Kitchel*

### Associate Managing Editor
*Cari Shaw Fischer*

### Acquisitions Editors
*Jessica Faust*
*Michelle Reed*

### Development Editors
*Phil Kitchel*
*Amy Zavatto*

### Assistant Editor
*Georgette Blau*

# Production Team

### Development Editors
*Amy Zavatto*
*Kate Layzer*

### Production Editor
*Robyn Burnett*

### Copy Editor
*Susan Aufheimer*

### Cover Designer
*Mike Freeland*

### Photo Editor
*Richard H. Fox*

### Illustrator
*John Bergdahl*

### Book Designers
*Scott Cook and Amy Adams of DesignLab*

### Indexer
*Angie Bess*

### Layout/Proofreading
*Angela Calvert*
*Mary Hunt*

# Contents at a Glance

# Contents

# Foreword

Creative weddings. What does that mean? The dictionary would describe them as a productive, inventive, or artistic way to conduct the act or ceremony of marriage and the festivities that follow. Weddings are celebrations, reunions, parties, and an intertwining of lifestyles.

Every wedding has importance, if only to the happy couple. Brides constantly search for ways to make their receptions stand out, to leave fond memories in the minds of the guests. Brides want uniqueness and individuality. They want to show their guests that they can entertain and be inventive. A wedding is a rite of passage, a transition from one stage of your life to another. You might as well make this journey pleasant and have it reflect the personalities of you and your intended spouse.

In my 25-plus years in the wedding industry, I've seen a lot of creative weddings and receptions. Here are some examples:

One bridal couple invited their guests to the golf course on a weekday. They played nine holes of golf, retired to the country club, changed into their wedding attire, had the officiant perform the ceremony, and then celebrated with food and music for the rest of the afternoon. Their reception was dotted with golf paraphernalia. And their wedding cake! Well, it was a golfer's dream. The cake was four staggered layers representing a golf course, complete with sand and water traps. The entire day fit the couple to a tee.

Another bride was a striking young woman who wanted to step out of the mold. She had a formal event. Her attendants wore red satin and black velvet gowns, the men were in black tuxedos with red cummerbunds and red boutonnieres. Unbeknownst to anyone, the bride had a formal wedding gown (complete with chapel length train, lace, and beadwork) designed and made in a bright red. She was gorgeous! She was kept hidden from everyone until she walked down the aisle—she received the stir she was looking for!

An industrious couple decided not to tell their family and friends they were tying the knot. Once they decided to get married, they didn't want to wait to plan a more formal event. They invited specific people over for a back yard bar-b-que. About 50 of their closest friends and family members showed up. About an hour into the party, the bride and groom disappeared to change clothes. A small altar was set up on the patio. Suddenly, wedding music started to play. As the guests looked around to see what was happening, the bride and groom made their appearance. The clergy smiled and asked the guests to gather around to witness the marriage of these two people. Bet there was no lack of conversation for the remainder of that party!

These are just a few examples of how brides and grooms have made the day uniquely their own. And you'll find much more in *The Complete Idiot's Guide to Creative Weddings*. This book provides wonderful information for both brides and professionals. A lot of thought and research has gone into the preparation of this resource. It's easy to mix and match helpful hints in any category to create the event that both reflects your dream and one that meets your budget. This is a book that every library should stock and every new wedding consultant should read. For the brides who want to step out of the box and entertain on a different level, this book is for you!

Renee Grannis

Education Director, Association of Bridal Consultants

# Introduction

Welcome to a book on creative weddings. You're probably bubbling over with ideas right now—a romantic spot you're hoping will work as a ceremony site, a wedding favor you'd love to give, a special song you want sung. But just how do you bring all these ideas together? How can you be sure they'll work?

Putting together a wedding takes a lot of hard work. Sometimes it seems way too complicated. Sometimes it seems overwhelming. And that's assuming you're planning a run-of-the-mill wedding. A wedding that includes some unique touches—from vows you pen yourself to a hot-air-balloon ride—takes some extra legwork. This book tries to make the whole process more manageable.

To keep you on track, I spoke with lots of different experts in their fields—bridal consultants, event planners, caterers, floral designers, bakers, and photographers—people who deal day in and day out with brides and grooms like you. They all told me that couples today are looking for something different, something that makes their wedding days stand out. Brides and grooms aren't afraid to show a little spunk and originality these days. They want the ceremony to represent who they are and who their families are. Across the board, the experts I spoke with were full of fresh ideas and great stories about what they'd seen and done. I've tried to pass all that wisdom and creativity on to you.

Perhaps most important, this book is about ideas. I want to get you thinking about all the possibilities out there. As I wrote about all the little ways to make a wedding special, I got excited about each and every one of the ideas. I fantasized about each type of wedding, every theme, and every season. That's the fun of a book like this! It helps you dream…and it helps you find a way to make those dreams a reality.

I also had the chance to reflect happily on my own wedding. You, too, will soon have the day behind you, as a cherished memory. I can remember vividly what it felt like to be the bride, to search for reception sites, to gently tell parents and in-laws about a few "alternative" ideas, and to wonder how every decision I had made would be perceived by my guests. The good news is: I survived it, I enjoyed it, and I love to think back on it. It was a great day and I know yours will be, too. By no means was my day perfect (my bridesmaid showed up without her shoes, we forgot to tell the band what song to play for the first dance, and the bouquet I wished to save never made it home), but looking back now, I wouldn't change a thing.

The purpose of this book is to give you the freedom to choose a more interesting path to the altar, the courage to pursue your dream day, and the know-how to make it happen. By the time you've finished reading this book and are well on your way to the wedding, you won't feel like such a complete idiot anymore. You'll feel comfortable and confident with your wedding style and the ways you choose to express it.

## How to Use This Book

There are two ways you can approach this book. You can go immediately to the chapter that describes exactly what you want—a winter wonderland wedding, for example, or a nautical theme. Read everything I have to say on one topic and take it from there. Easy!

However, I encourage readers to spend some more time with the book browsing, the way you would in a great clothing store. Maybe you went in looking for a little black dress, but when you saw that slinky silver number, you just knew that's what you had to get instead! It works the same way with weddings. You may start out thinking small and informal and end up at the opposite end of the spectrum. So check out all of the chapters even if you think they're not for you. Maybe a medieval wedding doesn't appeal to you, but the hearty fare mentioned gives you an idea for your reception menu. Feel free to borrow from many areas of the book to create your perfect wedding.

In the front of this book is a tear-out card that lists some basic steps to planning a creative wedding and includes a checklist for counting down to the big day. You can tear it out and carry it with you or stick it up on your refrigerator or in your office at work if you need to. At the back, there's an appendix listing my resources for this book, as well as Web sites and suggestions for further reading.

**Part 1, Get Ready!** tells you what a creative wedding is and helps you discover some personal touches you may want to include in yours.

**Part 2, Get Creative,** talks about how to plan a weekend wedding, a destination wedding, or a travel wedding.

**Part 3, Theme Weddings,** explains how to find a theme that suits your style—from the historical (a Renaissance festival) to the seasonal (a New Year's Eve bash).

**Part 4, Making It Your Own,** covers how to write your own vows and how to make the most of music, flowers, and more!

**Part 5, Survival Tactics,** offers advice to the couple on how to reduce the stress levels while planning your wedding.

## Extras

For a little added fun and information, boxes filled with useful tidbits and clever ideas appear throughout the book. They are:

**Creative Corner**

Fun, offbeat ideas you can use to enhance your wedding day.

### Consultants Say

Expert tips to help make your day better or easier.

### Bridal Blunders

Common problems couples face, and ways to avoid making mistakes.

### Something True

Surprising or interesting little-known facts about wedding history or lore.

## Acknowledgments

Thanks to my editors Jessica Faust, Kate Layzer, and Amy Zavatto, and to my hard-working copyeditor, Susan Aufheimer. An additional thanks to my agent, Linda Konner, for hooking me up with the wonderful folks at The Complete Idiot's Guide series of helpful books.

A special thanks goes to Nicolaas van der Meer, my son and Internet aficionado, who retrieved lots of information on weddings for me and found some fabulous Web sites for the book.

I could not have written the book without the generous advice and suggestions of the following people:

Charrisse Min Alliegro, Preston Bailey, Patricia Bruneau, Bev Dembo, Cetta Fessett, Gary Fong, Dianne Forbis, Diane Gedon, Audrey Goldstein, Renee Grannis, Joann Gregoli, Bill Hansen, Lance Holland, Maggie Kennedy, Andy Marcus, Stephen Morris, John O'Mahoney, Elaine Parker, Lois Pearce, Meredith Waga Perez, Carl Pickhardt, Brenda Rezak, Gloria Teague, John J. Tunney III, Gail Watson.

# Special Thanks to the Technical Reviewer

*The Complete Idiot's Guide to Creative Weddings* was reviewed by an expert who not only checked the technical accuracy of the information in this book, but also provided valuable insight to help ensure that it tells you everything you need to know to have a beautiful—and creative—wedding that you'll never forget.

Our special thanks are extended to wedding consultant Patricia Bruneau of L'Affaire Du Temps in Milpitas, California. Patricia has owned and operated L'Affaire Du Temps, a wedding consulting company, since 1992. Prior to opening her business, she achieved the title of Professional Wedding Consultant through The Association of Certified Professional Wedding Consultants (ACPWC). She is also a Certified Wedding Consultant through June Wedding, Inc. (JWI), and is currently the Northern California Regional Director for this organization, conducting workshops for professionals in the wedding industry. Through this organization, Patricia has been awarded the Wedding Consultant of the Year 1995 Award and the JWI Marketing Award in 1997. Patricia has also been spotlighted in *Modern Bride* magazine and has appeared on *The Caryl and Marilyn Show* on ABC.

# Part 1
# Get Ready!

*You've finally decided to get married! This should be the happiest time of your life, a time to savor. Unfortunately, it often feels tense and rushed. Slow down! You can handle the ups and downs of wedding planning with the help of this book.*

*To get you started on the right foot, read Part 1. This section paves the way for a creative wedding. It tries to answer the question, "Just what is a creative wedding, anyway?" It helps you determine what kinds of personal touches you might want to include. It includes advice on creative invitations (this is usually the first glimpse guests get of the type of event you're planning) and on modern etiquette, especially relevant to couples planning to bend the rules a little.*

*The information presented in Part 1 should give you a solid platform on which to build a truly fabulous wedding!*

# Chapter 1

# Paving the Way to a Creative Wedding

> **In This Chapter**
>
> ➤ Finding your creative wedding style
>
> ➤ Incorporating your family's style
>
> ➤ Researching your family history
>
> ➤ Utilizing the library and Internet

When I got married, I did a lot of traditional things. I had something borrowed and something blue. But I also added a few creative twists that surprised some of my family and friends. For one thing, my husband and I walked down the aisle together. No one gave the bride away. We liked the symbolism of both of us entering into this marriage—and the church—together. Not all of my creative touches were appreciated by everyone in attendance, but they were what made my day special. Creative weddings speak volumes about who you are as a couple.

Before you spend your first dollar, or draw up your first guest list, you need to think about what kind of wedding you want. Will you tread the straight and narrow path to the altar, or are there a few twists and turns you're just dying to explore? Just what *is* a creative wedding—and is it for me? Once those great ideas start flowing, you can start working on how to make them a reality.

## What Is a Creative Wedding?

When you think about weddings, do you see what everyone else sees? Or do you, perhaps, dream of something a little different? You may want your German shepherd to be the ring bearer. Or maybe you've always dreamed of being married on the ski slopes of Vermont. Maybe you're wondering about wearing a pastel gown in lieu of a white one. Perhaps you have a special situation, such as children from a previous marriage and you want to include them in the wedding vows. These are all creative touches to a traditional day.

Of course, in a way, all weddings are creative ones. After all, they are the ultimate expression of a couple's unique love for one another. Although imbued with tradition and often steeped in formality, your wedding can be truly personal. You *can* write your own vows, get married with bare feet, or wear a period costume. There are so many choices out there, and if you dare to be creative they're all yours!

A creative wedding is a celebration that stands apart. It breaks away from the idea that there is only one right way to get married. A creative wedding gives you the freedom to say you've seen what everyone else has seen, but you'd like to add some new things to your day that no one else has thought of before. This book will provide a springboard for those ideas and give you the courage to incorporate your innovative additions into your wedding day.

"Creativity" is described in *Webster's Collegiate Dictionary* as "the ability to invest with new form; to produce through imaginative skill; to design or invent an original work of art; and to have the power to create rather than imitate." Are these words you would love to hear a guest use when describing your wedding day? Original! Imaginative! Skillful! Inventive! If so, then a creative wedding may be just your style.

To have a creative wedding, you must be willing to let your ideas flow. Wolfgang Amadeus Mozart, one of the great creative geniuses of all time, explained it this way: "When I am...completely myself...or during the night when I cannot sleep, it is on such occasions that my ideas flow best and most abundantly. Whence and how these come I know not, nor can I force them...."

So go ahead and dream. Free-associate. Be creative. After all, if you think about it, your love for each other and this impending marriage is a new creation—a creation of oneness out of two people. Your wedding should reflect this fact.

# Mild Mannered, Wacky, or Wild—What's Your Wedding Style?

There's no trick to finding your wedding style. It just takes a little time and a little thought. Before you get started, you'll want to expose yourself to as many ideas as possible. Get your party antennae up and tune in to the thousands of ideas swirling around you. What's out there? What are other couples doing right now? What are brides wearing? Couple serving? Musicians playing? Who's entertaining and how? To get those creative juices flowing:

➤ Read local newspaper accounts of weddings in your area.

➤ Ask friends to describe delightful and interesting weddings they've attended.

➤ Ask married friends what the most meaningful part of their wedding day was. The most fun? The most surprising?

➤ Make a list of the five best parties you've ever attended and what made them special.

➤ Flip through bridal magazines, looking carefully at all the pictures for creative details you'd like to borrow.

➤ Spend some time exploring other magazines for entertainment, decorating and food ideas: *Travel and Leisure, Gourmet, Martha Stewart Living,* and more.

➤ Attend a couple of bridal shows. You'll meet vendors, find out about bridal services in your area, and probably see a fashion show.

➤ Rent some movies that have great wedding scenes in them.

➤ Watch a little cable TV! The Learning Channel (TLC) offers "A Wedding Story" weekdays at 3 p.m. and 3:30 p.m. (EST). Real-life couples let you have a behind-the-scenes look at their courtship, wedding preparations, and big day.

➤ Read wedding books.

➤ Check out the soaps! There's always somebody getting married (usually for the 15th time, and to the evil twin by mistake). No time for TV? Grab a copy of *Love Honor & Cherish: The Greatest Wedding Moments from All My Children, General Hospital, and One Life To Live* (Hyperion) for some really wild wedding dress ideas.

➤ Borrow CDs from the library and expose yourself to a wide range of music.

➤ Talk to a bridal consultant. She's seen lots of creative and unique weddings.

Once you've started to see and notice a variety of ways to wed, you can start thinking about which way could be your way.

### Creative Corner

Keep a folder of wedding-ceremony and reception ideas. Any time you read about an unusual wedding that strikes your fancy (a ceremony held around a campfire) or notice a photo with an intriguing detail (fresh-cut wild flowers arranged in old-fashioned watering cans), cut it out and pop it into your folder. Also make note of special music you may hear on the radio. Periodically review the contents of your file with your fiancé to see if any of the same ideas appeal to him. If they do, these are creative options you'll want to explore further.

## Who, Me? Creative?

There are many reasons couples choose a creative wedding over one that is run strictly by the book. Without even thinking about it, you may be one of them if:

**Consultants Say**

If you have something you collect, or a special story about how you and your groom met or became engaged, Patricia Bruneau of L'Affaire du Temps in Melpitas, California, encourages couples to share it with their wedding consultant or party planner. There is usually a way to work a meaningful aspect of your life into your celebration. According to Bruneau, one couple who got engaged at the Eiffel Tower elected to place ice sculptures made in the shape of the famous edifice on each guest table as a centerpiece. Another couple who loved to watch professional boxing hired Michael Buffer of "Let's Get Ready to Rumble" fame to record a personal introduction to their first dance as husband and wife. He introduced each with "In this corner...."

➤ You have a strong feeling that a wedding should say something personal about who you are (for example, you want the wedding to reflect your love of skiing, so you marry at a winter mountain resort).

➤ You have a desire to break away from the ordinary or expected.

➤ You are trying to blend two very different cultures, such as Greek and Mexican or Indian and Jewish (read Chapters 3, 14, and 22 to find ways customs and traditions can be included in your day).

➤ This is a marriage of two very different religions.

➤ This is a second or third marriage for one or both of you.

➤ You have complicated families (stepparents, stepsiblings, and so on; see Chapter 22).

➤ You have financial limitations (see Chapter 8 for great cost-cutting ideas).

➤ You have geographical limitations (perhaps the bride and/or groom live abroad or far away from the rest of their families and friends; see Chapter 7 for information on the wedding that travels to its guests).

➤ You are looking to achieve something fun and memorable!

## Adding Your Family's Wedding Style to Yours

You have some great creative ideas you're just dying to try. Will your families like the ideas as much as you do? Do they, perhaps, have some suggestions that are even more appealing or practical?

Don't discount what they have to say. Sure, it's your wedding but there's a real social dimension to making a public commitment as a couple. After all, people grow up, meet, fall in love, and marry in a social context of family, friends, and associates. Unless you and your fiancé plan to live on a desolate island somewhere, cut off from human civilization, it's important for you to consider those who will be most affected by your decision to marry, and to be considerate of their feelings and desires. This is especially important when it comes to the creative wedding. Expect that you'll need to do some compromising, accommodating, and, most important, *listening,* and be gracious about it. You might just find that you like what you hear.

# Ask Your Parents

Before you get wild and crazy with your creative wedding ideas, talk with your parents and your future in-laws. How do they envision this day? What were their own weddings like? Do they have certain expectations for the ceremony or the reception? Is a certain ethnic tradition especially important to your fiancé's mother? Is your father looking forward to a church ceremony? Are the groom's parents made uncomfortable by a lot of formality? Would either family be greatly inconvenienced by a distant locale for the wedding? Is there a specific date you have in mind for the wedding? How does it fit with your family's plans?

Of course, most parents will understand that this wedding celebration has to be your own, but they still will want to feel a part of the planning. By demonstrating that you care about their wishes and desires, you'll help them feel appreciated. Remember, if the parents are happy, your day will go more smoothly and feel more like a celebration. If they're nursing hard feelings…well, who knows what could go wrong? On the plus side: stirring in a few ideas from both sides of the family can really add to the creativity of your day.

Go to each family member (by phone or in person) and ask for their ideas. Jot them down in a spiral notebook or other place where you'll be keeping wedding ideas. Get some specific questions answered:

➤ Do you plan to contribute financially to our wedding? And if so, what sort of budget do you envision? (See Chapter 2 for more on budgeting.)

➤ How many guests are you hoping we'll have?

➤ If there were one element you would hope to see incorporated in our wedding ceremony, what would it be?

➤ If there were one element you would hope to see incorporated into the reception, what would it be?

➤ Do you have strong feelings about where the ceremony or reception should take place?

➤ What was the best or most meaningful part of your own wedding and reception?

If you keep an open mind, blending the wishes of both families may not be that difficult. And since you're looking for creative ideas, asking future in-laws and your own parents about the elements of their own wedding days may give you some surprising and useful answers.

**Bridal Blunders**

Think carefully before presenting your guests with any kind of physical challenge. Getting on and off a small boat, for example, can be unnerving if not extremely difficult for the elderly or disabled. Even an uneven path or a flight of steps can be a serious barrier for some.

# Picking Ideas from the Family Tree

Actually, the engagement period can be a great time to find out about your roots. There may be hundreds of plum creative wedding ideas just waiting to be picked from the family tree. Was there a Scottish grandmother on your father's side? A confederate army general in your fiancé's past? A suffragette in yours? Consider incorporating some of these facts into the food, music, decorations, or theme of the day. To find out about your family genealogy, try the following:

➤ Ask an older relative such as your grandmother about her parents and grandparents—their nationalities, their occupations, and so on.

➤ Look through old photo albums or scrapbooks that your family may have kept. See how relatives dressed, where they lived and vacationed.

➤ Contact a foundation associated with your particular cultural background, such as The Irish Family History Foundation (**www.mayo-ireland.ie/Roots.htm**), which can help you trace your roots. Or, go to **www.askjeeves.com** (a search engine) and ask for information on a particular country and its wedding traditions. Within seconds, you'll be on your way to some helpful sites.

➤ Research your own ancestry. Some possible places to start: the Family History Library in Salt Lake City, Utah, or the National Genealogical Society (**www.ngsgenealogy.org**).

Once you have a few family ideas, you can run with them. Perhaps you'll decide to have your flower girl wear wooden clogs and an old-fashioned Dutch dress, or you'll hire bagpipers to make an appearance at your garden reception. You may discover that both you and your groom have Italian heritage and that you'd like to honor your roots with a special dessert of cannoli at the reception. Simple nods to the rich past from which both of your families come are not only meaningful but moving! You can use a wedding program (see Chapter 18) to explain these wonderful additions—and the reason for them—to your guests.

### Something True

Genealogy is a record or account of the ancestry of a person or family. It is the study of family histories. If you go back far enough, you may even find your genearch—the chief of a family or tribe.

# The Library: Check It Out!

Family research is a great place to start, but it's only the beginning when it comes to gathering information and ideas for the wedding of your dreams. The rest of this chapter will focus on where to go to learn what you want to know. I recommend that you spend a few hours in the early stages of planning just browsing in the library or on the Internet (or both). Time spent on research is never wasted, even if you end up using your own ideas. The more you learn, the more confident you'll feel about making your own decisions—whether the subject is wedding cake or the subtleties of the Greek Orthodox marriage rite.

Remember where you went when you had that research paper to do for American Civilization? Well, it's time to go there again. Grab your coat: We're heading for the library to spend an afternoon with a friendly librarian and a pile of books. Don't forget pencils and paper. Oh, and a pocketful of change for the photocopier wouldn't hurt.

You'll find lots of bridal books and magazines to flip through, of course. But don't stop there. Wander through the aisles of reference books. These are usually found in a special area of the library and they remain at the library—they don't circulate. You'll find books there like *Holiday Symbols 1998* by Sue Ellen Thompson (Omnigraphics Inc., 1997) and *Celebrations: The Complete Book of American Holidays* by Robert Myers (Doubleday, 1972) If you're planning a holiday-theme wedding, at Valentine's Day or Christmas time, for example, imagine how many good ideas you might find in their pages!

Many libraries also have CDs and records you can check out for wedding music ideas. Chat with the reference librarian: There may be other avenues you haven't thought of. Libraries often have resource guides listing local places to have a party, or bridal consultants in your areas.

# Information Central: the Internet

You may feel more familiar using a library than using a computer for your research. Don't wait any longer to get with the program! More information than you ever dreamed of is waiting for you online. It may take a little effort to find exactly what you're looking for, but with a little bit of patience, you'll be amazed to discover what's out there. "Oh, yeah? Like what?" I hear you ask. Like over 6,000 wedding-related Web sites, to start with. No kidding—as a research tool, the Internet is hard to beat. So get ready to let your fingers do some walking!

## Getting on the Net

You can get online very easily these days, if you aren't already connected. Many PCs have built-in modems. If not, you'll need to purchase a modem, connect it to a phone line and to your computer, and get some Internet software from an internet service provider such as America Online, CompuServe, or AT&T. Most offer a flat-rate monthly fee, which may be worth it if you plan to be online a lot.

Some readers may feel daunted by the challenge of getting set up and connected. If you find yourself in this category, perhaps you have an experienced friend who would be willing to help out in exchange for a home-cooked meal or some free tax advice.

**Consultants Say**

If you don't have a computer at home, check out your local library. They may be set up to allow you to do Internet research right there!

## Finding What You Want

To help you search, most Internet access providers offer Web browser software. Two popular browsers are Microsoft Internet Explorer and Netscape Navigator. Netscape navigator, for example, can be downloaded from **www.netscape.com**. Depending on your computer and your Internet access provider, you may or may not need to get a Web browser.

Search engines help you find exactly what you want on the Web. Using **www.webcrawler.com** or **www.altavista.com** (to name just two search engines), you can search for a particular topic of interest, such as diamonds, honeymoons, or Hawaiian weddings. Take a quick look at some of the sites that come up in the search and see if any of them are for you.

### Consultants Say

You can buy books about weddings without ever leaving your chair. Go to **www.barnesandnoble.com** or **www.amazon.com** and search the subject index for the word "wedding." Drop the books you want into your virtual shopping basket and they'll be sent to you. It's easy!

You can also try **www.askjeeves.com**. Just type in any question you have and in seconds you'll have tons of Web sites to choose from. Just scroll down until you find a site that sounds appealing, click on it and poof! You're there. Don't like what you find? Go back to Jeeves and find another.

Check the Appendix in the back of this book for some fun wedding-related sites.

Now you know what a creative wedding might include and where to look for meaningful and inventive additions to your day. But what about the etiquette of weddings? Is it really possible to have a wedding that's unique and special while simultaneously trying to comply with a strict code of wedding conduct? Check out the next chapter and see for yourself.

### The Least You Need to Know

➤ Spend some time dreaming before you start planning. Browse through magazines and this book, collecting ideas and finding out what you want your wedding day to be.

➤ Start getting organized. File folders and notebooks are useful for keeping track of research and ideas.

➤ Talk with your families to determine how comfortable they might be with some of your creative additions.

➤ Explore your family histories for meaningful themes and creative wedding ideas.

➤ Use your local library and the Internet to begin the process of exploring wedding ideas and services.

# Etiquette du Jour

Weddings can be strange animals. To many brides and grooms marriage traditions seem driven by an unfamiliar, even daunting code of etiquette. Sure you know what R.s.v.p. means, and you've written thank-you notes before, but otherwise you may be feeling a little out of your league. Don't worry! First of all, the creative wedding isn't ruled by rules. You can feel a little freer than you would with a traditional wedding. Secondly, this is your day. Although you don't want to insult anyone or make a guest feel uncomfortable, you are the one who gets to say what's "proper" today.

## Emily Post Ain't the Same Gal She Used to Be

The world has changed a lot since your grandmother's day—or for that matter your mother's. Even formal weddings have loosened up a lot to accommodate different styles, backgrounds, and tastes. Rigid rules are out. Good taste and common sense are in.

Etiquette today is about being considerate of others. You can read hundreds of pages in etiquette books, but that is the bottom line. As the wedding couple, you want to make yourselves and your guests comfortable. Whether you send engraved invitations or call on the phone, wear a gown or a mini skirt, serve poached salmon or fish sticks, the main thing is that you display good manners and thoughtfulness throughout.

# Elements of Style

Weddings tend to have compatible parts. A formal ceremony is heralded by a formal invitation and followed by a lavish sit-down dinner, while an informal ceremony is anticipated by an informal invite followed by a simple buffet. One thing leads to another, and guests pretty much know what to expect.

Although a creative wedding can mix styles in some personal and surprising ways, once you and your fiancé decide on the type of wedding you want (large/small, formal/informal, indoors/outdoors), other decisions will start to fall into place. You will develop a wedding style that carries you through the day, from ceremony to reception.

Weddings tend to fall into a few basic categories.

➤ *The Formal Wedding.* Think of a long, dressy gown with a train and veil for the bride, formal attire for the groomsmen, and long gowns for the bridesmaids. Imagine an engraved invitation to a noon, late afternoon, or evening ceremony, followed by a party at a lavish reception site with a sit-down meal. The formal wedding is a glamorous four-star affair. Crowds of 200 or more are not unusual. There are bridesmaids aplenty.

➤ *The Semiformal Wedding.* Picture a lovely floor-length wedding gown worn by the bride, dark suits worn by the groomsmen, and cocktail dresses by the bridesmaids. Imagine an intimate reception with light refreshments or a gracefully laid out buffet. The semiformal wedding is tasteful and elegant.

➤ *The Informal Wedding.* Think of a beautiful suit for the bride, business suits for the groomsmen, fancy street clothes for the maid or matron of honor (usually there are no bridesmaids), a daytime ceremony (perhaps at city hall), handwritten invitations, and a lively reception with light refreshments. The informal wedding is fun and freewheeling.

➤ *The Creative Wedding.* Mix and match! The creative-wedding planner is free to pick and choose among the elements of style. There's really no reason why an informal beach ceremony (shoes optional) can't be followed by a seated dinner on a deck overlooking the ocean…or why a traditional church wedding can't precede an informal barbecue and square dance reception…or why a couple marrying at city hall can't treat themselves to all the sophistication and flair of engraved invitations, formalwear, and a remarkable dinner.

"There are no hard-and-fast definitions of style any more. Just use your common sense," counsels Charrisse Min Alliegro of Princeton Wedding Consultants in New Jersey. The overriding theme should always be consideration of your guests.

# Who Pays: Romeo or Juliet?

Unfortunately, the couple who think this is the love of the century can sometimes end up facing bills that take a century to pay off! It's important to find out early on how much your wedding day is going to cost and who will be responsible for the bills.

No one wants to start a new life together in debt—yet couples seem to spend more and more every year. Today the average wedding costs a startling $19,000.

In the past, the bride's family paid for the ceremony and the reception. The groom's family was usually responsible for the rehearsal dinner and the honeymoon. Although many continue to follow these general guidelines, leaving the bride's family with the lion's share of the expenses, more and more couples are finding creative ways to foot the bill. Some pay all the expenses themselves. Others find that both sets of parents are willing to help. In some cases, grandparents, godparents, and even close friends have been known to pitch in. The advantage of sharing expenses like this is that the financial burden is not placed entirely on one party. A possible disadvantage, depending on your point of view, is that those who are contributing may feel entitled to some say about what happens on your wedding day.

No matter who's paying the bills, tension around decision making is common. Spread the word among all interested parties that decisions need to be made diplomatically, with everyone in mind—not just the bride and groom or their parents. Be polite; let others make some decisions; take the feelings of both families into consideration. "It's good practice for marriage," points out wedding consultant Charrisse Min Alliegro in Princeton, New Jersey.

Naturally, the first thing the two of you will need to determine is how formal and extravagant your wedding day will be.

Sit down with your groom and have a preliminary discussion of your dreams —and your financial realities. Then have the same discussions with your

**Something True**

The most expensive place in the world to get married? Japan. The average cost of a wedding there today is about $28,500! If they're lucky, the bride and groom may make some of that back. Guests traditionally give couples cash, in the amount of $150 to $200 and up per person. According to *Something Old, Something New* by Vera Lee (Casablanca Press, 1994), one VIP bride reportedly raked in $140 million in cash and gifts at her wedding.

**Consultants Say**

If both sets of parents live near enough to you, call a meeting at your home or in a restaurant. Discuss the budget on neutral territory with everyone present so there are no misunderstandings. If the parties live too far apart, consider scheduling a conference call or entering a private online chat room.

parents, stepparents, future in-laws, or anyone else who may be financially involved in the wedding. I realize that few people look forward to this kind of conversation. I'm sorry, but there's no good way around it. Don't put it off until money is already flying out the window. Make some sound financial decisions now and save yourself a lot of heartache later.

**Bridal Blunders**

Whoa! Beware of getting carried away. If projected expenses seem to be getting bigger than the national debt, pause and ask yourselves, "If we had to cut back on one thing, what would it be?" The number of guests? The type of food? The size of the band? Make a list of your wedding elements in order of their importance to you. It will help you figure out where you're willing to negotiate and where you want to stand firm.

To get a general idea of how much a wedding might cost you, start by asking yourself the following questions:

➤ How many people do you want to invite?

➤ Do you want to serve a three-course meal or just hors d'oeuvres?

➤ Is dancing at the reception a top priority? Do you want live music or a DJ?

➤ What kind of reception site are you hoping to use?

➤ Will the site require a lot of decorations, rental items (such as tables and chairs), and so on?

➤ Will you be hiring a professional photographer? A videographer?

➤ Do you have your heart set on any unusual extras (exotic car rentals, hot air balloon rides, over-the-top floral designs, fireworks)?

➤ Do you plan to have an open bar?

# Invitational Etiquette

Invitations set the mood for the ceremony and reception to come. Make sure they reflect the theme or style of your wedding day so that your guests will be able to dress appropriately. If you're planning a relaxed outdoor beach ceremony, for example, it is not a good idea to send an invitation that looks as if the crowned heads of Europe may show up.

I cover invitations in detail in Chapter 4 and give lots of ideas for color, paper, shapes, and enclosures there. In the meantime, however, there are a few things you should know about the etiquette of inviting guests.

## *Setting the Tone*

If you are doing something creative and unusual, your invitations will probably reflect this in some way. For a wedding reception that takes place weeks or even months after the actual ceremony is held, you may decide to lead with a wedding announcement, followed by a party invitation, and enclose a photo of the two of you tying the knot. If you are planning a theme wedding, you'll probably want your invitations to reflect the theme. You don't have to stay with the formulaic, "Mr. and Mrs. X request the pleasure…." If you're having a Cinderella-theme wedding at Disneyland, why not begin with "Once upon a time…"? For a garden wedding, why not include pressed flowers? A little confetti could fall out of the envelope when guests open an invitation to a New Year's Eve wedding. A favorite love poem could grace the cover of a Valentine's Day invitation. Use your imagination!

## How Shall I Put This…?

Choose whatever words you wish. It doesn't matter if the bride and groom are paying for the event themselves; the bride's parents can still be the hosts of the party, if that is how your family would like to approach it. The invitation can still read:

> Mr. and Mrs. William Smith
> request the honour of your presence
> at the marriage of their daughter
> Joanne Tyler Smith
> to
> John Robert Jones.

If both sets of parents are helping to defray the costs, then you may wish the wording on your invitation to reflect this arrangement:

> Mr. and Mrs. William Smith
> and
> Mr. and Mrs. Peter Jones
> request the pleasure of your company
> at the marriage of their children
> Joanne Tyler
> and
> John Jones.

With a creative wedding, the design and wording of the invitation are dictated by what is tasteful and comfortable for you and your family. If the traditional wording on an invitation doesn't sit right, toss it out and start again. Choose wording that you think is clear, warm, and beautiful.

Do make sure you discuss the wording with all parties involved—especially those who are paying. Some people care very much about having their names appear on the invitation. For example, if your parents are divorced and your mother is paying the wedding expenses by herself, she may feel strongly about top billing for herself, even if your father is going to "give you away."

Need help? Stationary stores can show you hundreds of examples of the way people have worded their invitations to the ceremony and the reception. So can online wedding-invitation printers. (Bridal magazines are littered with ads for such services.)

Feel free to be creative about printing methods, too. For very small or informal weddings, some couples prefer a handwritten, hand-delivered note or even a telephone call, to professionally printed invitations.

Nowadays some couples do their invitations at home on their personal computers. If this appeals to you, there are lots of programs to choose from. With the right paper and a creative mind, you'll be on your way.

## That's Honour with a "U"

If your invitation is on the formal side, there are a few traditional points of etiquette you may wish to be adhere to:

➤ All names are spelled out in full (no nicknames).

➤ The date is written out in words, not numbers (the fifth of September).

➤ The time is also written out in words (six o'clock).

➤ "The honour of your presence" is the typical wording for an invitation to a wedding ceremony.

➤ "The pleasure of your company" is the typical wording for an invitation to a reception.

➤ Guests are asked to respond by the addition of "R.s.v.p." at the end of the invitation (formal invitations use uppercase R, lowercase s.v.p. with periods after each letter).

➤ Assuming the bride's parents are hosting, the bride's last name is not given unless it differs from her parents.

➤ A reception card is usually a separate invitation within the same envelope, but the two invitations can be printed together on one card, assuming all guests are invited to both the ceremony and the reception.

➤ If the ceremony and reception are in the same location, a sentence at the bottom of the invitation is all that is needed, such as, "Reception immediately following the ceremony."

# Here Comes (and Goes) the Bride

The etiquette of processionals and recessionals can be confusing for couples who are having a nontraditional wedding, or whose families don't fit the traditional mold. Don't worry: It's okay to bend the rules to make them work for you. Figure out what you and your family feel most comfortable doing and then go with it.

To start, let's take a quick look at the most traditional route to the altar. The bride's father walks her down the aisle. (Remember, the bride usually walks on the right.) When they reach the altar, dad places his daughter's hand in the groom's hand. Then he lifts the bride's veil (if she's wearing one) and gives her a kiss before seating himself in the pew next to mom.

Think through this scenario for a moment, imagining your own family situation. For many brides the traditional processional may be the perfect way to go. Others, however, will have problems. What about the bride who wants both her mom and dad to walk with her, or who wants to include her stepfather or grandfather along with her dad? What if the bride has a child from a previous marriage? To say nothing of what today's brides might think about being "given away" at all.

Happily, there are many ways you can choose to glide down that aisle on your big day. Ignore the script and include those you love in the way that gives you the most emotional support on your way to the altar. Certainly grandparents and stepparents can be part of the processional! Having children from a previous marriage walk with you is not only moving, it sends them a clear message that they are part of this new union. Even beloved pets, a spray of baby's breath tucked into their collars, have been known to be part of the processional. Of course, be sure to check with your location and officiant first. The parade to the altar can be beautifully symbolic of the blending of two families.

The bride may enter on the arm of her father, stepfather, grandfather, uncle, family friend, or older brother. She can walk with her father on her left and her stepfather on her right. She could be

**Something True**

In ancient China, a "good luck woman" was hired to carry the bride to a waiting sedan chair, which then carried the bride to the groom's house. The bride's feet were not supposed to touch the ground. Firecrackers were set off to frighten away evil spirits. That would certainly start the processional off with a bang! (For more information on ancient and contemporary Chinese wedding traditions, try **www.chcp.org**.)

**Something True**

The tradition of having your father walk you down the aisle is rooted in a time when a woman was essentially the property of her husband, father, or other male head of household. In walking her down the aisle to the waiting groom, the father symbolically transfers his absolute power over his daughter to her husband, who then becomes the new lord and master of the bride.

flanked by her dad on her left and her son on her right. She can walk with her dad on her left and her mother on her right. She can walk down the aisle alone, preceded only by her bridesmaids. She can even (as I did) walk down the aisle together with her groom rather than have someone give her away.

Some couples fret about having exactly the same number of bridesmaids as grooms-men. Relax. It's perfectly all right for you to have two bridesmaids and your groom to have four groomsmen, for example. Just give some thought to how the attendants will be paired. Either each bridesmaid walks in with two groomsmen (one on either arm), or each bridesmaid walks in with one groomsman, followed by two groomsmen walking together behind them.

Think of the processional as your very own ballet, choreographed by you. You're in charge here. As long as you and your groom are happy with the arrangements and feel the processional and recessional reflect who you are as a couple, everything should be fine.

# Falling into Line

Receiving lines are a convenient way for the bride and groom and the hosts of the reception to greet their guests individually. They are commonly held at the reception, but they can also happen just after the ceremony and before the party.

The way it's supposed to be isn't the way it has to be—but for the record, here's the lowdown on receiving lines. The mother of the bride is usually at the head of the line, followed by the groom's mother, the bride, the groom, the maid or matron of honor, and the bridesmaids. These days, bridesmaids very often skip the receiving line. They may find it awkward to greet guests, many of whom they have never met before.

What about fathers? If fathers want to be part of the receiving line, they can stand to the left of their wives, or head the receiving line themselves if there is no mother or stepmother in that role. The same goes for a grandmother, aunt, or older sister.

If the bride and groom are the hosts of their own wedding, they can place themselves at the head of the receiving line.

Families that have expanded because of divorce and remarriage take some extra consideration. If your mother is divorced, she should probably stand in the line alone, or, if remarried, with her new husband. If your father wants to be in the receiving line too, you may have to do some maneuvering to find him a comfortable spot away from your mother, depending on how everyone feels about each other. If you have a step-mother, you may wish to include her as well. So much depends on your particular family and how they all get along.

Small weddings typically have small receiving lines: just the bride and groom and their parents. Some weddings skip the receiving line altogether. The bride and groom and parents simply circulate among the guests, greeting everyone and helping to get the party underway. This is fine, but just make sure you know how your guests will react. As wedding consultant Charrisse Min Alliegro of New Jersey puts it, "Weddings are not just about what you want as a bride, but what your family and guests need. Will your relatives be insulted if they are not formally received? Obviously, you don't want to insult your guests."

Again, the point of the receiving line is to make sure each guest is greeted by the bridal couple and their families. If you skip the receiving line, there are other ways of accomplishing this.

➤ Speak to as many people as possible at the rehearsal dinner, especially out-of-town guests. Say, "We're not going to be having a receiving line tomorrow, so I wanted to be sure to talk to you tonight."

➤ After the recessional, the bride and groom might re-enter the church (or other ceremony site) and release each pew or row. This gives them a moment to say a quick "Hi, we'll see you at the reception" to everyone as they file out. Assuming you took photos *before* the ceremony, you may have time to do this. Otherwise, check with your church to see if they have a time limit after the ceremony.

➤ Stop by each table at the reception and say hello to your guests.

➤ Mingle, mingle, mingle. Don't get stuck in a corner.

➤ Pass out your favors so you are sure to say hello to almost everyone.

**Bridal Blunders**

No matter whom you decide to place *in* the receiving line, be sure you give some thought to *where* you put the receiving line. As you get closer to the big day, talk with your reception-site manager about this. He or she should be able to help you find a place that won't cause a bottleneck.

Just make sure everyone's comfortable with their placement (or lack thereof) in the receiving line. Then get busy with the task at hand: receiving your guests. To be polite, introduce each person to the next person in line, as in, "Mrs. White, I'd like you to meet Sylvia's college roommate and maid of honor, Elizabeth." This way, everyone feels they have been able to meet everyone else, as well as understand that person's relationship to the bride and/or groom. You can also do this in your wedding program if you have one, by listing attendants' names and relationship to you.

## Have a Seat!

At a creative wedding, your seating options are wide open. Depending on your reception style, you may or may not be having a seated meal. If you are, then you need to give some thought to the placement of your guests. The main idea in creating seating arrangements is to ensure that your guests have a good time at your party with people they already know, or people you think they'd like to know. Be sensitive to sensitive situations. If there are divorced parents, for example, you will probably want to seat them at separate tables. Put yourself in your guests' position! Think about who gets along with whom.

If your meal is not a seated affair, you should still take guests' comfort into consideration. Always plan on having enough chairs for everyone. Don't expect people to be able to stand the entire time, balancing plates and drinks.

Of course, you will also want to give some thought to where you and your groom will sit. Do you like the idea of a head table for the bridal party? If not, you may opt for the sweetheart table, the bride and groom alone at a table for two—usually located at the center of the room, surrounded by traditional tables of 8 to 12 all around them.

Have some fun with the seating. Will there be a lot of children at the wedding? A separate kids table can be a lot of fun, as can tables of teens, tables for your college buddies, tables for cousins, and more. Your job in planning the seating is to make sure that everyone attending your party has the best time possible.

### Creative Corner

These days, the trend is to direct guests to an assigned wedding table, but not a particular seat at that table. They arrange themselves as they like. Instead of assigning a table number, which is a little cold, why not assign table names? You could come up with monikers like "The Boston Bombers" to describe a table of college chums. You could name tables after different cities you and your fiancé have lived in, or different sites and places you plan to go to on your honeymoon. If the reception site is a winery, naming the tables "Chardonnay," Beaujolais," and "Rosé" work beautifully. (You probably have to retain a table number in smaller print underneath your clever name, so that the wait staff doesn't get confused.) As an amusing icebreaker, one couple left a poem on each table that described all the guests at that table. You could come up with such couplets as "Here we have two lawyers from Yale... Sandy, tell Dennis a funny tale!" and so on. Use all their names and a little snippet of biographical information about them. It will certainly get everyone talking—and laughing!

A bride I know is throwing a long-weekend wedding (a ceremony surrounded by a few days of togetherness with guests) at an outdoor camping site in southern California. She has opted for no seating arrangements at all. "By the time of the ceremony and party, all the guests will have been together for a couple of days and should know each other really well...so they can sit wherever they like," she says. This free-for-all may not work as well for more controlling brides and grooms.

# Consultant of the Bride

If the etiquette of a wedding seems like uncharted (and unfriendly) seas to you, you may want to find someone to help navigate. For nervous or overworked couples a bridal consultant can be a lifesaver. "Consultants can offer simple reassurance. We have seen a lot; we hear a lot. If there's something you want to do, a consultant is going to know how to do it. Almost anything can be accommodated in a tasteful way," says Charrisse Min Alliegro of Princeton Wedding Consultants in Princeton, New Jersey.

Wedding coordinators and professional consultants can provide valuable assistance in a busy world where brides and their moms often work full time. Professional consultants will match couples with the appropriate vendors taking into consideration style, budget, and personality. They have resources at their fingertips that you might spend weeks or months tracking down on your own. According to Renee Grannis, Education Director for The Association of Bridal Consultants, it can take a bride working solo a couple of hundred hours to put together a wedding—longer if the wedding will be extended over two or three days. If this doesn't sound feasible, a consultant may be just what you need.

The consultant is there to answer your questions and calm your fears. Most have seen hundreds of weddings and have a pretty good idea of which rules of etiquette can be relaxed and which have a serious reason for being left in place. "A good consultant should be up on traditional etiquette as well as the meaning behind the rules, and know how to make them fit with your lifestyle," says Alliegro. Many coordinators will give advice not only before the day but during it as well, attending the wedding to help make sure your day goes as smoothly as possible.

## *How to Find a Bridal Consultant*

Some ceremony/reception sites have bridal consultants on staff to help you. They work only at their place of employment and recommend the vendors they know best. Couples seeking more creative touches may prefer to find their own *independent* consultant.

There are several ways to go about this. One is to attend a bridal expo or fair and meet some consultants at their booths. Another is to look in the yellow pages, or contact the Association of Bridal Consultants at 860-355-0464. You can also call another organization, June Wedding, Inc. at 702-474-9558. The best method of all is word of mouth. Do you know someone who married recently, with the help of a consultant or coordinator? If that couple was pleased, there's a good chance you might be, too. No matter how good the references are, however, make sure you do plenty of interviewing before you choose one.

When meeting with a potential consultant, ask the following questions:

1. Do you work full time or part time?
2. Have you been trained and do you maintain active membership in wedding organizations?

3. How long have you been in business?

4. Can I get references? (Check for vendor references, also.)

### Consultants Say

When it comes to consultants, you can get as much—or as little—help as you need. You may want anything from a one-time-only hour consultation to detailed help from conception through completion of the day. Let your consultant know how much assistance you need—and when you need it.

5. Could you explain the services offered in the contract?

6. How is payment arranged: hourly, flat fee, or a percentage?

7. Are expenses included in your fee (telephone, gas, mileage)?

8. Are you independent? (A consultant who also sells bridal products or services or who has a commission arrangement with vendors may not be completely objective.)

9. Which specific services are offered? (Some consultants may handle every detail, others may not be quite as accommodating.)

"I encourage clients to interview as many consultants as their schedule and stamina permits," says Alliegro of Princeton Wedding Consultants. "It's not just about finding someone with the right technical knowledge. You've got to *like* the person." Here's what to look for:

### Something True

The Association of Bridal Consultants started out with only a handful of members less than 20 years ago. Today, they have over 2,000 members in all 50 states and 17 foreign countries. Over 90 percent of them, you may not be surprised to learn, are women.

➤ A consultant with lots of resources and connections

➤ Good references (from both vendors and past clients)

➤ A consultant who doesn't just push *her* idea of the perfect wedding but who listens to yours (Though if a consultant has a very distinctive or signature style, and you know that's exactly what you want, go for it.)

➤ A consultant who is liked and respected by your florist, banquet manager, and others connected to the wedding. (They work with these people all the time and know who's talented and organized.)

## What's It Gonna Cost?

When interviewing a consultant, be sure to discuss fees and understand the contract. Consultants' costs can really run the gamut. Some offer package rates, meaning you pay a flat fee. Others charge an hourly rate based on face-to-face meetings, phone, and e-mail time with you. "Understand what it is you are getting for that money," says Renee Grannis of The Association of Bridal Consultants. Will the consultant be keeping track of wedding invitation responses? Finding a florist? Attending your wedding? If an hourly fee is being proposed, try to get an idea of how many hours the consultant is imagining you will need to spend with her to do the things you want. Remember, besides saving you time and effort, a consultant can sometimes save you money as well, either through discounts or simply by being savvy enough to know where to go for the best price.

Find out how the consultant wants to be paid. Many ask for a certain amount down at the signing of the contract and the rest later. Most couples find it easiest to pay as they go, with monthly bills that are more manageable than a lump sum.

## When to Call in the Troops

Not everyone dials the bridal consultant right after their fiancé hands them the engagement ring, but some do. (Others call their mothers first and the consultants immediately after!) You can find a professional consultant to walk you through the entire planning process, and through the wedding and reception itself, right up to the time you leave the reception. (There's probably no need to take the consultant along on your honeymoon.) If this is more personal attention than you need, arrange to have less. Fees can be tailored to the exact amount of coverage and assistance you need.

For the couple who needs only one or two sessions with a consultant for reassurance, advice, and a few resources, the best bet is to find someone who will work for an hourly fee. Some couples like to see their consultant for an hour once a month, like a monthly checkup at the doctor's. This keeps them on track while still leaving them in charge of most of the legwork.

Occasionally consultants see couples who have done all the planning and arranging themselves and who are now ready to step back and enjoy their day. "They don't want to end up playing the role of wedding consultant on the actual day of their wedding, so they call in a professional, usually about a month before the big date, says Charrisse Min Alliegro of Princeton Wedding Consultants. As the couple heads into the home stretch, hiring a professional to put the finishing touches on the wedding and steer it to its completion can be a real relief!

You now know how to create a unique wedding style while still respecting your guests. You've discovered how a consultant can help you handle

**Bridal Blunders**

If you call in a consultant to finish what you started, step back and let her do her job. You'll need to hand over copies of all contracts and let the consultant know about everything you have put in place so far. If you're still running around and doing things on your own and not informing the consultant, it will end in chaos.

the etiquette of your situation. In the next chapter, you'll start to discover some novel ideas for personalizing your wedding. It'll get those creative juices flowing.

---

### The Least You Need to Know

➤ Today's etiquette is less about rigid rules and more about good taste, consideration for others, and feeling comfortable with your choices.

➤ The bride's family may still pay for most of the wedding and reception costs, but more and more couples are finding the costs to be a "family affair" with everyone pitching in to make the party a success. Today, in fact, most couples pay for their own weddings, or at least a portion.

➤ In the wording of your invitation, be clear as well as respectful of each person's role in the wedding. Use the invitation to give an idea of your wedding theme and style.

➤ Arrange the wedding processional and receiving line to reflect your personal wedding style.

➤ Hiring a bridal consultant as etiquette advisor and wedding organizer can save money and time, and reduce stress.

# Personal Touches

The creative wedding is all about personal touches—those special elements that set your celebration apart from every other couple's. It may mean a little more work for you in the beginning, but the payoff at the end can be tremendous. You will have succeeded in putting together a day that truly reflects who you are as individuals and as a couple. And the result will be as personal as it is unforgettable. You will find some fabulous ideas as you read through this book. For specific ideas check out the chapters on flowers, music, long-weekend weddings, theme weddings, and more. The details can make all the difference in your day. Here are some small ideas that can be incorporated into almost any style of wedding. This chapter shows you ways to take what you love in life (or about each other) and turn it into fabulous wedding ideas and memories.

## Incorporating Your Interests

A couple's hobbies, interests—even their love of sports—can be used creatively to personalize their day. Think about what you and your fiancé love to do in your free time. Is there anything there that can be used for a party or theme? What about for decorating?

Consider the way you and your groom spend your time. Does he love building model ships? Do you sail or windsurf? Consider a nautical wedding theme. Are either of you avid golfers? Show your style with a wedding at a country club overlooking the 18th hole. Plan on a day of golf the day before the wedding and give out tees with your names and wedding date printed on them. Tennis buff? Why not marry in June, with a Wimbledon theme. Strawberries and cream for everyone! The score will always be love–love.

### Consultants Say

If you have a wedding consultant, tell her how you met and how and where you got engaged. List your hobbies, occupations, and loves. Your consultant will be happy to help you think of creative ways to incorporate these things into your day.

*Is golfing your bag? Why not get married at a country club and have your photographs done on the green?*
®Monkmeyer/Ploeger

Is rock climbing your thing? Imagine a beautiful illustration of a mountain expanse behind the words of your invitation—something about the heights this love has taken you. A mountaintop ceremony could be followed by a reception a little closer to earth (for guests who prefer it down there).

Take what you love most and find a way to put it into your ceremony. Do you both adore animals and wildlife? Have the family pet walk down the aisle with you, or release butterflies at your garden reception. Does the bumper sticker on your groom's car read, "I'd rather be fishing"? Serve fish as the main course. Send announcements or invitations that explain what "lured" you to him. Put a bunch of flowers in a tackle box as a centerpiece for the head table.

A hobby or past time can be reflected in the getaway. For example, if you are both accomplished horseback riders, why not ride off into the sunset together after the ceremony and reception? If you're looking for something a little less athletic that still incorporates your love of horses, ride to the reception site in a romantically decorated horse and carriage. Does your dad have a thing for old cars? Think about renting some exotic cars for the wedding party to travel in from ceremony to reception site.

*No matter what your hobby, there's a way to make it part of your day.*
© Index Stock/Chris Briscoe

Use a talent to give a little something of yourself to the party. Do you or your groom sing or play an instrument? Have the groom join the band for one number. Let him serenade you with his best love song. Decorate your wedding invitation with musical notes.

Even if your hobby is more sedentary, you can find ways to make it work at your wedding. Suppose a bride and groom love reading books. Could this be reflected in their day? Absolutely! The bride might present her groom with a special gift of antique books. Guests could receive beautiful bookmarks with the bride and groom's names and wedding date printed on it. Everyone could take a tour of a beautiful library-museum, such as the Morgan Library in New York City. Instead of being numbered, tables at the reception could be named after favorite books or beloved authors.

### Creative Corner

Do you collect anything? One bride collects giraffes, another, frogs, a third anything with ladybugs on it. Any of these motifs could be used on unusual invitations, napkin rings, wedding programs, jewelry, and more. For a whimsical nod to a bride's collection, the groom might sport ladybug cufflinks and studs with his traditional tuxedo. Guests will notice the fun and funky style first...then later find out about how it related to the bride, the groom, or their relationship. It's almost as though you have left little clues everywhere as to your personality or the groom's. Such touches are fun for the guests and meaningful for you.

# The Way We Were (and Are)

You may be young, but already you and your fiancé probably have lots of history behind you. Some of the personal aspects of your relationship—how you met or what the two of you love to do together—can give you some great creative ideas.

Delve into your past as a couple. Did you two first meet at summer camp when you were nine? So maybe you didn't know back then that this was the man of your dreams (in fact, you only remember him as the crazy kid who ate 24 marshmallows at one campfire sitting), but now that you are getting married, it may make a fun reference. Perhaps you can all sing the camp song at the reception. (Give the band the music in advance.)

If you met at college, you might want to take a trip down memory lane by toasting in champagne glasses engraved with your college emblem. Many couples who meet in college actually like to return to the campus for the ceremony. University chapels can be a lovely setting for a wedding. A few college songs sung at the reception (perhaps by an a cappella campus group) can round out your reminiscence.

Were you a cheerleader for his football team back in high school? How about a witty arrangement of flowers in a football helmet? A game of touch football for guests the day before the wedding? A casual rehearsal dinner held in a sports bar with big-screen TVs?

Did the two of you meet on a blind date? At the rehearsal dinner, have a blind seating arrangement. Guests pick a table number out of a hat and sit with whoever else is there. Alternatively, make everyone find a seating partner by cutting a deck of cards in half and asking each guest to pick up a card and then go and search for his mate. An added benefit: Everyone will be forced to make a new friend!

Perhaps you fell in love with the help of the Internet. Set up a Web page to keep guests posted on your wedding plans. Send invitations you designed yourself on your computer. E-mail guests with your wedding news.

Did one of you grow up on a farm, the other in the city? Offer a few special guests a bandana in a Tiffany's bag. Run a tape of Green Acres in an anteroom during the reception. Decorate your glittery city-slicker reception site with a few bales of hay.

*There's no better way to mark the occasion then going back to where it all began. If you met in a unique spot that's special to you and your fiancé, add it in to the festivities.*
®Richard B. Levine

These wild and wacky ideas are meant to help you start thinking about who you are as a couple—and how your past can be reflected on a day that marks the beginning of your future together. The bottom line is: The things you love about life—and each other—can be worked into your wedding day in humorous, touching, and meaningful ways. These personal touches are at the root of every creative wedding.

## Reel Love: Turning to Your Favorite Movies for Creative Ideas

Since movies are a favorite venue for the dating crowd, you and your groom may well have a few movies you remember with special fondness. If you're a real movie buff, or have fallen in love with a particular movie (or with each other *at* a particular movie), you might consider incorporating movie memories into the theme of your wedding.

Perhaps, like most of America, you were swept away by Titanic. The romance! The adventure! Consider marrying on a cruise ship in turn-of-the-century dress. Romantic music from the movie could be played at the reception. In fact, many favorite movies have wonderful music soundtracks that you can incorporate into your day. What's your favorite?

Little touches here can be amusing (almost secretive) reminders of intimate cinematic moments you and your groom share. From *It's a Wonderful Life*—bells can decorate a tree at a Christmas reception. From *Back to the Future*—a Delorean can whisk you away from the ceremony to the reception. From *Cinderella*—a horse and carriage ride is a must. From *The Wizard of Oz*—the flower girl can carry an adorable (and hopefully extremely well-behaved) terrier down the aisle in a basket instead of flowers. Use your imagination.

---

### Wedding Classics of Film

In the mood to watch others getting hitched? See if you can find and rent the following movies. Now that you're a bride yourself you'll have a greater appreciation for the fashion, the flowers, the venues.

➤ *The Love Parade*, starring Maurice Chevalier and Jeanette McDonald. You'll love the twenties gown and bouquet!

➤ *It Happened One Night*, starring Claudette Colbert and Clark Gable. Check out the thirties look in this movie about a lavish high-society wedding.

➤ *The Graduate*. It's a sixties romp ending in an interrupted wedding, as Dustin Hoffman steals the bride from the altar!

➤ *Gone with the Wind*, starring Vivien Leigh. What a dress, Scarlett!

➤ *The Philadelphia Story*, starring Katherine Hepburn, Cary Grant, and Jimmy Stewart. A fab forties flick.

➤ *Father of the Bride*, starring Spencer Tracy and Elizabeth Taylor. It may help you keep your sense of humor.

➤ *My Best Friend's Wedding*, starring Julia Roberts. If you're inviting any of his past girlfriends to the wedding, this may help reassure you (or maybe not). Plus, Cameron Diaz throws a great garden party before the wedding. You may pick up a few ideas.

---

At a long weekend or honeymoon wedding, when you and your guests have more time together, there are more ways to incorporate the fun of movies into your celebration. For example, the two of you might want to share comedy classics with your guests one evening before the wedding with a showing of old Abbott and Costello or Marx Brothers features. Play a trivia game related to the movies. The prize? A bicycle horn, of course! If it's going to be a Star Trek night instead, play Star Trek Trivia and make the prize a replica of the starship Enterprise. Star Trek attire is appropriate. Go where no couple has gone before! Serve Mars bars and decorate tables with silver lamé table-cloths. Guests can toast to the bride and groom with, "May they live long and prosper!" (According to *Off The Beaten Aisle: America's Quirky Spots to Tie the Knot* by Lisa Primerano [Citadel Press, 1998], one couple actually had a Star Trek theme wedding in a Las Vegas chapel, complete with swirls of white fog, squeaking tribbles, wedding vows in which they promised to "care for each other when your dilithium crystals are low," an assortment of crew members, and Captain "Quirk" officiating.)

Have fun with a prewedding party based on a dance movie like *Grease* or *Saturday Night Fever*. Think of women in poodle skirts and saddle shoes dancing to fifties music alongside guys in letter sweaters, or a roomful of people in seventies disco attire.

The point is to have some fun, make your day personal, and remember the things you share. Let your love speak!

## You Say Potato...Celebrating Your Differences

When two different cultures meet, the results can be electric. And all those interesting differences can give a couple some wonderful ideas for celebrating. Can Italian antipasto, Chinese dumplings, Spanish music, English tea, Russian wedding rings, and a Saki toast really all coexist happily at the same event? Certainly, most couples don't have quite that many different cultures to incorporate into their weddings, but if they did, they could probably find a way to handle it all. With a little planning, anything is possible! See Chapter 14 for a more complete look at the many and varied cultural and ethnic wedding traditions that exist.

The ethnic additions or cultural touches don't have to be large or pervasive to be worthwhile. Even a nod to the heritage of bride or groom can be a grand gesture. Families appreciate having their cultures recognized and respected. Since this is a day about unions, what better way to celebrate than by including as many different cultural and ethnic additions as possible?

### Something True

The Top 10 Movies of the eighties were (in order): *E.T., Indiana Jones and the Last Crusade, Batman, Rain Man, Return of the Jedi, Raiders of the Lost Ark, The Empire Strikes Back, Who Framed Roger Rabbit?, Back to the Future,* and *Top Gun.* The top 10 movies of the nineties so far include *Jurassic Park, Independence Day, The Lion King, Forrest Gump, Home Alone, Terminator 2, Ghost, Twister, Aladdin,* and *Pretty Woman.* (Source: *The Top 10 of Everything 1998* by Russell Ash, [DK Publishing, Inc.])

### Something True

At a Russian orthodox wedding, the bride and groom stand under crowns held by their attendants and drink wine from the same cup as a symbol of their willingness to share experiences. In Thailand couples might wear a "Brahman rope" around their heads symbolizing the ties that bind them together. At an Indian wedding, newlyweds often wear garlands of fragrant flowers around their necks.

A beautiful huppah (canopy) used in Jewish ceremonies can be held over the couple and their family, even in a mixed religion marriage. A historic Ketuba (Jewish marriage contract) can be turned into a work of art for both families to enjoy. A bride can wear an ornate, silk Indian sari worked with gold thread to a Western wedding. To honor an Austrian heritage, fiddlers can lead the wedding procession (an early nineteenth-century custom).

A wonderful place to include ethnic and cultural touches is in the food. Italian wedding knots (Farfalette dolci) can be placed on a dessert table; Mexican wedding cookies (pastelitos de boda) can make a delicious favor. If your family has a special favorite or an old family recipe for a traditional dish, discus it with your caterer or bridal consultant to see whether it can be offered at your reception.

Music, too, can be a wonderful way to span the ethnic backgrounds of your two families. Bagpipers can celebrate a Scottish heritage; flamenco music can salute someone's Spanish roots. You might consider hiring a special group to perform at a select portion of the party.

**Consultants Say**

Talk to your parents about what cultural traditions, if any, were a part of their wedding day. Ask about your grandparents' and great-grandparents' weddings as well. You may find some beautiful or interesting cultural touches that you can add to your own day. For more information on ethnic traditions from yesteryear and today, read Chapter 14.

# The Crazy Quilt

Quilts have long been a symbol of love and comfort. With many colorful pieces stitched together into a single piece, the quilt can also be a symbol of the family and friends united on one special day to bless the union of two people. The quilt can be included as a personal touch and kept as a lasting memento.

Think about asking friends and family members to supply you with one square each for a quilt. Give exact measurements so that everyone's square is the same size. Guests can supply an unadorned piece of fabric, or better yet come up with a lovingly designed square (two appliquéd oars crossed over each other, to remember a canoeing weekend you shared, for example). Later, all the squares can be stitched together to make a fabulous wall hanging in your new home.

If a large quilt seems too ambitious, think about a smaller, more manageable quilting project, such as a pillow case cover, or for a Christmas wedding, a quilted Christmas tree skirt that could be passed down for generations.

A simple quilt that involves little advance preparation can be created during the reception itself. Leave pieces of fabric out on a table, allowing each guest to choose his or her own. With indelible ink pens in a variety of colors, guests can sign their names or add a goodwill message. These squares can later be stitched together to form a lovely collection of memories. For more about quilting ideas and practical advice, read *The Complete Idiot's Guide to Quilting* by Laura Ehrlich (Alpha Books, 1998).

---

### Creative Corner

The quilt can do double duty as a huppah (a Jewish wedding canopy). One bride plans to use a quilt made by friends and family to create a huppah for her wedding ceremony. She and her fiancé look forward to a warm and intimate ceremony under the shelter of these expressions of love. Later they can put the quilt on their bed, display it as art on the wall, or put it away as a treasured family heirloom. Another bride used as her wedding canopy the quilt she had on her bed since childhood. For her it represented her past and her family home.

---

## Guess Who's Signing the Guest Book?

What makes your wedding different from anyone else's? The guests, of course. The guest book is one time-honored tradition you may wish to incorporate into your creative wedding. A guest book can lovingly record who is in attendance, and their wishes for you. It makes a charming and sentimental keepsake.

Begin by purchasing a beautiful guest book in white satiny fabric or leather—or decorate the cover of a hardbound blank book, if that's your style. Place the book where it is accessible to all your guests. You might even post a couple of teenagers nearby to remind guests to "please sign in."

Have a little fun with the book, if you wish. A straightforward list of names, one right after the other, while "historically accurate," is less interesting than asking each person to contribute something of themselves. One Connecticut family I read about asks visitors to their home to sign their names in the guest book, then shut their eyes and draw a pig without peeking. You could try a variation on this theme by asking guests to sign in, then close their eyes and draw a heart with an arrow through it. After all, they say love is blind!

### Something True

The guest book originated in the eighteenth century. From its place of honor on a table by the front door, it kept track of who had visited in the days when exchanging social calls was de rigueur for members of the well-to-do classes. Some pretty impressive lists could be built up in the old days at homes of great social standing! At a wedding, the guest book is less of a "who's who" and more of a "we were there."

## Creative Corner

Do you want guests to get wordy? People often have trouble thinking of anything more profound to say than "Best Wishes!" Help them to get a little more personal by giving them a topic to write about. For example, you could ask guests to "Tell us where you think we'll be in 10 years." Or suggest that they answer, "What are your wishes for us today?" You could even say, "Please leave us your definition of *love*." You'll get remarks that are sentimental, witty, ribald, intimate, and meaningful. What fun *this* guest book will be to read later! Be sure to give guests clear instructions related to the guest book. Type or print these directions neatly on a heavy white card and place them next to the guest book.

## The Least You Need to Know

➤ Personal touches are what make a wedding unique and memorable.

➤ Think about what hobbies, interests, sports, books, and films you and your groom enjoy, and consider ways to represent some of these loves on your wedding day.

➤ Special memories and places the two of you share can be incorporated into a moving wedding celebration.

➤ Celebrate the ethnic and cultural backgrounds of your two families. Pick and choose the traditions that work best for your wedding style.

➤ Make beautiful memories. Quilts and guest books can be used creatively to express your individuality, your past, your future, and your relationship.

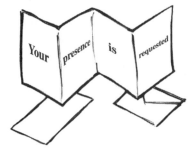

# Chapter 4

# Creative Invitations

---

**In This Chapter**

➤ Sending out engagement and wedding announcements

➤ Choosing an invitational style

➤ Finding the right words

➤ Creating your own invitation

➤ Adding the extras that make your invitation creative

---

The first impression most people will get of your wedding will be through the wedding invitation. The invitation sets the scene for a formal or informal event, reveals the theme of the wedding, if there is one, and most of all reflects your style, creativity, special poetry, and love. There is a formula and etiquette to invitations, but your invitations don't necessarily have to follow the straight and narrow path. This is one area where you may want to think about adding some individual touches.

## Hear Ye! Hear Ye! Announcements That Get the Word Out

Engagement and wedding announcements tell the world a story. They make your love and commitment known to the outside world—traditionally about six to ten months before the wedding is scheduled to take place.

The usual way to publish the engagement, of course, is in your hometown newspaper, which you can do by contacting the lifestyle editor. Some papers have very specific rules for how an engagement or wedding announcement must be filed, and about photo use. (Certain papers, for example, will print a picture of the bride, only.) Some charge a fee, some don't.

As with wedding invitations, the convention is for the engagement announcement to be made by the bride's family: "Mr. and Mrs. Robert Reynolds announce the engagement of their daughter, Laurel Anne to...." However, it can also be made by both sets of parents or by the couple themselves.

A college or high school's alumni news section is another avenue for getting the word out. Just send your school a few lines that can be reprinted. Have a little fun: "Bart Summers '87 and Mary O'Reilly '86 never took the same side in debate club, but there's one thing they now see eye to eye on: an April 17, 2000 wedding date."

### Creative Corner

Spread the news yourself among friends by sending a silly spoof of a chain letter over the Internet. Insist that they send your announcement on to the 5 names whose e-mail addresses appear below. In typical chain letter fashion, explain the good luck that comes to those who comply (for example, they receive a lovely invitation to a terrific party). Remind them that terrible luck can befall those who do not pass it on: they may be hit by flying rice at a friend's wedding!

Wedding announcements are traditionally placed in the bride's hometown paper. As with the engagement announcement, there may be certain standards for submission of the information. You may be given a form to fill out. Call the paper in advance of your wedding day to find out what its rules and requirements are, and don't forget to submit the information by the deadline.

The paper may ask for a description of your gown or other aspects of your day. You may wish to highlight a few of your more creative and meaningful wedding moments. "The bride wore her great grandmother's twenties wedding dress...." or "The bride and groom were married on a yacht...." Wedding notes usually appear in the newspaper the day after the ceremony. For this reason you'll want someone back home to save the paper for you if you're not home to get it yourself.

# Inviting Invitations

Be sure to give yourself plenty of time to get the invitations out. Plan to be at the printer with your order about three to six months before the wedding. Most wedding invitations are sent a month in advance. If you are throwing a long-weekend wedding or would like guests to join you at a far-away destination, you will probably want to offer at least two months' advance notice.

Start now with a good look around at what's out there. What mood do you want to convey? Elegant? Romantic? Artistic? Funny? With thought, your invitation can stand apart from the crowd because of the way it looks, the way it's delivered, or what it says.

## From Trendy to Traditional (and Everything in Between)

"These days, everyone wants something different and unique," says JoAnn Gregoli of Elegant Occasions in Denville, New Jersey. The hottest trend right now? Boxed invitations. Instead of using envelopes, brides place the invitations in little gift boxes and wrap them in a heavy tissue paper that can be written on and sent through the regular mail. What a special and unique way to say, "Please come!"

Other hot trends, according to Diane Forbis of Rexcraft, a mail-order catalog specializing in wedding invitations:

➤ Large or small square-shaped invitations

➤ Long and narrow invitations

➤ A layered-look (translucent paper over a heavy stock card)

➤ Handmade looks

➤ Dark, jewel colors

➤ Personalized statements or poetic verses added to the traditional wording on a facing page

As you can see, the creative possibilities are pretty much endless. To help you get started, I suggest you sit down with your fiancé and discuss two basic questions:

1. How much do you wish to spend?

2. How formal do you want to be?

## Ouch! Deciding How Much to Budget

When it comes to choosing or designing invitations, the first thing you'll need to consider is budget. Invitations can really run the gamut, from fairly inexpensive to $1,000 or more, depending on where you have them printed, the quality of paper, style, and so on. Special envelopes, extras (such as a bow tied through the card), handcrafted elements, and custom designs will add to the expense. Once you decide how much of your budget to commit to the invitations, deciding about specific elements will be much easier.

## Setting the Tone

The other basic issue is formality. If you choose to go the traditional elegance route, the creative options will, of course, be fewer.

A traditional invitation looks and reads something like this:

> Mr. and Mrs. Roger London
> request the honour of your presence
> at the marriage of their daughter
> Louisa Christina
> to
> Francis Scott Winter
> on the sixth of August
> nineteen hundred and ninety nine
> at three o'clock
> Our Lady Church
> Newton, Massachusetts

A separate card is ordinarily enclosed inviting the guest to join you at the reception as well. It can be as simple as this:

> Reception
> immediately following the ceremony
> at Newton Country Club
> Country Club Road
> r.s.v.p.
> Sixteen Laurel Drive
> Newton, Massachusetts

This elegant, simple style is perfect for a formal or semiformal wedding and remains one of the most popular ways to word a wedding invitation. If your day is going to be quite informal however, this kind of invitation is likely to send your guests the wrong message. Remember, guests will take their cue about how to dress from the tone of your invitation. Help them know what to expect with a clear invitation that accurately represents the type of day you have planned. If your wedding takes place outdoors, on a dock, beach, field, or hillside, let your guests know so they can plan on appropriate footwear and outerwear.

### Creative Corner

The most informal invitation style is in the form of a personal note. Writing your invitations by hand is time consuming, but probably quite manageable with' a small wedding. You might write:

*Dear Aunt Mary,*

*I'm so excited to tell you about my plans to marry John Fairly on the Fourth of July at the beach house in Maine. There will be a small ceremony outside at noon, followed by a luncheon reception in the house. Mom and Dad say there's plenty of room at the house for you to stay with them over the weekend. We really hope you can be with us on that day. Please call us and let us know.*

*Love, Christine*

## In Your Own Words

Even if you're planning a formal affair, there are many reasons to depart from traditional wording. Maybe it just doesn't feel right. Maybe it doesn't work with your family circumstances or wedding style. Couples who are marrying for a second time, whose parents are divorced, who already have children, or who are paying for the wedding themselves, all may feel more comfortable creating their own wording for the invitation. Again, the best advice is to try to match the style of the invitations with the style of the wedding.

Many couples choose to break out of the box with wording that includes:

➤ A famous quotation

➤ A favorite poem

➤ Heartfelt words from the bride and groom

➤ A fairytale story

➤ Meaningful quotes from their kids

➤ An amusing play on words

➤ A takeoff on a newspaper report, theatrical program, or ad

### Consultants Say

Are some of the guests from a different country or culture? Make them feel welcome by printing a bilingual invitation with, for example, French on one side and English on the facing page. The foreign language invitation could also be printed on an insert.

Creative wording can reflect your theme. A couple might write, "The greatest show on earth—one performance only" when hosting a country-fair wedding. A play on words can tie the invitation to the theme in a clever and humorous way: "Be swept away on June 3 when Bob and Leslie tie the knot on board The Norwegian Princess." Or "Celebrate a marriage made in heaven with Adam and Eve."

The traditional "request the honour of your presence" can be changed to "invite you to share in their joy" or "ask you to join them for a day of new beginnings."

Remember, wording can be tricky. If the two of you plan to come up with your own, it's a good idea to sit down and work on a few different versions until you get it just the way you want it. If it would help you to look at what others have used, there's no shortage of examples out there. Most stationary stores and printing services have hundreds of samples you can look at.

### Bridal Blunders

Proofread! Proofread! Proofread! Make sure your invitations are free of typos, that every word is spelled properly, and that all numbers are correct. Before hiring a professional printer, make sure they guarantee their work and will correct any mistakes for free.

### Something True

According to *Something Old, Something New* (Casablanca Press, 1994, 1998) by Vera Lee, in one small Greek village the custom is for two friends of the bride and groom to go door to door, inviting all the guests. They travel with a bottle of wine, sharing it along the way with all invitees. In a town in India, emissaries reportedly are sent to spread the word of an upcoming wedding. Guests are each offered a small coin. By accepting it, they are agreeing to come.

## Response Cards: Is Anybody out There?

As you well know, wedding invitations can be extremely elaborate affairs—outer envelope, inner envelope, tissue paper, reception card, response card, dinner preference, map, self-addressed stamped return envelope. If this fits your wedding style, great. If not, you might still wish to include a separate reception card giving the date, time, and place of the party—especially if more guests will be attending the reception than the ceremony.

Many couples these days tuck a response card and stamped, self-addressed envelope into the invitation to make it easier for guests to reply. The card may be as simple as "_____ will _____ will not attend ."

Printing r.s.v.p. on the invitation means that guests should respond; so does "The favor of a reply is requested" above the address. A very informal invitation may simply give a phone number. Most often, however, couples tuck a response card into the envelope to make replying by mail easier.

# Enclosed Please Find

A creative wedding may call for any number of enclosures. If your ceremony or reception venue, for example, is typically off limits to the general public (such as a yacht or historic site), you may want to include cards that permit entrance by the bearer. A rain card might be advisable for a non-tented outdoor wedding. The rain card tells where to go in case of rain. Separate cards can also give guests the heads-up on anything from suggestions for appropriate footwear to a request for costumed attire, to special transportation arrangements.

# Form Follows Function

Once you decide on the style and content of your invitations, the next step is to choose the perfect medium for your message.

### *Puttin' on the Ritz*

For formal invitations, the selection process is relatively straightforward. Rectangular sheets of heavy-weight white, off-white, cream, ivory, or ecru paper are folded in half and the lettering engraved on the front. The invitation is placed inside an unsealed envelope, which is placed inside a second envelope to be addressed and stamped.

Engraved invitations convey fine quality and tradition. They are also very expensive. If you choose this method, ask your stationery store to save the engraving plate for you as a keepsake. Some couples have it made into the lid of a pretty box.

**Something True**

Engraving is a centuries-old printing process in which an individual plate is engraved with your wording and pressed onto the paper, resulting in slightly raised lettering. Thermography, a much newer printing process, mimics the engraved look and is less expensive than engraving.

### *Choices, Choices!*

For those who choose a less formal style, creative options abound. Consider:

➤ An unusual type face—script, bold, shaded (explore them all at your stationers' to determine which one is right for you)

➤ Handwritten invitations using calligraphy

➤ Translucent paper

➤ Shiny paper

➤ Sparkly paper

➤ Colored paper

➤ Bordered paper

➤ Kente-cloth inspired border

- ➤ Parchment paper
- ➤ Handmade paper
- ➤ Colored ink
- ➤ Gold or silver lettering
- ➤ Stenciling
- ➤ Floral designs
- ➤ Traditional African-American tribal symbols
- ➤ A ribbon tied through the card
- ➤ Cutouts or silhouettes (perhaps with wording that says "…are truly cut out for each other"
- ➤ Tulle or lace decorations

You can also play with the size and shape of your invitation. A large square or long rectangular card could be a real stand-out. Just make sure you put enough postage on oversized envelopes, and on invitations being mailed abroad. It's a good idea to take all items, in their envelope, to the post office to verify the weight.

### Creative Corner

Why send a card at all? Some couples send a message in a plastic bottle! This clever and unique idea can work perfectly for a destination wedding on an island ("Cast away with Bob and Misa….") or a nautical theme wedding. If the bottle you use resembles a split of champagne, it can be perfect for a New Year's Eve wedding. Guests uncork the bubbly and find out about a smashing celebration!

Another alternative to the traditional card is a scroll. Seal it with wax, tie it with a bow, and place it in a small tube for mailing. A scrolled invitation can be perfect for a Renaissance-wedding theme.

Many brides like to use the invitations to make visual reference to their themes. Pressed flowers can adorn an invitation to a garden wedding, white confetti can be tucked into a winter wonderland-weekend wedding invitation, a heart-shaped reception card can be sent for a Valentine's Day marriage, or red, white, and blue borders put on a Fourth-of-July invite. For a Victorian wedding, consider using Old English wording and typeface.

# Making Your Own Invitations

If you are artistic, you may even wish to design your own wedding invitations. The easiest way to do this is on the computer with a program designed for that purpose, but there are many other hands-on approaches. Is calligraphy a specialty of yours? Depending on the size of your guest list, you might want to create personalized wedding invitations. (Just be sure you have the time to make it through the entire guest list. It would be a shame to give up halfway through!)

Alternatively, you can create your own invitation and take it to a professional stationer to be printed. This would allow you, for example, to add a pen-and-ink drawing or watercolor to your design. Or what about hand-applying pressed flowers to invitations to an outdoor wedding? There so many options to consider.

Photos can be used to great effect. Think about affixing a photo of the bride and groom or the church where they will marry on the front of the card. A photo lab can easily create a wedding photo card for you.

Use your imagination. A silhouette (cutout) of the bride and groom can be an elegant, if untraditional, addition. A caricature of the couple can set the stage for a ceremony with a sense of humor. A cartoon-strip version of the courtship or wedding can tickle the funny bone. If you have young children from a previous marriage, you might even want to ask them to make a drawing for your wedding invitations.

Invitations can be whimsical and playful—printed on a balloon or on the back of a puzzle photo of the bride and groom. For a very small wedding, door-to-door singing telegrams can announce the date and time. Printed or handwritten invitations can be hand delivered.

There are thousands of options out there. It's up to you to find the one that best reflects your style.

---

### The Least You Need to Know

➤ Have invitations made three to six months in advance of the wedding. Send them at least one month in advance of the date. Give guests two months' notice if you are planning a long weekend or holiday event.

➤ Include response cards if you think your guests might need some encouragement to respond.

➤ Find ways to let your wedding invitation give guests a taste of what is to come.

➤ Choose wording that reflects who you are as a couple, as well as the style of your day.

➤ For a unique invitation, feel free to play with the color, size, paper, or method of delivery.

---

# Part 2
# Get Creative

*There are so many different types of weddings these days. How can a couple choose?*

*Part 2 presents some of the more popular creative wedding ideas in detail. There's the weekend wedding, which involves a few days of festivities surrounding the wedding. For those thinking of running off to get married, consider this: Take close friends and family with you and make it a destination wedding! For couples whose families are far flung, Part 2 also covers the two-for-the-road wedding which travels to its guests.*

*For couples who need to be budget wise, this section also has tons of ideas on how to host a low-cost party that's still fabulous.*

# Chapter 5

# The Weekend Wedding

---

**In This Chapter**

➤ Choosing a site for your weekend wedding

➤ Helping your family understand your weekend

➤ Planning for perfection

➤ Getting the word out

➤ Making sure there's room at the inn

➤ Picking your parties

➤ Dressing for success

---

Is your wedding the social event of the decade? Well, it is as far as you and your groom are concerned, but you may not be the only ones who think so! Are some of your friends and family planning to put their lives on "pause" and travel long distances to celebrate with you? Why not take advantage of their presence and treat them to a whole weekend of wedding fun? Long-weekend weddings are increasingly popular these days because they allow more time to savor the moment, for guests to get to know one another, and for the bride and groom to visit with long-time (but not often seen) friends and relatives.

## Why Have a Weekend Wedding?

Nowadays, marrying the boy next door is more the exception than the rule. Gone are the days of the small-town wedding where the guests are all residents of the place you grew up. Women from LA are marrying men from NYC, and the guests are coming from all over the country—if not the world!

Part reunion, part party, and all wedding, the long weekend promises two to three days of fabulous festivities. From a cozy brunch for 20 in the home of a friend to a full-blown backyard barbecue for 100, from tennis matches to scavenger hunts to pool parties, the long weekend provides many delightful opportunities to meet, greet, compete, and eat. Guests feel welcome and wanted at this extended celebration.

### Something True

Long-weekend weddings were a regular part of life in ancient Greece and Rome. Medieval marriages also went on for days, complete with feasting and jousting. Then, as now, friends often had to travel hundreds of miles to get to the wedding. (At least we don't have to make it there on horseback!) In colonial times guests might come for a fortnight or two, hunting, fishing, and partying with the group before heading home.

The message is clearly one of inclusion. The bridal couple is saying, "We want you to be part of our celebration and our lives." Perhaps just as important, the couple is asking that both sides of the family spend some time getting to know one another, uniting themselves into one big happy family that will be better able to support the bride and groom in the coming years of marriage. For couples who want to be married in a remote setting with all their loved ones in attendance, the long weekend is often the only way to go. Once everyone makes it to the top of the mountain or the chapel nestled deep in the woods, they're going to want to stay awhile.

For the couple, the long weekend offers the chance to relax and really have a good time. Too often the wedding ceremony and reception can go by in a blur. After nine to twelve months of planning, five or six short hours of revelry may not seem like very much. A long weekend wedding may take more time to plan, not to mention the help of friends and neighbors, but in the end the time together is worth it.

## Choosing the Site for Your Weekend Wedding

Most weekend weddings take place in the bride or groom's home town, or in the city or town where the bride and groom currently reside. For a bride who grew up and moved away, a hometown wedding can be a chance to remember roots and revel in happy memories. Some couples return to the college campus where they met, or to the bride's summer home. What place holds special meaning for you?

You probably want to choose a place that will be easily accessible to most of your guests. (Proximity to a major airport helps.) Some couples, however, do opt for remote locations requiring hiking or boating to get there. Be sure you have taken the physical requirements of all your guests into consideration before deciding on this particular option.

In Chapter 6, we'll explore another route, taking your guests away with you to a vacation location.

# Coordinating the Comings and Goings

As soon as you decide on the long-weekend wedding, get the word out to all the invitees with a quick Save-The-Date postcard. Your guests will need plenty of time to plan for their arrival and departure. Broadcast the dates, especially if the weekend you have in mind is a popular one.

Next, send some flight information. It can be helpful for people to know the name of the airport nearest your home, as well as which airlines fly there. Sample airfares may be particularly helpful for young professionals who are trying to budget. Train and bus schedules can also be mailed to guests who live within a reasonable distance of the long-weekend wedding site. Also send some preliminary hotel information including a variety of rates.

Some airlines offer special rates for wedding groups. Call around and see what programs are available. American Airlines, for example, has a wedding program. Call 800-548-8193 or go to their Web site at **www.aafirstcall.com**. They will give you a special reservation code which your guests can use when making reservations to receive 5 to 10 percent off airfares. If 10 or more guests book this way, the bride and groom can earn benefits or upgrades.

As guests make plans, they'll need to let you know all their arrival and departure times. Consider starting a Guest Travel Log to help you keep track. It's important for you to know whether cousin Sydney needs a place to stay on Friday or Saturday, or whether your old college chum will still be in town for brunch on Sunday.

**Consultants Say**

Consider starting a guest travel log to help you keep track of guests' arrival and departure times. Write down the names of all out-of-town guests. Leave space beside each name for arrival date, arrival time, and mode of transportation (example: American Airlines, flight 763), as well as departure date and departure time. Note whether they will be arranging for their own transportation to the hotel. If you're providing any kind of shuttle service, note whether they would like a ride.

# Family Concerns

When you and your fiancé first suggest a long-weekend wedding, your family may be worried. Among other things, they may wonder:

➤ Who will have the time to do all the planning?

➤ Will it be too expensive?

➤ Isn't three days a little too much?

Here are some possible answers:

➤ We'll do a lot of it, but we need your help...and we need to be super-organized! (A travel agent and bridal consultant can take some of the burden off your shoulders as well.)

➤ In reality, a long-weekend wedding may not cost too much more than a traditional one-day event. Guests pay for their own travel and lodgings. (Guests who have trouble with the expense might be hosted at the homes of friends and relatives in the area.) Neighbors and others typically pitch in and help out by throwing parties in your honor. The groom's parents might get involved as well (even if they're out-of-towners) by hosting a Friday night sock hop at a local restaurant you know about. Some of the events can cost next to nothing, such as a volleyball game on the beach, a communal run in the park, or a nature walk at the arboretum.

➤ With advance planning and plenty of nice events for guests to attend, two to three days should be just right. Let your parents know that the events calendar will include time to relax and rest. As an added incentive, you can remind parents how great it will be to have both families together for an extended time. There aren't many chances like this to get together with family and friends for a joyous occasion. When was the last time your dad had time to play golf with his brother from Arizona? How often does mom get to sit down and have a heart-to-heart with Aunt Bridget from Ireland?

**Bridal Blunders**

Hosting a wedding over a popular vacation weekend such as the Fourth of July can mean crowded flights and booked hotel rooms. Be sure you're on top of this situation by making all arrangements as early as possible, including blocking off a group of hotel rooms even before you know who's coming.

## The Quest for Guests

Who should be invited to a long-weekend celebration? It really depends on how many people you want at your ceremony and reception, and how many you realistically think you can handle at surrounding events. You'll probably have the same guest list that you would have had at a one-day celebration. The difference is that your most distant guests may be more likely to come knowing that they will be feted and cared for over the period of a few days. They may even decide to combine the event with a small vacation to surrounding areas. A long-weekend wedding may actually help to balance family attendance at the wedding, so that neither side is over-represented.

As you would do for any type wedding, you'll need to think long and hard about budget and location before you begin inviting anyone. How many guests can you realistically accommodate? How many will your reception site hold? Ask both sides of the family to come up with lists so you can see how many names you have to work with. Then cut down or add to it as needed.

## Welcome to "Planning Central"

In order to get a whole weekend of events off the ground, you'll need to be fairly organized. That means notebooks, file folders, computer files—whatever system works best for you. Set aside one day a week when you will spend an hour or two concentrating on pulling this weekend together. This is the time to work on a newsletter, touch base with a neighbor who has offered her home for a party, and call hotels to block off rooms at a favorable rate.

Think of planning the wedding the way you might plan a meal, only on a larger scale. The roast may take hours, but the salad doesn't have to be tossed until the last minute. In the same way you can lay out a timetable that breaks your many jobs into manageable chunks.

Step one, for example, is choosing the ceremony and reception site and reserving your dates—preferably at least a year in advance. Don't be surprised to learn that your first choice of site is already booked on Memorial Day weekend. Be ready with ideas for alternative dates or locations.

As soon as you've got the date and place nailed down, alert as many people as possible—especially key figures like bridesmaids and groomsmen—that they should hold the date.

**Bridal Blunders**

Wait! Before you get any further, call the chamber of commerce nearest your wedding site to make sure your date doesn't conflict with a major civic event. You don't want to find out at the last minute that a parade is going to block various entrances and exits to your wedding site, or that a huge convention of out-of-town insurance salesmen is going to make you and your guests feel crowded out and lost in a sea of blue suits.

## Countdown

Once the main event is scheduled, you can relax a little...but not for too long. It's time to start thinking about the activities and parties surrounding the wedding ceremony. Begin by outlining some of the festivities you hope to have, keeping in mind the ages and interests of those who will be attending. Do you live in an area where outdoor activities would be easy to arrange? Or is the wedding taking place in a season or city more conducive to indoor activities? Think in terms of lunches, afternoon activities, dinners, and late-night parties. What will work best for your crowd? If someone has offered to host a party, it's up to him to get it off the ground. If you are arranging an activity yourself, however, you may have to start looking for and reserving the site soon after you book the reception site.

About five months before the wedding weekend, consider sending out a newsletter to keep folks up-to-date on plans in the making. Two months before the wedding you might want to send another, along with the formal invitation. (Invitations to a long-weekend wedding need to go out earlier than a traditional wedding, since guests need to finalize travel and lodging arrangements.)

Otherwise, much of your planning should be the same as for a traditional wedding. Feel free to use the kinds of time charts and organizational lists found in almost any bridal magazine or book.

## The Fine Art of Delegating

Planning is easier, of course, if you are efficient about the use of your time. A large staff doesn't hurt, but unfortunately few brides have that luxury. What most brides do have are lots of friends and relatives who are probably eager to help make this the best weekend ever.

A number of the events you are dreaming of may be dependent upon the kindness of others. Will your neighbor let guests swim at her pool one afternoon? Would Aunt Cecily's oldest daughter mind babysitting for a few young ones during the wedding rehearsal? Call and let your closest friends, relatives, and neighbors know about the weekend you're planning. Tell them about some of the events you are working on: a volleyball game on the beach, a breakfast buffet at your house. Explain that you are trying to fill the weekend with low-key activities for the wedding party and guests. Someone will be sure to offer her services.

Whatever help is being offered, say yes! You'll need it. One or two talented entertainers might even offer to throw a party in your honor. A breakfast, lunch, or afternoon tea at someone's home would be truly appreciated.

**Consultants Say**

Whenever you can, ask someone else to do it for you—whether it's picking up the invitations from the printer or checking out bridesmaid's shoes at a store. Always thank everyone profusely for their help. Make a phone call, send a card, or stop by with a bunch of flowers. Give small gifts to those who are hosting parties or who are putting people up in their homes.

Sometimes a close relative or future in-law who doesn't live in the area will offer instead to foot the bill at a restaurant or bar. Be prepared with the names and phone numbers of a couple of establishments you think would work particularly well, in case you are asked. Try to give the prospective host an idea of what such a party might cost in each place; then let that person make a decision that fits in most comfortably with his or her own budget and style, while still respecting your likes and dislikes.

Just because someone can't host a big party doesn't mean he can't be a major help to you. A friend with a large van might be called upon to pick people up at the airport. A neighbor with a few extra bedrooms might be willing to host a wedding guest or two. Someone else might put himself or herself in charge of finding contributors for a potluck picnic. A high-school friend might be willing to lend her superior organizational skills by keeping track of all the comings and goings of guests. Remember: *You will drive yourself insane if you try to do it all.*

## Scheduling Times for All the Weekend's Events

Write down events and their times as they fall into place. You are basically in charge of the ceremony and the reception. Let those who have offered to host other events be in charge of running them. Remember that you are an honored guest at these parties; you do not run them. It *is* up to you, however, to coordinate all the events—to keep guests informed and in touch with the hosts so the hosts know how many people are coming and you know what type of event they are hosting. A three-day weekend may start to look something like this:

**Friday 3 p.m.:** The first guests begin to arrive. Larry will make two trips to the airport with his van to pick up 14 guests. Others will arrive by taxi, train, bus. Welcome and buffet-style snacks at the bride's house between 3 p.m. and 6 p.m. On tap: coffee, soda, and juice. For the hungry: quartered sandwiches, cheese wheels, crackers, cookies, cut fresh veggies, fruit.

**Friday 6 p.m.:** Rehearsal at the church.

**Friday 7–10 p.m.:** Rehearsal dinner for the wedding party and out-of-town guests at Ye Old Tavern.

**Sat 9–11 a.m.:** Sit-down breakfast at Aunt Millie's in her garden.

**Sat 4 p.m.:** Wedding Ceremony at Our Lady Church.

**Sat 5–10 p.m.:** Reception at The Fine Arts Mansion.

**Sun 8–10 a.m.:** Breakfast buffet at The Hilton, where most of the guests are staying. Croissants, muffins, fruit, juice, jams, coffee.

**Sun 1 p.m.:** Pool party and badminton at Marilyn's house. She's serving an informal luncheon of cold salads.

**Sun 5 p.m.:** Soccer game on Blakely Field. Teams will be divided based on birthdays: Odd numbers are on the groom's team; even numbers line up on the bride's side.

**Sun 8 p.m.–midnight:** Barbecue and live music at Rusty's, hosted by the groom's parents.

**Monday 7–10 a.m.:** Breakfast buffet at the bride's house as people depart and return home.

# Parties, Parties, and More Parties

A long weekend offers you plenty of opportunities for creative get-togethers. Think of activities that will appeal to all ages and sexes. Later you can narrow down the list based on the availability of hosts and sites. Certainly you'll need to take a number of variables into consideration: the season, the location, the ages and abilities of your guests, and so forth. Offers to host specific parties will also play a big role in what you're able to fit into your weekend.

**Bridal Blunders**

No matter how many parties get scheduled for the weekend, you and your groom should plan to attend them all. Your presence is expected. While you don't have to stay to the bitter end of any, it is your responsibility as either honored guest or host and hostess to come and greet everyone who has come to celebrate with you.

Here are some party ideas you might want to consider:

➤ A clambake at the beach or a friend's house

➤ A barbecue

➤ A bowling game

➤ A tennis match

➤ A golf outing

➤ A nature hike

➤ An ice cream sundae party

➤ A pool party

➤ Line dancing

➤ A fifties sock hop

➤ A karaoke bar

➤ A piano bar

➤ An afternoon tea at a private home or cozy country inn

➤ A museum excursion

➤ Beach volleyball

➤ Lawn games (bocce ball, archery, croquet, horseshoes)

➤ A soccer game (bride's team versus groom's team)

➤ A minimarathon (the winner gets to kiss the bride)

➤ A scavenger hunt (include clues that relate to the wedding or to the bride and groom)

➤ Carnival games (dunking booth with the groom's or bride's father as dunkee)

➤ A trivia game (each group of four guests makes a team—include questions about the bride and groom)

➤ Home videos of the bride and groom growing up

➤ A slide show of the bride and groom growing up

➤ A film festival (be sure to have appropriate titles on hand such as *Bride of Franken-stein, Father of the Bride, The Wedding Singer, Four Weddings and a Funeral, Philadel-phia Story, My Best Friend's Wedding*)

➤ A sightseeing tour (by boat or bus)

➤ A party at which guests are entertained by a palm reader, magician, or astrologist

➤ A country fair (hopefully it will have a Ferris wheel, cotton candy and all the trappings)

➤ A trip to an aquarium, outdoor museum, or other area attraction

➤ A spa afternoon for the women in the bridal party (complete with manicures, pedicures, hot tubs)—be sure to contact the spa in advance for reservations

➤ Disco, ballroom, or swing dancing

➤ Caroling (at Christmas time), ending up at your house for hot cocoa

➤ A hay ride (or sleigh ride, depending on season)

➤ An ice skating party

➤ A pops concert

➤ A sing-a-long (just hire the piano player)

➤ A skits night (teams take on topics of your choice—they can relate to the bride and groom, or the weekend festivities)

➤ A casino night (set up your very own casino with poker tables, backgammon, 21, bingo)

➤ A square dance (hire a band and a caller)

➤ Entertainment by a barbershop quartet

➤ A Caribbean-themed dance party on the beach complete with steel-drum band

➤ A Mexican-themed backyard buffet complete with strung lights and a mariachi band

➤ Helicopter tours

➤ Boat trips

➤ Old-fashioned steam train rides

➤ A gondola ride to the top of a mountain to see the sights

➤ Cross country skiing or snowshoeing (complete with winter picnic packs on every back)

### Creative Corner

Little remembrances can be given out to guests attending satellite parties. JoAnn Gregoli of Elegant Occasions says she knows of couples who have had fanny packs made up with the bride and groom's names and wedding date on them. Guests off on day hikes immediately recognize one another as members of the same wedding party. Likewise, golf balls can be printed with wedding information for a golf outing. Plastic beach buckets can be painted with the same. Or bandanas can be given out at a square dance, or goggles at a pool party (write the wedding date on the strap!).

➤ A biking trip to see the sunset (have someone drive to the appointed spot with "mocktails" for the bikers)

➤ A backgammon tournament

When planning parties over a weekend, be sensitive to the needs of your guests. "Know your guests' demographics!" warns consultant JoAnn Gregoli. "Take their likes and dislikes into consideration—not just your own."

**Bridal Blunders**

Beware the overcrowded, over-planned weekend. Don't forget to build in a little down time—a few hours when guests can go back to their rooms and take naps, for example. Variety is also important, since not all events will appeal to everyone. It's important to make Great Aunt Edith as happy to be celebrating with you as your younger college-aged cousins.

**Something True**

According to *The Top Ten of Everything 1998* by Russell Ash (DK Publishing, 1977), the average American reads through about 105 pounds of newsprint. Your newsletter should add only another ounce or so to that load!

# The Weekend Wedding Newsletter

Reunion excitement is in the air. There's a whole smorgasbord of events for guests to choose from. Why not keep everyone posted with a wedding newsletter or Web site? JoAnn Gregoli of Elegant Occasions in New Jersey says the newsletter is a popular method of communicating with weekend guests. "The newsletter might list happenings, tell how the bride and groom met, or highlight people important to their lives. When guests arrive, they've already read about each other in the newsletter, and there's an 'Oh, you're so-and-so' feeling."

Another function of the newsletter is to provide guests with information and advance notice on the various events. Including the results of your hotel and airfare research is particularly helpful. Include a tentative weekend schedule so guests can plan when to arrive and depart, and note any packing suggestions they might not have thought of. If you are offering cross-country skiing, horseback riding, nature hikes or swimming, your guests will want to be prepared with ski hats, riding boots and jeans, hiking boots, swim suits, and so on. Don't leave a guest kicking himself or herself for not having brought along that pair of jeans or second cocktail dress. The wedding newsletter is a good place to alert guests to the dress code.

Will Saturday night's party be a jacket and tie affair? Say so in the newsletter. Also note any extra costs, such as museum admission fees. If a particular party will be closed to everyone but the bridal party, state this clearly and, if possible, offer others an alternative. (Something as low-key as a chess or checkers match on the front porch of the lodge where many of the guests are staying is fine.)

## Let 'em Know, Let 'em Know, Let 'em Know

Whether by Web, wire, or snail mail, the point is to keep your guests fully informed—and to build a little excitement while you're at it. A typical newsletter might include:

➤ A choice of hotels in the area (with descriptions and rates)

➤ A deadline for telling you their arrival and departure plans

➤ Bulletins on low fares between major cities and your weekend wedding location

➤ A list of the weekend's events

➤ A poll to gauge guest's preferences about something

➤ A "wedding guest spotlight" on a particular person, such as your 90-year-old great-great aunt who says she *will* be attending; perhaps you could reprint the note she sent you about your upcoming wedding, or include a little information on what she's doing now: "still driving, still baking cakes," for example

Your newsletter might end up looking something like this:

---

### THE WEDDING BELLS CHRONICLE

Edited by your very own bride and groom, Cindy and Ted

Hi, everybody! Some of you may still be reeling from the news, but we want to get you back on your feet and thinking about being here with us on the big weekend. Mark your calendars for April 1–3. Yes, we know it's April Fool's Day…but no, we're not kidding! We're really getting married, but we don't want to do it without you, so start making your travel arrangements! Read this newsletter to find out what fun things are going to happen that weekend!

**Friday Night Flyers**

Are you planning to fly into National Airport on Friday night? You're not alone. Lots of our guests will be there, and we're hoping to provide transportation for as many of you as possible. Please call Sandy at 000-111-1234 as soon as your know your flight numbers and times.

**Fairer Fares**

My Uncle Bob assures me that Airline ABC currently has some of the best fares for the Chicago-Washington route ($99 round trip). Call the airline directly or contact our wedding travel agent Cindy Smarts at 000-555-7223. She knows of an interesting one-way train, fly-back fare—not for everyone…but it might work for you.

**Poll**

Okay, everyone, now is the time to make your wishes known. On Sunday, are more people interested in:

a) A soccer game

b) A tennis round robin

E-mail Bob "Mr. Athletic" Schwartz at bschwartz@xyz.net

*continues*

---

*continued*

**Best Dressed**

Don't forget to pack:

➤ Sneakers and shorts or warm ups

➤ Bathing suit

➤ Hiking boots and jeans

➤ Hats (Optional: But what's a garden party without them?)

➤ Sunscreen

**Who Can Identify This Photo?**

Hint: Cindy and Ted met here.

Hint: The ceremony will take place nearby.

Answer: We'll print it in the next issue of the *Wedding Bells Chronicle*

**A Place to Lay Your Head**

There are two hotels in the area that we are recommending for the weekend:

The Lancshire Arms, 800-111-0000. ($99 a night, one block from reception site)

The Milton, 888-000-0000 ($150 a night, this is the reception site)

Please make your hotel reservations by March 1. Be sure to tell them you're with Cindy and Ted's wedding.

Anyone who would like to ask for a free bed in the home of one of our many very generous neighbors should call me directly at 202-555-0000. I am setting up as many people as I can.

See you in April!

# High-Tech, Low-Tech

For the technologically minded, a wedding Web site is a great way to make information available to your guests at all times—provided they're plugged into the Internet. Some brides and grooms are old hands at creating web sites; others will need some help getting started. Try **www.angelfire.com** or another home page provider to find out how to set one up.

What you include on your site is up to you. Anything suitable for a newsletter is also suitable for a Web site. You can even have some extra fun and post photos—of the church, the reception site, or the bridal party. If all of this is too high-tech for you, you can still take advantage of computer technology by writing a newsletter and then e-mailing it to guests. Suggest that everyone who has questions or would like to confirm travel arrangements can meet you online in a chat room at 8 p.m. on Fridays.

Of course, you will need to make the same information available in printed form for the computer-illiterate. Today's computers make it easy to create an appealing-looking newsletter at home. This may be the time to invest in a decent desktop-publishing program, especially if you also plan to make your own invitations on the computer. Or go the low-tech route with a handwritten photocopied newsletter you pop in the mail. Whatever gets the word out.

# Lodging Logistics

Long weekend guests need a place to stay, one that is comfortable for them and easy for you. It's a good idea to offer people the choice of a couple of hotels, especially if there are big differences in prices. Most guests, however, will probably appreciate being all together in the same location. It will make your job easier, as well, if most of your guests are coming from and returning to the same place. You'll probably be able to use the main hotel as a "wedding center" for some informal get-togethers (such as breakfast buffets), or as a reception center. Holding your reception in the hotel where most of your guests are staying makes everything that much easier for you and for them. As an added plus, you don't have to worry about any of your guests drinking and driving.

Call the local chamber of commerce for a list of hotels in the area, if you don't already know. It's a good idea to call and ask for brochures offering rates, services, and maps showing proximity to your wedding site. If at all possible, go to see the hotel in person or have someone you trust do it for you. Your guests are depending on your judgment.

Think about the amenities each hotel offers. Does it have 24-hour room service? This can be a real boon for late-arriving guests. Is there a pool or spa? Most guests these days look for some sort of exercise facility to help them keep up with their usual regimen while away. Are there large lobbies or good gathering spots where guests can meet and greet? Guests without cars will appreciate hotels that are within walking distance of the ceremony or reception site.

**Bridal Blunders**

Prices change depending on what the hotel considers its high season. You should be aware of these time blocks when arranging your date. Having your wedding a week earlier or later may make a big difference in how affordable your weekend will be for your guests.

Ask each hotel about renting a block of rooms for your guests and how that affects the price. Usually you can get a reduced rate for large groups of 10 or more. You can ask the hotel to hold a block of rooms for the wedding party. This is especially important at hotels that tend to fill up. You may be wise to start blocking off rooms as early as six to twelve months ahead of time, depending on the popularity of the area, the number of hotels, and the season. Let your guests know the date by which reservations must be made to hold the room. Guests should use the name of the bridal party when they call the hotel to make their reservations.

In the case of a small inn, you may end up taking over the whole establishment. This can provide an especially intimate setting and a real feeling of togetherness. Each guest has both privacy and the chance to commune with relatives and friends in the common rooms of the inn. The owners of the inn may be able to do some special favors for you, such as placing goodie bags into every guest room, or arranging for a late check out for everyone.

# Teen Talk

What about the teens on your list? Some of the events you're planning may be great for all ages; a square dance, for example, can be as fun for teens as adults. Other events, however, may not appeal to teens. If you have a sizable group of kids ages 12 to 17 years of age, you might want to make some special arrangements for them. The teens might like to get together by themselves for an afternoon nature hike, country fair, mall adventure, or whale-watching trip. If most of them don't know each other well, teaming them up for a scavenger hunt can work wonders at breaking the ice. Even something as simple as a video shown on a large-screen TV in a private room at the hotel, with plenty of popcorn, snacks, and sodas, lets teens know you're aware that one dinner spent seated next to Great Aunt Mary may be enough.

# Kids Korner

Long-weekend weddings often include families with small children, and you will want to find plenty of ways to keep the kids amused and content. Some of your events may be perfect for kids, without any extra work on your part—a beach or pool outing, for example, or lawn games.

If kids are invited to the ceremony, you'll have to count on their parents to keep them under control. Be prepared to face the occasional shout or cry with good humor and patience. Your day needn't be totally silent or uneventful to be perfect.

Kids who are coming to the reception deserve a little extra attention when it comes to place settings and menus. One bride and groom decorated a table at the reception specifically for the kids, with an oversized teddy bear sitting at each place. Other couples have had the band play songs from *The Lion King* and *Sesame Street* during the evening. Most importantly, make sure their culinary needs are attended to. Kids' meals should definitely be offered to those on whom salmon and filet mignon are going to be wasted. A good caterer should have some ideas for festive foods that kids will actually eat; just make sure the caterer knows how many children you expect.

If there will be events to which children are not invited, let guests know by designating them as "adults only" occasions in the newsletter. Provide a list of reputable babysitters or the name of an agency you trust, then leave it up to parents to make their own childcare arrangements.

# Welcome Wagons and Good-Will Ambassadors

For a long-weekend wedding, make your guests feel comfortable by going the extra mile for them. (After all, they've come the extra mile for you!) Show them how much you appreciate the effort they've made and how happy you are that they're here to share this special event with you.

As guests arrive by plane or train, it's nice to have someone there to meet them. A friend with a large van may be willing to serve as the welcome wagon for arriving guests, ferrying them from the airport to their hotels. If a number of guests are arriving on the same flight or at similar times, this van service can work especially well. A refreshing beverage can be kept in a cooler in the van, and each guest can be offered a little celebratory drink as they get in. Already they will feel pampered and well cared for, relaxed and ready for the festivities to begin.

Some couples even set up a "welcome center" where guests can check in, get coffee and light snacks, and pick up a folder or envelope full of weekend information. The folder should include maps, a schedule of events for the whole weekend, and local tour information in case guests wish to use their free time to explore the area's sights. Contact your local Visitor's Bureau or Chamber of Commerce for free brochures advertising local attractions. If possible, let guests know about such things as museum hours, bicycle rental locations, babysitter agencies, lists of movie theatres, and more. As an extra inviting touch, include a list of all invitees with information on where they are staying (hotel or friend's home) and their accompanying phone numbers. This way cousin Fred can find second cousin Ted.

### Creative Corner

As each long-weekend guest arrives, have a little fun with him or her. For example, you could ask her to fill out a quick survey about the bride and groom and drop it in a box. Ask funny questions like: "The bride and groom remind me most of (a) Laurel and Hardy, (b) Cupid and Persephone, (c) Fred Astaire and (d) Ginger Rogers, Beauty and the Beast." Or, ask: "Within a week of the wedding, who do you think is more likely to have control of the clicker? (a) Ann (b) Dennis (c) Charlie, their dog. Tally up the results and report on them during one of the informal weekend parties. They should be pretty funny!

Create welcome packages for each guest and ask the hotel if you can place them in the guests' rooms ahead of time. If this proves too complicated, ask that bags be kept at the front desk or at a welcome table to be given to each guest upon check-in. Use your imagination and sense of humor to stuff the bag with such things as:

- ➤ A comb
- ➤ A travel toothbrush
- ➤ A split of champagne with two plastic glasses
- ➤ A bag of peanuts
- ➤ Antacid tablets
- ➤ Aspirin

- ➤ An herbal tea packet
- ➤ Bubble bath
- ➤ Suntan lotion
- ➤ Chapstick
- ➤ A squirt gun
- ➤ Chocolates or fruit

➤ A bandana

➤ Breath mints

➤ Nail polish (in your wedding colors)

➤ A little plastic toy (for children)

➤ Soap bubbles and blower

# A Weekend Wardrobe

One last word on long-weekend weddings. Remember that you're taking center stage all weekend, not just at the wedding ceremony. Give some thought to what you will be wearing to the various parties. An ankle length cream-colored dress with straw hat for the garden party? A little black number with spaghetti straps for the late-night dance party? Walk yourself through each event in your mind and plan your outfit right down to your shoes. With all the excitement and high emotions of the weekend, the last thing you'll want to be doing is standing in front of your closet moaning that you have nothing to wear.

Plan your hairstyles as well. Will you be at a pool party prior to the rehearsal dinner? Then allow for a little extra time to put yourself back in order, or schedule an extra trip to the hair salon. Some stylists will come to you, making your life that much easier— but find out what it will cost you before you count on this kind of royal treatment! Many brides like to play with a few different styles over a long weekend of events— loose and curly at a sock hop, a tidy twist at Aunt Hilda's breakfast buffet, an elegant blown-dry look for the ceremony.

---

### The Least You Need to Know

➤ Plan a date well in advance and tell guests what it is as soon as possible.

➤ Arrange the ceremony and reception first, then think about accompanying events.

➤ Enlist the help of friends, relatives, and neighbors for your many and varied weekend activities. Learn to say yes!

➤ Find a pleasant, convenient, and reasonably priced hotel nearby. If possible, arrange for some of your guests to stay in the homes of friends and neighbors.

➤ Be sure guests feel welcome and wanted and that all ages and abilities are taken into consideration when you plan events.

---

# Chapter 6

# And Away We Go!

---

**In This Chapter**

➤ Locating your dream destination

➤ Using a travel agent

➤ Planning long distance

➤ Finding the right lodging

➤ Incorporating local customs

➤ Carving out some private time amidst the crowd

---

The destination wedding, or honeymoon wedding, takes place at a typical honeymoon spot such as Disneyland, the Bahamas, or Jamaica. The idea is a simple one. Instead of going off alone to some romantic spot after the wedding, the wedding couple brings their guests with them and ties the knot right there. For some of the participants the festivities can last as long as a week.

The honeymoon wedding is a lot like the long-weekend wedding described in Chapter 5. The two main differences are the location and the length of time guests may choose to stay.

## Romance, Travel, Adventure!

With a honeymoon wedding (also called a destination wedding) you can marry in a thatched-roof chapel, cruise through a fern grotto on a riverboat, or meet atop a Colorado mountain. The world is your oyster. All the pleasures of a vacation in the paradise of your choice are combined with the beauty of a wedding ceremony and party. Your dream day takes place in your dream wedding setting—on a beach at sunset, alongside a waterfall, in a botanical garden, by a torch-lit lagoon, on a boat, or in a waterfront gazebo.

The key to the honeymoon wedding is choosing the right site—one that can accommodate both the ceremony and reception, and where you and your guests will be happy staying and playing for a few days. As with a long-weekend wedding, the benefit of the honeymoon wedding is that it enables you to spend more time with your friends and relatives who have traveled so far to be with you. It lets you savor your public commitment to one another over the course of a few days instead of a few hours. It enables far-flung families to have the reunion they may have dreamed of for years but never got off the ground.

With a honeymoon wedding, all your activities are conveniently close together. If you stay at a hotel boasting a pool, beach, shuffle board, gym, movies, manager's cocktail parties, free boat rental, and so on, all the activities you would need to plan might be built into the cost of the hotel. On-site staff will help turn your dreams into realities with a minimum of fuss: They're used to dealing with parties of this size.

Once you choose a location and figure out how to get everyone there, the honeymoon wedding can be anything you want it to be. It can be formal or informal, lavish or simple, large or small. Honeymoon weddings can be tailored to fit any bridal budget. Usually guests are responsible for their own travel and lodging expenses.

# Location, Location, Location

Are you a beach bum deep down? Hawaii awaits. A skier? Picture a wedding in a winter wonderland resort in Colorado. The history buff may gravitate to the colonial town of Williamsburg, Virginia. Or if European history is your game, putting everyone up in a parador (an inn) in Spain can be romantic perfection. This is the beauty of a honeymoon wedding. You get to spend time in a place that you love, doing things that you love, with the people you love.

Before you begin scouting locations, take your groom's travel temperature and see if it matches your own. Do you both crave sunny climes? Or are you polar bears at heart? Is weather more important than the historical or emotional significance of the destination? Assuming you can both agree on the same *kind* of destination (you are, hopefully, somewhat compatible if you're getting married), start doing a little research.

According to Doris Gedon, reservations manager at Vacation Home Rentals Worldwide, there are plenty of exotic sites to choose from. "Couples today are looking for places where they can do their own thing," she says. She mentions an eight-bedroom castle in Jamaica—big enough for you and some, if not all, of your guests. Then there is the beautiful villa in Treasure Cay with a private dock, which she found for a couple who wanted to be married on a dock. The bride and her mother gathered flowers from the grounds and decorated the dock with island flowers for the ceremony. "With 3,000 villa locations to choose from, Gedon says, she can always find something wonderful.

Before you contact a travel agent or villa rental agency, however, you may want to do a little research on your own. Narrow the search by finding general areas of interest. Go to your local library and search the travel section by region—"Caribbean,"

"Scandinavia," "Florida"—whatever appeals to you. Flip through a few books that describe an area you're considering. Check out the pictures, the travel notes, and the descriptions of some of the resorts.

*Have a storybook wedding at a castle of your dreams.* ©Lyn Hughes/flowers by Belle Fleur, NYC

While you're there, read a few travel magazines. They often contain the most up-to-date information, along with great pictures that can help you decide if this is the place for you. Buy a few recent issues on the newsstand and pour over them with your fiancé. Even if you don't end up actually booking that destination, you will have done a little fun armchair traveling together.

Is there a specific spot you have both been to and would like to visit again? Perhaps there is a destination that has special meaning for one or both of you. The site of your first vacation together as a couple, for example, can be a very romantic choice for a wedding site. The city where a favorite movie was shot or a favorite book was set might be a playful but meaningful pick. Going to the same resort where your parents had their own honeymoon 35 years earlier can make an especially sweet and touching wedding site.

Depending on your taste, you may end up choosing an out-of-the-way spot others often overlook; or you may end up traveling a more familiar path to a popular honeymoon destination. If you want to find out if you're going with the flow or bucking the trend, check out this list of the Top Ten favorite destination wedding spots (according to *Modern Bride,* December, 1998):

1. Jamaica
2. Hawaii
3. Las Vegas
4. Mexico
5. U.S. Virgin Islands
6. Florida
7. Bahamas
8. Italy
9. Bermuda
10. St. Lucia

**Consultants Say**

Here are a few phone numbers for some popular honeymoon wedding destinations. These numbers can get you on your way to a fabulous wedding away:

Disney World, 800-370-6009
Hawaii Tourist Network, 800-599-9902
Las Vegas Visitor's Information, 702-892-7575
Poconos, 800-762-6667
Caribbean, 800-356-9999

You can find more by reading travel books, contacting agents or calling information.

**Something True**

According to *Modern Bride* magazine, 55 percent of couples who get married in Hawaii are actually from out of state!

# Dealing with a Tourist Board

As you begin to narrow down your search, you should contact the tourist board or local chamber of commerce in the city you are considering. Ask questions, explore concerns. A good tourist board should be able to field questions such as: What's the hotel situation like in New Orleans during the big jazz festival? What are some other attractions in Nashville, Tennessee, besides Opryland? Ask for brochures and resort or hotel information. Many cities can also send you a "What's going on in the month of…" news release informing you about any conventions, festivals, and celebrations you might want to either avoid or embrace. Ask, too, about average temperatures and rainfall for the time of year you're planning your visit. You don't want to find out that your beautiful outdoor event has a dark cloud hanging over it, or that hurricanes are common occurrences at that time of year (and we don't mean the tropical drink).

Once you begin to think seriously about a particular location, your next step is to find out if any of the resorts or hotels there are really set up to handle large groups, a wedding ceremony, reception, and surrounding parties. Some will naturally be better equipped than others. Depending on how much work you want to do, and whether you think you'll be able on your own to find a florist in Fiji or a DJ in Dallas, you might want to concentrate on finding a hotel that handles lots of wedding parties. If the hotel staff is capable and experienced, you'll be able to relax a little and leave some of the running around to them. You can get names of resorts from a tourist board, but then you'll have to explore each one to determine what's best for your group. Ask each resort you contact what kind of wedding services they offer.

### Creative Corner

Better think carefully about where you go to tie the knot. Some states have some pretty strange regulations. Check out these, from *Loony Laws and Silly Statutes* by Sheryl Lindsell-Roberts (Sterling, 1994):

➤ In Kentucky, it's against the law for a woman to remarry the same man four times.

➤ In Delaware, if you marry on a dare, you can have it annulled later.

➤ In Halethorpe, Maryland, it's against the law for a kiss to last longer than a second.

➤ In Chillicothe, Missouri, it's against the law to throw rice at a wedding.

# Using a Travel Agent

For many couples planning a destination wedding, the travel agent offers the surest route to success with the least amount of headache. "A travel agent can search and get you the best value for your money. A couple might be thinking of only one resort but the travel agent can say, 'Just up the block there's another place with better rates [or different rooms]'. Without an agent, people often don't know the questions to ask," says Audrey Goldstein of Shenandoah Travel in Ft. Lauderdale, Florida.

Although any travel agent should be able to help you plan a honeymoon wedding, some advertise this as a particular area of expertise. Ask around and see if anyone knows a really good travel agent. Has your future mother-in-law used the same agent for the last 10 years? Do you know another couple who arranged a similar wedding weekend? Ask if they were happy with their agent.

When you contact a travel agent, tell him or her what you have in mind. It helps to know the destination you want, but a good agent can help guide you to the right spot by asking you a few questions about your preferences. Perhaps you've decided you want your ceremony held on a beach, followed by a reception on a boat. After the party, perhaps you want to sail away with your new husband and leave the others to continue the party on dry land, enjoying their vacation for the next few days.

*Find your heart in San Francisco.*
©Joshua Ets-Hokin

Does the agent seem to understand your vision? Is she willing to work hard to find what you want, even if it doesn't come in a tidy package? Has she been to the location or the resort herself? (This is helpful, but not necessary.) Has she handled wedding parties this size before? Will she be able to help you with some of the local customs or laws regarding marriage at that site? Does she know how you can find an officiant there to perform your ceremony? Most good travel agents can help with all these aspects of planning a destination wedding.

### Consultants Say

If you are traveling through time zones, you may wish to arrive a day or two before your guests. You'll have time to recover from jet lag—and you'll look a lot fresher at your wedding!

## Have Guest, Will Travel

As you draw up your guest list, think about who you really want to have with you on your big day. Think, too, about which of your family members and friends can feasibly attend. Given the distance, time involvement, and expense, honeymoon weddings often have a much smaller guest list than traditional hometown weddings. According to Audrey Goldstein of Shenandoah Travel, 15 guests are about average for a honeymoon wedding. But some couples decide to have it both ways: They celebrate their marriage at their honeymoon destination with an intimate circle of family and friends, then return home to throw a larger reception for friends close to home. This can be done weeks or even months after the actual wedding ceremony has taken place.

## Please Join Us at the South Pole...

Before you make too many plans, think about whether your special loved ones will be able to join you at the destination you're considering. Will grandma really be willing to get on a tiny plane for the short hop between Puerto Rico and Tortola? Will your sister be able to get a direct flight to Arizona from London where she works? Can your best friend, the one who wants to be a playwright, afford to join you?

If you do have some concerns about the guest list, don't despair. With a little creative thinking and some compromise, you should be able to make your honeymoon-wedding idea work for everyone. Perhaps Florida would be more convenient for your grandparents than the Caribbean. A simple change of location—while adhering to the same general theme—could mean the difference between a doable event and disaster.

Think about where most of your guests are coming from. A destination on the East Coast, for example, may beat out the one you had originally considered on the West Coast if you have a lot of guests flying in from Europe.

**Bridal Blunders**

Do you, your groom, or any one of your guests have a disability? If so, ask your travel agent to help you identify hotels and wedding sites that are accessible to all. There are travel agents who specialize in making travel arrangements for people with disabilities.

## Can They Get There from Here?

For the good friends or close relatives who have trouble affording the trip, consider a few options. You could choose a site that is accessible by car or train rather than by plane. A resort in the Pocono Mountains in Pennsylvania, for example, might be only a couple of hours away for your East Coast guests, yet a world away from the city lives you lead. Guests could even drive to the Poconos together to defray the costs of car rentals, gas, and tolls. Acres of beautiful trails, cross-country skiing, ice skating, and great rooms with roaring fires might provide the perfect late-autumn fest for your family without any of the high fares associated with flying. You can also offer the option of doubling or even tripling up with other singles in one room to minimize expenses. Reduce costs further by choosing an "off season" date for your visit and finding a hotel where guests get a lot of bang for their bucks (more amenities).

As with the long-weekend wedding, once you and the groom know your plans and have a guest list, get the word out as early as possible. People need plenty of advance notice for a wedding that may take them out of state or even the country for a period of days. Give as much advance notice as possible about:

➤ The kinds of travel papers they will need (proof of citizenship, a passport or visa, for example)

➤ Plane or train fares

➤ Hotel rates

➤ Dates

This information will help guests determine whether or not they're going to be able to join you.

## Making It Legal

Be sure to check the local marriage license requirements. Each state is going to have slightly different laws regarding the necessary paperwork and tests. You can search for your answer online, or phone the marriage license bureau in the city where you will be tying the knot.

If you're planning a wedding ceremony abroad, write for information from the American Embassy in that country well ahead of the date. (If foreign regulations are complicated or lengthy, you may choose to circumvent any difficulties by officially marrying in the U.S., right in your own home town. This takes care of the legalities—before you head off to your site for a more festive ceremony.) You might have a few special guests at this event. Whatever you choose to do, give yourself plenty of time to comply with all the rules and regulations. You may be asked to collect such items as passports, birth certificates, blood tests, proof of citizenship, and proof of death or divorce (in the case of a previous marriage).

To find an officiant at your honeymoon destination, talk with the hotel. They will have lists of synagogues and churches of many faiths in the area. You can contact them and take it from there. A wedding-friendly resort (one that handles lots of honeymoon weddings) can probably also give you the names of officiants for nondenominational services. They will surely be people who have married "out of towners" many times before. At the very least, a hotel should be able to give you the names of wedding consultants in the area who in turn could help you find an officiant for your ceremony.

**Bridal Blunders**

Some locations, such as Jamaica and the Bahamas, for example, require couples to be physically on the island a certain number of hours prior to the marriage. Make sure you are familiar with such restrictions when making your plans and that you have allowed yourself the right amount of time between touch-down and the "I do."

## What Your Family Will Be Most Worried About

When Mom and Dad hear that the wedding they've always dreamed of is not going to occur in the *place* they've always dreamed of (under a big white tent in the backyard), there may be a certain amount of grumbling, if not all-out conniption-fitting. If your dad is like a lot of dads, he'll be worrying about the expense—or maybe wondering why he has to uproot himself and leave the comfort of his den when the whole shebang could just come to him. Mom will be fretting about how she's ever going to help run a wedding that is taking place 2,000 miles from her front door.

If you and your groom are serious about doing this, be prepared to quell some fears. The more research you do beforehand, the easier that will be. You may actually know how much a couple of different resorts cost. You may have discovered a "package" deal at a place like Walt Disney World that includes the wedding ceremony and reception. Make it clear that you've thought through the practical difficulties as you explain some of the reasons behind your choice. ("We love the idea that this is where you two started out on your honeymoon!" or "Won't it be great to actually have a vacation at the same time you give your daughter away?")

Let them know how many guests you're hoping to have. Ask who they think would like to be included, making it clear that guests will be paying their own way. Encourage them to think how nice it will be to spend some time with close relatives while making new friends among your in-law's family.

If the reception for 200 is a dream they just can't part with, suggest that such a reception could still take place a few weeks or even months after the actual wedding. This is a common practice and can provide the bridal couple with the best of both worlds—a special, distant setting for the wedding ceremony and a big party in familiar territory where everyone can be included.

# Oh, Didn't We Mention...

Actually, your mom has a point. Planning from afar *can* have its pitfalls. A hotel gives a glowing description of a room for your reception but forgets to mention one thing: It has no windows. The resort you chose looked great in the brochures; too bad you didn't know about the major (and very noisy) construction going on next door. The hors d'oeuvres sound great—on paper, anyway. You like the tape a band sent you, but what does the group look like? Are they professional and presentable?

## *Don't Make Me Come Out There!*

If you can afford to, you might decide to make an advance trip to your destination, meet with a couple of consultants and an officiant, and make a few of the more important decisions on the spot. If this is not a possibility for you, don't worry—most couples do just fine without the extra trip. Again, those who are using a large resort with an experienced staff will have less to worry about than couples who are planning something a little out of the ordinary, or who are staying in a small inn or villa that's not really set up for wedding parties. For those in the second category, an advance trip may be especially helpful. (All others stay by those phones!)

If you are able to swing such a visit, this is your chance to measure fantasy against reality. Does everything look and feel as it was described over the phone and in brochures? Arrange to meet the hotel manager, the caterer, the florist, the officiant—whoever is playing an important role. One meeting can make the rest of the planning so much easier. Not only will you have achieved some small rapport with the hotel, you'll also have gotten a much better grasp of the space, logistics, and services available when you're discussing them over the phone back home. ("I love the way the pool looks at sunset. Can we set the buffet table up right under that big oak tree, overlooking the pool?")

## Get Help

A good bridal consultant in the destination city or town can act as your eyes and ears when you're far away. To find a bridal consultant in a distant city, consult the hotel or your travel agent, or try an online search using the keywords "wedding consultant" and the name of the city. You can get referrals from organizations such as the Association of Bridal Consultants in New Milford, Connecticut, or June Weddings, Inc. in Las Vegas, Nevada. (See the Appendix at the back of this book for phone numbers.)

Chances are you'll be doing all or most of your interviewing over the phone, so be ready with a list of questions. Ask the consultant what kinds of weddings she has worked on lately, and tell her a little about what you have in mind. Does she seem to understand your vision? Is she a good listener? How long has she been in business in that area? Can she give you a few names as references? (Be sure to actually use these numbers and call her clients.) Has she ever helped a bride long distance before? Will she be able to handle floral arrangements, music, photography, and food for you? Is there anything she won't handle? What can she do to make the whole planning process easier for you? Ask about the consultant's rates (hourly? flat fee? percentage?). She should send you a contract.

# Budget Basics

When it comes to managing your budget, the honeymoon wedding is no different from any other. You need to keep the larger picture in mind and have an idea of what the whole thing is going to cost before you get bogged down in the details of putting your wedding together.

Be prepared for the honeymoon wedding to throw a few curves into your budget, starting with long-distance phone bills and a possible advance trip (for yourself and possibly your fiancé or a parent). You may be able to keep costs down by using e-mail instead of the phone to correspond with hotel personnel, caterers, florists, consultants, and others, but plane fares are another matter.

Often couples arrange for a package, typically including the hotel room, wedding ceremony site, meals, and more. The all-inclusive resort helps couples get a handle on the costs and stick within a prescribed budget. Even if they don't offer such packages, many hotels today cater to the honeymoon-wedding crowd and can give you a pretty good idea of what you might end up spending.

Let's see how the costs might add up. Prepare a sheet something like the one below and fill in some numbers, based on your preliminary research.

## Honeymoon Wedding Budget Worksheet

| Item | Cost estimate |
|---|---|
| *Bridal consultant*<br>(You may decide this is worthwhile since you can't be at the site to oversee everything yourself.) | + _____ |
| *Phone bills* | + _____ |
| *Ceremony site*<br>(Sometimes a honeymoon location will offer a package deal in which there is little or no charge for the ceremony site. Of course, if you're tying the knot in a public park or on a beach, costs may be little or none, as well.) | + _____ |
| *Reception site* | + _____ |
| *Caterer* (resort's caterer or independent caterer)<br>Catering fee × number of guests | + _____ |
| *Bar Bill* (for reception) | + _____ |
| *Cake* | + _____ |
| *Two to three days of meals for guests*<br>(You may be offering to pay for some, all, or none.) | + _____ |
| *One advance trip for planning* (optional)<br>Air fare _____ + hotel _____ | + _____ |
| *Wedding trip for immediate family*<br>No. of people in<br>family ___ × air fare_____ = _____<br>No. of people in<br>family ___ × hotel_____ = _____ | |
| Total air fare + hotel expense | + _____ |
| *Car rental* (if desired) | + _____ |
| *Invitations, announcements, newsletters* | + _____ |
| *Wedding gown and shoes*<br>(May be simpler than for a traditional wedding, especially if you are marrying on the beach) | + _____ |
| *Photographer/Videographer* | + _____ |
| *Music* | + _____ |
| *Florist* | + _____ |
| Officiant's fee and marriage license | + _____ |
| ***Total Estimated Honeymoon Wedding Budget*** | = _____ |

Many of the larger resorts offer honeymoon and wedding packages. Find out what each resort is willing to include, and take this into account as you compare and contrast prices. Some, for example, offer limo pickup at the airport, champagne, the honeymoon suite, meals, and more, all tied into one tidy package.

# Lodging Logistics

Some couples book everyone (including themselves) at the same resort. This makes partying together so much easier. Others choose one hotel for themselves and a nearby hotel for the wedding guests. This allows both privacy and proximity.

Your lodging choice will likely be determined by your ceremony or reception's location. If the reception is going to be at a particular resort, you may want to stay there as well, with or without all your guests. If your reception site is not a hotel, then of course, you will have to look elsewhere, keeping in mind proximity to the site and ease of transportation. At a honeymoon wedding in France, for example, guests could be housed in a chateaux—a romantic choice.

### Bridal Blunders

Have the hotel put everything in writing, and make sure to confirm all reservations prior to arrival. Double check all the times for all your events, says Shenandoah Travel in Fort Lauderdale, Florida, and make sure the hotel hasn't mistakenly double booked someone else for the same pavilion, ballroom, or dining room.

Check with the hotel (either directly or through your travel agent) to see what kinds of rooms and services are available and what the rates are. Not everyone needs the deluxe ocean-front view. This is an area where your travel agent can be very helpful. "Room choice is very personal. The guest from Florida may not be as desperate for the ocean view," says Audrey Goldstein of Shenandoah Travel, Fort Lauderdale, Florida. A careful look at a map of the resort should help you to determine where rooms are located, and how far away they are from such central locations as the pool or dining room. Get specific. Find out as much as you can about the rooms: smoking or nonsmoking? number of beds and sizes? will kids fit?

Try to get a group rate when booking a number of rooms all at the same time. You aren't responsible for your wedding guests' expenses, but you do want to be conscious of how much they have to pay to be with you, and do what you can to keep those expenses down.

## Only as a Last Resort

A traditional resort or hotel is not for every couple. Perhaps you would prefer to rent a villa, complete with maid and chef and large enough to accommodate a dozen people. If your group is larger, you may have to rent a couple of villas near each other. This might be an economical way to go, as well as a family-friendly accommodation. There are many agencies that cater to people looking for villas. For example, you can find villas to rent in St. Barts and St. Marteen by calling WIMCO at 800-932-3222. You can also contact Villas of Hawaii at 808-735-9000. Try Vacation Home Rentals Worldwide at 800-633-3284. They represent villas in The Bahamas, Caribbean, Europe, Mexico, and more. Villas International at 800-221-2260 and Hideaways International at 800-843-4433 are two other places you could contact. You can easily find others by contacting the tourist board in the location that interests you. Many guidebooks now include villa rental information along with more traditional hotel listings.

For something a little more off the beaten path, you might want to think about a guest ranch, fishing lodge, camp site, or yacht charter. Check out a book of ranches. Contact a travel agent. Flip through a yachting magazine or call a charter company.

**Consultants Say**

Far away from home in a place where your curling iron won't work? Never fear! Ask your on-site bridal consultant or hotel liaison to arrange for someone to come and do your makeup and hair before the ceremony. That will be one less thing to worry about! If you're planning to do your own, make sure you know the voltage and have the proper converter or plug for your hairdryer.

## How Do I Get a 40-Pound Wedding Gown into a Carry-On Bag?

You're going to be married in Bali, but the gown of your dreams is sitting in Boston. What's a girl to do? Tell the bridal salon where you purchased the gown what your plans are, how far you're shipping the gown, and how you plan to get there (car, plane, boat, train). The bridal salon may be able to box and ship the gown for you. Just be aware that no matter how much tissue paper they use or how carefully they pack, it will arrive wrinkled. Give yourself time to have the gown pressed on site prior to the wedding.

To avoid any unfortunate surprises, most brides simply take their gowns with them. Checking it with the luggage can be risky (not to mention wrinkly). The best idea is to take the gown on board with you. Exclusives for the Bride in Chicago says they spend about two hours preparing each gown to hang on a hanger for the trip. Call the airline in advance and let them know that you will be traveling with a wedding gown and need a place to hang it. Most airlines are very accommodating and will put the gown in the first-class cabin, even though you may be flying coach!

**Consultants Say**

What are you packing? For travel-friendly items, check out the following mail-order catalogues: TravelSmith at 800-950-1600, Orvis Travel at 800-541-3541, or Magellan's at 800-962-4943.

Then again, some brides will buy or rent a dress to wear when they arrive. You may wish to go casual, or wear an island-style outfit in keeping with your locale.

# Incorporating Local Customs

Part of the fun of marrying in an exotic locale is drawing upon some local customs, traditions, music, or food to make your wedding even more memorable. Think about the many things you love about the place you chose. Is there a flower unique to this location? Use it in your bouquet or at the reception table settings. A special brand of music like reggae, steel drums, bluegrass, country or jazz? How do the locals dress? Perhaps you can incorporate some of this fashion into your wedding day attire. What is the food like? Is there something special that you and your fiancé love to eat when you travel there? Serve it up at the reception!

You could have a clambake or lobsterfest at a Maine wedding, or serve ribs (and plenty of napkins) at a Texas party. At a wedding in the South of France, serve specialties such as roasted pigeon with asparagus and foie gras. In the Caribbean or the Bahamas, why not put a little island flavor into your day with a seashell motif on your wedding cake? Opt for a luau at your reception in Hawaii, and be sure to have "The Hawaiian Wedding Song" played. Wear a maile lei, symbolizing long life and prosperity, or pikake, fragrant jasmine, which is a sign of love. Take a gondola ride in Venice. Dance to the beat of a steel drum band in Jamaica. Serve grilled fish on a stick on a Mexican beach, or the traditional mole poblano in a hacienda-style dining room.

By throwing a little bit of this and that into the mix, your wedding day will truly commemorate your romance with this special setting, as well as your romance with each other. Incorporating local customs and traditions will help you feel as though you are more a part of this place. After all, once you choose to get married somewhere, you're not just a guest there anymore. A part of your history as a couple will remain there forever.

## *Trinkets and Treasures*

Sure, you'll leave with memories—but a few three-dimensional mementos wouldn't hurt either. There's always room in the luggage for a few trinkets and treasures. Locally made products make perfect souvenirs.

Here are a few items, from the silly to the sublime, that you might want to consider taking home:

➤ T-shirts

➤ Hats

➤ Local produce, such as macadamia nuts from Hawaii, or jams, jellies, rums, whiskeys, wines, pineapples, and coffee

➤ Locally made pottery

➤ Hand-made jewelry

➤ A painting by a resident artist (or a painting of a local site—something that really gives you a feel of this place that you love)

➤ An antique

➤ Local attire, such as pareaus, muumuus, sarongs, shawls, wrap-around skirts

➤ Handicrafts, such as wood carvings, scrimshaw, ceramics, printed cloths

➤ A quilt

➤ A seedling of a favorite plant (Tulips from Holland or an exotic blooming plant from Hawaii, for example, can be shipped back home. Plant it and watch it grow as a daily reminder of your wedding and married life together.)

➤ A CD of local music (perhaps even the band that played at your wedding reception!)

➤ A book of beautiful photos of your wedding site

➤ A book of the area's history

➤ A framed map

**Consultants Say**

Unsure of where to shop? The concierge at your hotel is probably a font of information. Tell him what you're looking for, and he should be able to send you to the right store or local artisan.

Besides shopping for yourself, think of some small souvenirs you can provide for your guests. Great to have at each place setting at the reception, these little gifts say, "Thanks for coming all this way to be part of our day." What you will present will depend on your wedding location, of course, but here are some fun ideas for guest giveaways:

➤ Sea shells

➤ Small handmade whirligig toys for the kids

➤ Locally made candies (especially if this is a place known for its chocolates!)

➤ A tape of local music

➤ A little book of postcards

➤ Fancy tea bags

➤ A small (hopefully inexpensive) piece of china, glass, or pottery that depicts the wedding location and/or has your wedding date and names on it

➤ Cookies from a local baker, prettily tied with tulle and ribbon

➤ Little wooden boats with your names and wedding date printed on the sail

➤ A paper weight

➤ A tiny bottle of beach sand, decorated with a ribbon with your wedding date on it

➤ Foreign coins from your honeymoon wedding location

# All Together Now

Having family and friends around has been wonderful. You've had a fabulous few days leading up to a romantic ceremony and a smashing reception. Technically, however, this is your honeymoon as well as your wedding, so you may be feeling like you need a little space about now.

Honeymoon weddings can be arranged so that there is together time and alone time. Don't wait until you get there to realize that you didn't schedule in any privacy for yourselves. Plan ahead with your travel agent and your family so that quiet, intimate moments are built in to your honeymoon wedding. Here are some ideas for achieving time for yourselves in the middle of a crowd of friends and relatives:

➤ Book yourselves in one hotel, guests in another.

➤ Start out together but end by spending a night or two on a private yacht while guests continue to stay on dry land.

➤ Suggest that guests join you from Friday through Monday, while the two of you stay on for the whole week.

➤ Move to another nearby island for a couple of days if you are vacationing somewhere like Hawaii.

➤ Rent a nearby villa while the rest of the gang stays at the resort.

➤ Arrange a sightseeing tour for the family, while you and your groom stay back at the resort.

➤ Go out to dinner by yourselves off site.

➤ Have a boat drop you off on a deserted island for the day and pick you up again later.

➤ Rent a couple of mopeds and spin off on your own for the day, with boxed lunches packed by the hotel.

➤ Get lost in nature by taking a leisurely hike together, leaving the rest of your guests behind in the throes of a heated Ping-Pong tournament at the main lodge. If backpacking makes you and your groom happy, take your double sleeping bag along and spend the night in the wilderness away from everyone.

➤ Go out for a drink together in an intimate piano bar or a wild disco—whatever suits your taste. Guests may be back at the resort, hotel, or villa enjoying a "movie night" complete with popcorn.

➤ Stay at a resort that offers so many activities, you never have to worry about entertaining your guests. Everyone is free to do their own things during the day and then meet up at night for dinner!

### The Least You Need to Know

➤ Make sure your dream destination is within your budget and can accommodate a wedding party.

➤ Research your site carefully. An experienced travel agent and/or tourist board can help you get the most out of your trip.

➤ Contact wedding guests as soon as possible to tell them about your destination and dates.

➤ Use the resort, campground, or hotel's services, or hire an outside consultant to help you plan.

➤ Find out about all legal requirements for marriage in the location of your choice and get all papers in order as early as possible. Fax the details to your wedding planner in advance.

# Two for the Road

You have relatives in England. His family lives in New York. Your best friend's in Nevada. You both went to school in California, but now you live in Washington. Should you just call the whole thing off? No way!

When important guests are so far-flung, it can give you pause. It's probably unrealistic to expect so many people to fly thousands of miles just for a five-hour event (albeit an important one!). One solution is the weekend wedding, described in Chapter 5, which invites guests to come and spend a few days with you. Another solution is the honeymoon or destination wedding, described in Chapter 6, which allows guests to combine a fabulous vacation with attendance at your wedding. A third alternative may turn out to be the best one for you: the two-for-the-road wedding, in which bride and groom travel to family and friends, celebrating (and sometimes even remarrying) in a number of different cities across the country or even abroad.

With the two-for-the-road wedding, you can accommodate more people, have larger parties, and spend time with all the people who mean so much to you and your fiancé.

## What Is a Two-for-the-Road Wedding?

The two-for-the-road wedding travels to its guests instead of having its guests travel to them, thus rolling the honeymoon and wedding into one. A couple might marry in the presence of the bride's parents in New Orleans, then travel to Paris for a lavish reception in their honor given by the groom's parents. The bride might choose to wear her wedding gown again, and the couple could even reenact the wedding ceremony by renewing their vows in French at the groom's family chapel. Upon your return home, friends in New York throw you a lively dance party at a favorite club and toast you with champagne.

Whew! It's a lot of moving around, but it's a lot of fun, too. Stopping here and there to enjoy parties, people, feasts, and fetes in your honor will make you feel like royalty (or at the very least, like a visiting diplomat). If you have the time and can coordinate it all, your wedding may last a week or longer. In fact, Audrey Goldstein of Shenandoah Travel in Davie, Florida, recommends that couples not try to pack all the festivities into a single week. She says you'll feel like all your time was spent on a plane or train. You want to be able to have quality time with your family and friends. You need to leave some time to stop and smell the roses.

# Ten Good Reasons to Take It on the Road

To help you decide whether the "Traveling Road Show" wedding is for you, try taking a cue from David Letterman's Top Ten motif. Come up with your own list and see if you convince yourself.

**#10:** Family and friends are spread out all over the globe.

**#9:** You've put down roots in several different places (hometowns, college towns, and the town you currently live in) and feel an attachment to all of them.

**#8:** Many of your guests would not be able to afford to come to you, or are elderly and have difficulty traveling.

**#7:** You're a little schizophrenic. You like the snowy mountains of Colorado where you went to school just as much as the sunny deserts of Nevada where your parents live; you like the quiet of Maine where you and your fiancé vacation as much as the glitz of Miami where your future in-laws reside.

**#6:** You want to spend quality time with separate groups of friends and family, many of whom don't know each other at all.

**#5:** Your parents (or his) are divorced and don't want to be at the same event.

**#4:** Friends or relatives have offered to host parties in your honor if you visit them.

**#3:** You love to travel. You're always on the go.

**#2:** You love parties.

And the number one reason…

**#1:** You want a reason to wear your wedding gown twice!

# Party Time (Again)

The two-for-the-road wedding requires a little extra work on the part of your trusty printer or local stationer. You'll need to have invitations prepared for a number of different parties. Happily, if a friend or relative is hosting an event for you in another city, he or she will probably handle the invitations as well, working with you from an agreed-upon guest list, of course.

You can use any wedding invitation of your choice for the actual ceremony. For ideas, see Chapter 4. If you are tying the knot in front of only a handful of people (just your parents and sister, for example), written invitations will obviously not be necessary.

Once you are legally married, you may wish to send a wedding announcement to alert everyone else you know that your wedding day has taken place. A wedding announcement might look like this:

> Mr. and Mrs. Paul Casey
> have the honour of announcing
> the marriage of their daughter
> Natalie Marie
> to
> John David Schaeffer
> on Saturday, the twenty-third of May
> One thousand, nine hundred and ninety nine
> Our Lady Chapel
> New York, New York

Receptions that take place in the days or weeks following the actual event may be formal or informal. The style of the after-parties will determine how formal your invitations should be. For a large formal reception taking place a few days after the actual wedding, you may opt for a printed invitation with traditional language:

> Mr. and Mrs. James Dunne
> request the pleasure of your company
> at a reception in honour of
> Mr. and Mrs. William Ballantine
> Friday, the tenth of June
> at six o'clock
> New Haven Country Club
> New Haven, Connecticut
> r.s.v.p.
> 6192 Middlebury Lane
> North Haven, Connecticut 06473

Notice the use of the couple's married name. The bride is no longer listed separately from her groom in the invitation, unless of course she is keeping her maiden name, in which case she would be listed by her full name, not just her first.

For an informal reception, such as a backyard barbecue at a friend's house, use an informal invitational style. Any wording is fine, from the traditional (You are invited to a reception in honor of….") to the romantic ("Our two dear friends have begun a life of love together. Please join us to…").

### Creative Corner

You can wax poetic for an informal invitation. Try coming up with a fun little rhyme like this:

Bob and Samantha have done got hitched,
So in the yard a tent we pitched.
Now all are invited to toast and cheer,
With sticky ribs and glasses of beer!
Come on over—it'll be real neat
It's party time at 42 Maple Street!

r.s.v.p 786-8967

If your hosts in various cities prefer, invitations can be handwritten, even hand-delivered. Guests can also be invited by phone or e-mail instead of by regular mail.

### Consultants Say

Don't be shy! Tell everyone—from airlines to hotels to rental car companies that you're on a wedding or honeymoon trip. You can expect nicer service and maybe a few extras here and there (champagne? fruit?).

# And Miles to Go Before I Sleep

The sooner you start arranging your flights, the better your chances of snagging reduced fares. You can make the arrangements on your own, but you might save time and money by engaging a good travel agent. Travel agents rarely charge for their services, and they can often help you find better flights and hotel rooms than you could find looking on your own. Everybody wins.

Share the planning with your mate. Make sure both of you are comfortable with the flight times and the number of days spent at each location. You might be a night owl who has no problem with a late-night flight, but what about your groom? He might prefer to book an earlier flight so he can get a decent night's sleep at the next location. If both bride and groom are active participants in the decision making regarding the trip, things will go more smoothly. No one will end up feeling that the visit with their side of the family side was shortchanged.

## Fare's Fair

If you're able to be flexible about dates, you'll find even lower fares. Stay in touch with friends and relatives who are offering to host and toast you in a far-away town. If it doesn't matter to them whether the party is on a Friday or a Saturday, for example, you'll have a little more leeway in choosing airline carriers and fares. Keep an eye on airfares, because they can go up and down. A good rate on December 1 may no longer look so good when the airline drops its prices in February, for example. An experienced travel agent will have a fairly good idea of whether you should jump at a particular fare or wait.

A number of airlines offer packages that include the flight, the hotel, and a car rental. For the couple who would prefer the privacy of a hotel to staying with friends or relatives along the way, this may be the perfect way to go.

Since you're traveling to more than one city, you might ask your agent to find out about the possibility of stopovers. Can you stop in Atlanta for a few days before continuing on to Miami on the same fare?

Finally, if you are traveling to a foreign or distant destination like Europe or Hawaii, plan to arrive a couple of days before the party that is being held in your honor. This will give you some chance to adjust to the new time zone and recover from jet lag. You don't want to be falling asleep in the middle of someone's toast.

## Up, Up, and Away

When choosing a flight, make sure you get the best and most convenient flight for your money. Here are a few rules of thumb:

➤ Go for a direct and nonstop flight, if possible.

➤ Choose a flight that will be comfortable (avoid crowded charters).

**Consultants Say**

Be prepared for weather changes, no matter where you're headed. Watch a weather channel, check the listing in *USA Today,* or go online at **www.weather.com**.

**Bridal Blunders**

Even if you're anxious to be called Mrs. So-and-So, use your maiden name on all travel documents. The name on the airline tickets must match the names on your driver's license, passports, and other IDs, which are presumably still in your maiden name.

### Consultants Say

Before you get in that car and start that engine, log on to **www.mapquest.com** for driving instructions anywhere in the United States and some locations abroad.

### Bridal Blunders

Look out for hidden charges in rental car agreements, such as mileage limits and drop-off and late fees.

➤ Choose a flight that arrives and leaves at reasonable hours.

➤ Look for an airline that you have flown with before and know to have good service.

➤ If your groom is big or tall, ask your agent to find an airline with roomier seats or more legroom, or else to search for a reasonably priced business or first class fare.

➤ If you must change planes, make sure you've allowed enough time to make the next connection.

## On the Ground

To round out your travel plans, consider reserving a rental car at each stop on your journey. With your own set of wheels, you won't be dependent on others. Look for a company offering reasonable rates and a convenient location. (If you're flying in, that probably means the airport.) Perhaps you'd like to opt for something a little jazzier than usual in honor of your wedding—a sporty little convertible in a warm climate, a jeep for snowy mountains, an Alfa Romeo or Mercedes for buzzing around Italy or Germany. Look for the best rates. Some companies offer discounts to AAA members or other organizations.

Taking the train can be a great travel alternative for newlyweds. What more romantic way to see the countryside you are traveling through than by overnight sleeper train? In some places, vintage trains can lend a historical touch to your trip. Talk to your travel agent for more information.

## Where in the World?

Even though you'll be in town with a group of family or friends, make a point of researching the area as if you were a tourist. Suppose your groom's parents recently moved to Washington D.C., a city neither you nor the groom knows well. Contact tourist boards for information on restaurants, events, and sights. Spending time with other people is nice, but you're going to want some private sightseeing and time alone together as well.

# Pack It In

Think ahead as you plan and pack for this wonderful two-for-the-road wedding. If you're traveling from location to location and through two or three different climates and styles (city and country attire), you'll have a lot to take with you. Start making lists well in advance of the big day, remembering to include those little extras. Suntan lotion? Ski hat? Norwegian-English dictionary? Mosquito repellant? Get organized with a travel wallet or one of the new hip bags that take the place of a purse.

Ask your travel agent about the weather in the various destinations you will be visiting. It's nice to know in advance if the date you plan to arrive on is in the middle of the rainy season. Try to pack a few things that will work in all climates. For example, take a raincoat that fits in a pouch. Pack casual clothes for a day of hiking or sightseeing, fancy clothes for a night on the town (or a dinner party at a friend's house). Even if you normally pride yourself on taking only carry-on, this is the time to break out the big luggage—and check it through!

Toiletries and medications should travel with you in your carry-on bags. They can be expensive or hard to replicate at certain destinations, especially foreign ones. Keep other must-haves with you in a carry-on bag as well (travel papers, valuable jewelry, for example.).

Try to bring clothes that don't wrinkle easily and that don't need dry cleaning, and put shoes and heavy items at the bottom. Packing clothes in similar color schemes helps you to mix and match for greater variety without a lot of extra outfits. Seal toiletries such as a shampoo and lotions into double plastic bags before packing, in case they leak or explode. It's also a good idea to pack an electric-current converter if the voltage is different.

**Bridal Blunders**

All that traveling can sometimes take a toll on skin and hair. It's smart to find out in advance about a place that can do your hair and makeup for you in each town you visit. Just because you just got off a plane doesn't mean you have to look like you did!

# You Ought to Be in Pictures!

Are the groom's relatives unable to make it to the wedding ceremony? Then you'll probably want to treat them to the movie version. Have your wedding ceremony taped by a professional and then bring the tape along on your trip, if it's ready in time. The editing can take a month or two, however, so you may have to send the video later, depending on the timing of your trip.

A friend's amateur video could help fill the gap, giving something to take with you if the professional version isn't ready yet. It won't be as fancy as the videographer's version, but it may be enough to give friends and family in various cities a taste of your special moment. You can share the professionally made video with them another time. Lance Holland of Holland Video Productions in Atlanta, Georgia, gives some advice to the amateur videographer:

➤ Go to the rehearsal the night before to get the lay of the land. Test out a few angles and find the best place from which to film the ceremony.

➤ If the couple is getting married in a church or other place of worship, do NOT run around during the ceremony, stand in the middle of the aisle, or otherwise disrupt the service. Leave the camera running on a tripod. You can zoom in and out as you like.

➤ If you have the equipment and know-how, use a wireless microphone on the groom for better sound. It will pick up what the bride, groom, and other participants are saying. A microphone is less noticeable on the groom than it is on the bride.

➤ When renting a camera, ask for one that does well in low light. Ceremony sites are typically not very well lit.

**Bridal Blunders**

Some clergy do not allow photographs or videotaping during the marriage service. Make sure to ask about this when requesting the services of a religious professional.

Things have improved a lot since your parents first started filming you as a tiny tyke. The quality of the sound, the clarity of the picture, and the ability to add some special effects (slow motion, music, and graphics) have all combined to make video technology an exciting way to preserve your wedding memories.

Be as careful choosing your videographer as you would your wedding photographer or even your caterer! Remember: The videographer really has only one chance to get this right. He can't exactly yell, "Cut!" in the middle of your wedding vows or ask you to "take it once more from the top." Start looking for the right person as soon as you have a date and location. The best vendors tend to get booked early.

Choose a videographer with plenty of wedding experience. He or she should have a well-established business and be familiar with filming weddings in your area. Videographer Lance Holland suggests that you watch the demo tape they offer but ask also to see a recent wedding video they did, from start to finish. Ask if the videographer has worked at your ceremony site before; this would make him more familiar with the necessary lighting and camera angles. If the videographer hasn't filmed at your site before, Lance Holland says, "Suggest that he attend the rehearsal the night before." As you would with any wedding contractor, get references (and call them!) before you actually do any hiring. References can tell you what they liked best (and least) about the videographer's work. Sign a contract that spells out all the details: location, date and time, fee, any special effects or specific types of shots you want, and the number of copies you'll get of the finished tape. Be sure the videographer understands what you want. Will he be strictly in the background or will he take a more active role, interviewing the bride, groom and attendants?

Most videographers will give you three copies of the tape, so you'll be able to keep one and send one to each set of parents. If you need more tapes, you can usually buy extras for about $25 each. This will give you plenty of flexibility and allow you to offer the tape to extended family and friends.

# Once More, with Feeling

Yes, Virginia, you can wear your wedding gown again. Once makes it legal, but there's no law that says you can't put that gown back on and reaffirm your love for each other in another ceremony later. "Later" may be the next day, the next week, or even the next month.

Let's say you and your groom just got married by yourselves in Las Vegas in a very private ceremony just for the two of you. It was fun and funky and everything you and your groom hoped it would be. Now it's off to the small town in Connecticut where your parents and elderly grandparents live. You wanted the Las Vegas wedding, but you didn't want to impose it on your parents and grandparents—for whom the trip would have been a hardship. Besides, you weren't sure the Elvis impersonator would be your mother's cup of tea.

In a flash of genius, you suggested that you renew your vows in a small chapel near your mom and dad's house. Why shouldn't your nuptials be all things to all people? You may already be Mr. and Mrs. in your own minds (and in the eyes of the law), but for your mom, dad and grandparents, seeing is believing. Now everyone is happy, and what could be wrong with that?

If this scenario sounds good to you, discuss it with your family and with the officiant you would like to lead the renewal of vows ceremony. You can wear the same dress you wore to your original ceremony, if appropriate, and afterward enjoy a small celebration with your family at the family homestead or a local restaurant. Who knows? Two ceremonies might make your marriage twice as strong. Kind of like double knotting your shoelaces!

The double ceremony also makes good sense for couples who wish to marry both here and abroad. If only one of the two is an American citizen, for example, you may be wise to marry first on American soil. A friend who wanted her wedding in Japan (and who was not yet an American citizen) said she and her husband married at city hall first, making her status as his wife legal here first before they went abroad to a fancier and more ceremonious kimono-clad affair with her family in Japan. They returned to the U.S. still hitched, but without a hitch!

# The Traveling Wedding Scrapbook

As your wedding journey unfolds, make sure you don't leave any memories behind. Photos, cards, menus can all be tucked into a beautiful book of remembrances. Choose something sturdy and substantial before you begin traveling. It will become a treasured heirloom, so you want it to last. A book with pockets is handy for those little extras.

As you move from ceremony to party to party, from town to town, keep on "feeding" your scrapbook. You'll be hungry for these little mementos later. Some of the things you might want to pop into the book:

- ➤ Plane tickets
- ➤ Theater tickets
- ➤ Invitations for parties held in your honor
- ➤ Postcards
- ➤ Photos
- ➤ Programs
- ➤ Menus
- ➤ Handwritten notes by well-wishers
- ➤ Matchbook covers from restaurants
- ➤ Maps
- ➤ Dated journal entries describing your days away
- ➤ Drawings/cartoons/doodles by you and your groom

Take the scrapbook to parties so guests can see where you've been. You might allow guests to write in it as they would a guest book. The scrapbook spans the miles you have traveled and unites the ceremonies and parties you have been a part of.

### Creative Corner

Collect souvenirs from each of the locales you visit along the way. Items that represent the region will be the most meaningful. Paintings of a local site, wall hangings and handicrafts made by local artisans, specialty foods, T-shirts, CDs of local music, cookbooks with local recipes, coffee table books that lovingly describe the area you're visiting—all make great keepsakes. Unusual clothing or jewelry can also be charming reminders of your wedding trips.

### The Least You Need to Know

- ➤ Guests can't come to you? Then bring the festivities to them, with video footage, scrapbook mementos—and especially yourselves.
- ➤ Follow through on offers to host parties in your honor. Stay in touch with travel information and suggestions about the guest list.
- ➤ Make your travel plans as early as possible for the best travel times and rates. A travel agent is in an excellent position to offer help and advice.
- ➤ Pack carefully for all activities—from the casual to the elegant.
- ➤ Remember your two-for-the-road wedding by collecting souvenirs of the trip all along the way.

# Chapter 8

# Fabulous and Free (Almost)

---

## In This Chapter

➤ Finding inexpensive sites for expansive weddings

➤ Using your city's resources to your advantage

➤ Throwing a low-cost party

➤ Making a potluck reception special

➤ Getting help from friends

---

Weddings don't have to cost a mint to be meaningful or special. In fact, do away with all the glitz and the trappings and you may just find the most perfect wedding ever. A wedding held in a public park and a reception in your own home can be every bit as special as the big church and expensive hotel reception site, if not more so.

With creativity and ingenuity behind them, weddings don't need to rely on big bucks. They show off your own decorating and hostessing skills, not someone else's. Of course, it means you'll have to be bride, bridal consultant, banquet manager, florist, and sometimes even caterer, all rolled into one! "Whenever you try to save money, it's going to take you more time and more preparation," cautions Brenda Rezak of Affairs To Remember in New York City. "If you're willing to do the work, you can definitely save…but you have to be prepared to put in the time." You also need to be flexible and comfortable with a wedding that's going to be slightly eclectic. "It may not always match, but it will definitely be personal!" says Rezak.

Friends and family are also an integral part of the less expensive wedding, and that's a big part of the fun. So many people are contributing to your day—with food and drink and music and extra chairs—that you can truly feel their love and support for you. Sometimes simple pleasures really are the best.

# Tightening the Purse Strings While Tying the Knot

Assuming your wedding party is not large, there are many places where you can tie the knot without spending money, though there may be a fee for the officiant. Then again, you might have a friend who happens to be a judge, justice of the peace, or member of the clergy, and who would be delighted to marry you without charge. Being married by a friend of the family makes the whole experience that much more intimate.

The great outdoors can sometimes take a great load off your pocketbook. Picture a wedding ceremony alongside a stream, on a nature trail, or on a mountaintop. How about in a natural cave or cavern surrounded by beautiful stalagmite formations?

Call the department of parks and recreation, the National Forest Service, or the National Park Service to find out about using public sites for private ceremonies. They will provide you with information on parking and access to the site you have in mind and let you know of any fees, restrictions, or permit requirements. Find out whether the wedding needs to take place at a certain time of day or after official visiting hours.

**Something True**

By some estimates, as many as 70 percent of all couples are paying for their weddings. No wonder cost-cutting ideas are so popular!

**Bridal Blunders**

Getting married in a friend's yard or home may sound great at first—but be careful how much it will cost you to make the location usable. Rentals of tables, chairs, and linens can really add up. Are these items you can borrow or do without?

If nature's not your thing, there are lots of other options. Perhaps a historic lighthouse would turn you on. Fairs and festivals can be used in interesting and noncostly ways; so can amusement parks. Some people have even chosen to marry while on a roller coaster ride. What a way to take the plunge! Of course, depending on where the roller coaster ride is located, entrance fees and tickets can add up. Call your local chamber of commerce to discuss your plans and find out about fees or restrictions.

Private sites can also make for dramatic and inexpensive settings. Your own home, yard, or boat might well be the perfect place. Think about ways you can dress the place up—with prettily strung lights, freshly picked flowers from your own garden, garlands of evergreens winding their way up your staircase. Still not special enough? Talk to your friends. If a friend owns a pretty sailing boat or a large, beautifully decorated patio, ask if he or she would let you have your wedding ceremony there. Most friends would be flattered.

Is there a hobby or a sport that makes you a "regular" at a particular place? Perhaps you can marry without charge at the horse farm where you ride, the baseball field where you play, or the marina where you take sailing lessons. If you work in a particularly attractive office, you might even consider asking your boss to let you hold your wedding in the reception area or in a large conference room with expansive views of the city (Make sure the boss is invited, of course!)

What about your alma mater? Does it offer any free or low-cost sites where you can marry or host a party? A simple ceremony on the campus green, followed by a reception in a community center or on a school field, may be just what you're looking for.

Planning to host the ceremony in your own home or apartment? How will it work? Think about the layout of your home and pick a place where you will stand for your vows. (If space is tight, you probably won't be walking up the aisle.) Barbara Rezak of Affairs To Remember suggests that you face your guests when reciting your vows and that you keep the ceremony short for their comfort. To dress up your home, use seasonal flowers you arrange yourself. You can also use a portable huppah (a Jewish marriage canopy), available from certain florists.

**Consultants Say**

Make a separate folder for each aspect of your wedding day—ceremony, photos, transportation, food, reception, flowers, music, decorations. Keep careful lists of what everything costs, or better yet, how you plan to achieve your goal without spending!

## Low-Cost Locations

Renting a reception hall at a hotel can cost big bucks. Happily, the great outdoors offers many other spaces that can be even more beautiful for free—or at a fraction of the cost. The village green or a public park may be perfect for your party plans. Picnic blankets can be dressed with silver candelabra. Traditional picnic hampers with gaily checked cloth napkins could set the stage for a delightful super of cold chicken, green grapes, and champagne. If picnic tables are available set them with pretty tablecloths and decorate them with helium balloons or flowers in pots. Some towns and cities might charge a permit fee for the use of a city-owned park; others might let you use it for free. Again, check with your parks commission or town hall for more information before you proceed.

**Bridal Blunders**

Be sure guests know they will be sitting on the ground! Guests won't appreciate your picnic style if they're not properly prepared—and dressed. Enclose a note with your invitation.

### Cold Reception

Hearty souls might consider a beautiful winter wedding party on ice! A local pond that is safely frozen over can play host to a fabulous skating party. Replicate turn-of-the-century ice fashions, with long woolen skirts, toasty capes, and warm, furry hats, or stick with jeans and a sweater if that's more your style. A picnic table decorated with white and gold ribbons can be placed in the middle of the pond with hot mulled wine, warm ciders, or cozy hot chocolates, and a bonfire can be built on shore—local ordinances permitting.

Make sure your town has checked out the suitability of the ice and okayed it for skating. *Never* skate on ice that is thin or melting in spots or has not been checked for safety by a city official.

Summertime? Beach party reception! Break out the volleyballs and Frisbees and have a sun and sand gathering. Barbecue on the beach. Bring ice chests with canned sodas, beer, wine, and champagne. If you have a friend with a pool, have a pool party. Play water volleyball or water polo. If that's a little too athletic and informal for your big day, simply use the pool as a glimmering backdrop. Host the party in the early evening and light hundreds of candles around the edge of the pool. Make your own gourmet pizzas or ask each guest to bring a salad big enough for six to eight people.

## Local Resources

Even though you're not a tourist, contact your town's tourist board or local chamber of commerce. Find out about civic events being planned in the month when you wish to marry. You may be able to coordinate a little inexpensive or free entertainment with your wedding. Perhaps your local downtown hosts lunchtime entertainment in the Main Square or village green. Why not time your ceremony at city hall to correspond with a local choir's free performance? Big doings in your town can mean big fun for your wedding party. Are the tall ships coming into port? What better backdrop for a wedding on a city pier? Is there a country fair opening? You and your friends can dance the night away at the community square dance, or be entertained by local bands hired for the occasion. (Entrance fees are usually nominal.) Is there a free theatrical production coming to town? Shakespeare in the park *(Much Ado About Nothing? A Midsummer Night's Dream?)* or other productions put on by the town can be a great way to spend the evening before or after the wedding. Free symphonies in public parks can also mean instant (free) entertainment. Bring blankets and silver candelabra for a "formal" wedding picnic. Does your summer weekend wedding coincide with a local fireworks display? Start your marriage with a bang! This setting can be perfect for the ceremony itself, or for a fun picnic-style or barbecue reception afterwards.

**Bridal Blunders**

When you coordinate with an important civic event, be sure to book hotel space early for guests and think carefully about the extra traffic that may be created by the event.

## Getting Lucky with a Potluck Party

The potluck wedding reception can have all the elements of a good time with good food, without any of the expense. A couple can marry on the village green, in the backyard, at town hall, or in a church, then return to their own home or apartment for a feast provided by friends.

The key to a successful potluck is putting someone in charge, either yourself, or, better yet, a willing friend. Without organization you may end up with twelve loaves of bread and no main course, or lots of salads but no desserts. Determine first how many people are coming and how many items you need; then make a list including everything from appetizers and drinks to main courses and desserts. "Analyze your guest list. Find out who's good at making what. Make a list of the foods you want and have people sign up. It's like a bridal registry for food," explains Brenda Rezak of Affairs To Remember in New York City. Your list might include such specific foods as heart shaped cookies. "Always ask, 'Would you enjoy making this food?' It should be a joy, not agony, for the guest," says Rezak.

### Creative Corner

You don't need fancy silver platters to make a buffet table look beautiful. More creative containers could include:

➤ White cupcake liners (fun if filled with colorful M&M's or bright red heart-shaped candies, for example)

➤ Small, plain brown or white paper bags (filled for example with pistachios and tied with brightly colored ribbon or yarn)

➤ Ceramic bowls

➤ Baskets you have around your house (lined with a cloth napkin or pretty dishtowel)

➤ Wooden or lacquered trays

➤ A giant waxy green leaf (can be used just like a tray—make sure, of course, that it's not from a poisonous plant)

Each guest should be requested to bring one item. Be specific. For example: 100 paper cups and 200 napkins in red, white, or blue. Two bottles of red wine. A pasta salad large enough to feed 10 people. When preparing a main course, guests need to know how many people they are cooking for. (P.S. Don't forget the serving spoons!!!)

Another way to organize a potluck would be to ask everyone to cook something with the same theme in mind, such as "Hot-N-Spicy" (chili or Cajun-style cooking) or "Sweets for the Sweet" (an all-dessert party). Suggest that contributors make up names for their creations, such as, "Marital Mousse," "Wedding Bell Blintzes," or "Bridesmaid's Brownies." Write the names on place cards in front of the serving dishes.

For an elegant but easy evening, plan your wedding reception around wine and cheese. Ask each guest to bring one bottle of wine (or champagne) and a favorite cheese (with the appropriate crackers or bread). A sparkling grape juice or cider could round out the offerings for children and nondrinkers.

A couple of days before the wedding, the person in charge should call around, reminding guests of what they have signed up to bring. This is a also a good time to give instructions on where to bring the food and by what time. If everyone bringing a main course shows up late, lots of people will go hungry. To get everything set up nicely and on time, you might want to specify a drop-off time some time prior to the party. Ask a couple of other friends to oversee set-up and to warm up foods as necessary.

For a nice extra touch, ask guests to include an index card with the recipe for what they made. Assemble the cards in a hand-painted box with your wedding date on it. This recipe index makes a great keepsake—and you can always recreate your wedding banquet on subsequent anniversaries.

# The No-Liquor Party

Liquor can be a very expensive proposition, and one you may not be terribly interested in having at your party anyway—especially if your guests are driving long distances to and from your wedding. Happily, there are plenty of festive drinks that don't rely on alcohol. Consider:

➤ Exotic fruit punch

➤ Sparkling waters

➤ Iced tea

➤ Virgin piña coladas (have blenders and ice at the ready)

➤ Sparkling ciders (great for toasts in place of champagne)

➤ A coffee bar

### Creative Corner

If you're borrowing wine glasses from different people, you're likely to find yourself with an interesting assortment of shapes and sizes. What about buying a few spools of pretty ribbon in your wedding colors and tying a piece of ribbon around the stem of each glass? Presto! The mismatched set matches!

Similarly, with the serving spoons, try tying big white satin or gauze bows around each one for a festive and unified look.

You can have some fun by adding little paper umbrellas to the drinks or, for an informal party, buying paper cups in your wedding colors.

Even at a no-liquor party, many couples like to buy enough champagne for a toast. By limiting it to the toast, you can keep this lovely tradition without going overboard on the budget.

# Reception Reducers

You've chosen the reception site with due care and thrift. Here are a few extra ideas for trimming the fat off your reception bill, while still having a festive party.

➤ Piggyback on another event at the reception site. The reception manager may be willing to offer you a better deal if there's another party at the site that same weekend. Rentals and decorations already in place, both parties should receive a price cut.

➤ Change your day for a less pricey time. Sunday afternoon is going to cost less than Saturday night.

➤ Buy Christmas lights (they're cheap) and use them to decorate trees in your back yard. They're wonderfully festive, no matter what the season.

➤ Use lots of candles (instead of lots of flowers). Candleholders don't even need to match. Different heights and shapes can look beautiful together in an arrangement at the center of the table.

➤ Buy or bake a very plain cake. If you have the culinary ability, make it tiered. Dress it up with fresh flowers.

➤ Nowadays some supermarkets offer cakes suitable for wedding celebrations. Check out styles and prices. Dress up a plain cake with fresh flowers or whatever you like.

➤ Buy a plain, inexpensive shortcake. Decorate with mounds of heavenly whipped cream. Offer bananas, peaches, or strawberries as toppers. Several of these, artfully grouped on platters of different heights, create a lovely effect.

➤ Keep your guest list small. Obviously, the fewer guests, the more manageable the costs will be.

➤ Instead of throwing rose petals, have guests blow bubbles for more youthfully exuberant (and less expensive) fun.

➤ Hire a photography student from a local arts college to take the wedding pictures. (Post a sign in the art department). Better yet—use a professional photographer but contract for a shorter period of time. He doesn't need to be there for five hours to get good shots.

➤ Arrange for a house-swap honeymoon. Trade your apartment in New York for a cabin on the Cape or a pied-à-terre in Paris!

➤ Use your computer and printer to create the wedding invitations.

## Low-Cost Music

You've made all these wedding plans—now it's time to pay the piper. Save notes—bank notes, that is—by hiring players from a highly respected high-school orchestra program. A nearby college or grad-school orchestra or wind ensemble can be another source of inexpensive talent. Be sure to hear them play first and agree on musical selections.

Looking for something a little livelier? A talented friend with a good sound system might be happy to make a dance tape for your party, using the sounds and songs you and your groom like best. You could also purchase or borrow CDs offering a mix of dance songs by theme—love songs from the eighties, for example. Be careful, though—you don't want your friend's tastes or personality to take over the party. If you have the money, it would be safer to hire a DJ.

If you prefer live music and have musicians among your circle of friends, ask if they'd be willing to put together a few arrangements for your party. Even if they don't normally play together, with a few advance discussions about the material and a few practices before the big day, they should soon be making beautiful music together. Be sure the music you want to have is playable by your friends, says Rezak of Affairs To Remember. If you can, listen to them practice to make sure this idea is going to work out. Afterward, be effusive in your gratitude. More than their time, your musician friends have given you a significant part of themselves.

## Low-Cost Flowers

Are florists' prices making you wilt? There are a number of ways to prune costs. For example, you might be able to share the cost of flowers with another couple. Say you're getting married at the Jewish Community Center at 2 p.m., shortly after someone else's noon wedding. Ask your officiant for the name of the other couple, contact them in advance, and offer to share the expense of floral decorations. Two weddings' flowers for the price of one!

If you marry in a Christian service during the Easter or Holiday season, you may not need to spend a dime on church decorations. Your church may already be so beautifully decorated with Easter lilies or Christmas trees and poinsettias that more flowers would be—well—gilding the lily. Many reception sites are also decorated for the holiday season. At my wedding, I didn't have to order a thing for the rooms where we had cocktails. There was a decorated Christmas tree, lots of pretty potted poinsettias, and garlands of evergreens hanging from the mantelpieces.

If your city has a flower district, go there and pick out your own cut flowers. Better yet, send a trusted friend with a car to choose and carry your blooms home. Buying direct can literally save you thousands! Know in advance, though, that this is a big job. You or your friend should be comfortable arranging flowers—and leave yourselves time to do it.

Have a friend with a large car transport the ceremony flowers to the reception site. Why waste them? One couple, whose ceremony took place within walking distance of the reception site, brought their huppah with them to the party. Friends and family held it over their heads as they walked. The huppah found a resting place at the reception site, where it continued to beautify the location and warm hearts.

Keep flowers to a minimum. A few pretty branches or evergreens lying on a table can make a beautiful statement of casual elegance at a fraction of the cost. Votives can add to the look. As an added benefit, says Rezak of Affairs To Remember, "guests will actually be able to see each other across the table!" Another idea: Place small potted flowering plants on the table, which guests can take home with them as favors

Do you have a green thumb? Pick your own flowers! For your personal bouquet, a lovely bunch of wild flowers can be the perfect alternative to a fussy, fabricated, overly stiff bouquet of roses—and with none of the cost. Wire, florist's tape, and beautiful ribbon are all you'll need to keep it tied together. Hand-picked flowers can also be arranged at the reception site—in pitchers, vases, glasses, jelly jars, watering cans, or whatever strikes your fancy. Since my wedding was around Christmas time, I wanted something seasonal for the pew markers, but I had already spent my flower budget. The solution: My mother-in-law offered to make them for us from greenery found in her own back yard. She and her sister created beautiful fans of evergreen with white satin bows. They were not only beautiful (and cheap), they also conveyed far more intimacy and meaning than a store-bought arrangement ever could have.

Pick your neighbor's flowers! If you know someone with a beautiful garden or a green thumb, ask her if she'd be willing to let you cut some fresh flowers from her little piece of Eden. She'll probably be honored. She may even offer to do the cutting and arranging for you.

**Consultants Say**

Ask the bridesmaids to encircle your wedding cake with their bouquets after the ceremony is over. This makes a beautiful floral display at the cake table at no extra charge.

One more idea: Ask each guest to bring a single long-stemmed rose to the service. As guests arrive, the roses can be placed in large vases, creating a bountiful display and decorating the site with a clear sign of everyone's love and support. You can do the same thing with tulips or another flower of your choice.

## Best-Dressed for Less

Finally, what about The Gown? There are so many ways you can look drop-dead gorgeous without the killer sticker.

Sewing your own, if you are extremely talented in this area, is certainly one way to go. Another is to wear your mother's dress, if you can do so without ordering expensive alterations. This is a meaningful and beautiful choice for many brides.

Borrowing a friend's dress is still another possibility. Of course, it will work only if you are exactly the same size, or if she is willing to let you alter the dress. Remember that there will be a dry cleaning and preserving bill to pay before you return it.

A number of savvy brides are shopping for their wedding dresses in the prom section of major department stores. A little addition here and there (a train, a fancy lace hem), and the prom dress is magically transformed into a bridal gown. Some of these dresses, already full of fancy beading, poufs, and tulle, actually need no work at all. You can find some great prom dresses for under $200 that look every bit as lovely as wedding gowns. Once you've purchased the dress, of course, you can stop referring to it as a prom gown. Its status has been elevated to bridal gown, and there's no reason for anyone to know differently!

Another sneaky place to look for a wedding dress is among the bridesmaids' dresses. While at the bridal salon, check out the bridesmaids' dress selections. Many of these gowns are available in white or ivory and look a lot like wedding gowns—without the wedding gown price tag. As with the prom dress, you can add lace, beading, or sequins to the dress to make it fancier. A long veil will enhance the look of lavish splendor.

If you don't feel compelled to have a wedding gown taking up space in your closet for the next 50 years, consider renting one. Yes, like Cinderella, you'll have to return it when day is done… but without it, you might not have been able to look like Cinderella at all. Rentals start as low as $100. Renting is an inexpensive and practical option. Look in the yellow pages under bridal wear or rentals to see if this is an option in your area.

Veils are a one-size-fits-all item, so the best bet may be to borrow a veil or tiara from a friend. Alternatively, you can make your own veil. They're really composed of very simple pieces of tulle, lace, and a headpiece, possibly costing you as little as $25 for materials. This is what I ended up doing for my wedding. I'm all thumbs with a needle and thread, so I asked a good friend, who happens to be a costume designer, if she would create a veil for me. She swept in and out of a couple of fabric shops one afternoon and put together a fabulous veil with Juliet cap for me. It was very inexpensive, and more importantly, I felt truly honored to wear my friend's creation instead of a store-bought veil.

# A Friend Indeed

Low-cost and no-cost weddings can't happen without a few friends. Don't be shy. Make the most of their willingness to help.

Give friends plenty of advance notice of your wedding date. Let them know you're going to try to put the whole party together yourself—without spending your entire inheritance. If a friend has a particular talent, don't be bashful about asking for help in that area: "You have such beautiful handwriting. Would you be able to help me hand write the invitations?" If a friend offers to help (but isn't sure how she can be useful) be sure you're ready with some ideas. "Do you have a big coffee pot you could lend me?" or "Could you come over the day before and help me decorate the house?" Friends will be happy to have found ways to be helpful.

Borrowing is a great way to sidestep additional charges. Need more chairs? Start calling for extras. Friends and neighbors can start dropping things off at your house in the days and weeks before the wedding: large serving platters, linens, lanterns, folding tables, chairs—whatever is needed.

Even bridal attire can sometimes be borrowed. While dresses can be hard to hand down because of differences in taste and size, veils, gloves, and even shoes should present no problem. "I've had four offers of veils from friends already," says one bride who plans to take one of them up on the offer.

With so many friends lending helping hands, you'll probably want to find little ways of thanking everyone who was part of your day. From heartfelt handwritten notes to a little wedding favor, saying thanks takes only a few moments, but means so much. Gifts don't have to be lavish to be appreciated. For inexpensive favors, consider:

➤ A packet of seeds ("Thanks for helping our love to bloom.")

➤ A single candle ("You bring light into our lives.")

➤ A kazoo ("You made our day hum. Thanks!")

➤ Spices ("Thanks for helping to spice up our day.")

➤ Cute notepads ("Your wonderful contributions to our day have been duly noted.")

➤ Funky shoelaces ("Thanks! We couldn't have tied the knot without you!")

➤ Bookmarks ("You could write the book on what it means to be a good friend!")

➤ A lottery ticket ("Your help was worth a million!")

---

### The Least You Need to Know

➤ Low-cost and no-cost weddings take a lot of time and planning. You have to be willing to do a lot of the work yourself.

➤ The ceremony site need not cost much—or anything. There are lots of lovely cost-free or low-cost spaces, from your chapel or synagogue to an area park.

➤ Your house, a public park, a nature preserve, your own backyard, a beach, or a friend's pool are just some of the possibilities for a free reception site.

➤ Be organized. Research every avenue, keeping careful records of quoted prices, permit requirements, and promises of help or goods.

➤ Enlist plenty of help from friends, relatives, and neighbors. Together they may be able to provide everything from the flowers to the food.

# Part 3
# Theme Weddings

*A wedding that centers on a particular theme can be fun to plan, entertaining for guests, and truly charming. Part 3 covers a number of different theme ideas, including advice on tying in everything from the flowers and the decor, to the menu and your wedding attire.*

*Discover the pleasures of the country wedding. Cast off for a fun nautical theme. Or choose from among a celebration of one of three different winter holidays: Christmas, New Year's, or St. Valentine's Day. Seasonal weddings (like a Fourth of July wedding date) often cry out for a theme approach. This section shows you how to have fun with it, without overkill.*

*Historical weddings can lend beauty and drama to your day. Find out how to arrange for everything from a Renaissance festival to a roaring twenties party. For those who wish to honor their ethnic heritages at the ceremony or reception, Part 3 also includes a host of traditions, customs, and ideas for celebrating the marriage melting pot.*

# The Country Wedding

The country wedding is a breath of fresh air. Not for you, the boxed-in feel of a church ceremony or the canned air conditioning of a hotel reception site. You want to be where the grass grows green and the breezes blow gently, bringing the scent of wild-flowers. Working hand in hand with nature, you can arrange a truly creative wedding that's unique to your chosen site and a clear announcement of who you are as a couple. Whether you choose a ranch, a valley stream, a mountaintop getaway, formal gardens, or your own backyard, the country wedding will always have a feel of easy elegance and spirited fun.

## Choosing Your Site

A country wedding can be all things to all people—from a country western hoedown to a British garden party. For a country wedding with a western flair, the bride and groom might tie the knot at a dude ranch and ride off into the sunset on horseback. For a country wedding with the elegance of a day at the races, the bride and groom might marry beneath a bower of roses, followed by a sit-down dinner for 100 on the lawns of a country estate.

Your country site should be one that reflects who you are, one that works well for the type of ceremony and reception you have in mind. Many couples choose a site for its sentimental significance. One couple who met at summer camp as children returned to that camp to marry there. Guests stayed in cabins, swam in the lake, and ate in the camp dining hall. Some couples return to places where they grew up or places where they used to summer. Others choose a country location simply because they like it. A horse farm where the bride or groom stable their horses can be a charming location. An old ghost town out West (some come complete with actors to liven things up a bit) can be all fun.

If your own backyard is large enough to accommodate your guest list, you might consider having your very own country wedding close to home. Perhaps you could rent the lawn of a nearby mansion for a day. A beautifully situated gazebo, fountain, bubbling brook, or goldfish pond might be the perfect place to tie the knot. Equally idyllic might be a summer home on Nantucket, Martha's Vineyard, or the like. Think of a setting where you have always felt happy, at peace, and full of life. If your own property wouldn't be right for your party, look for a nearby public site, or ask a close neighbor.

In considering the best site, ask yourself whether it would be accessible to all of your guests. If it involves a long walk over uneven terrain, for example, it may be out of the question for some of your more elderly guests. There are other considerations as well. For example:

**Bridal Blunders**

If you've chosen a site that is open to the public during the day, such as a botanical garden, be sure to find out not only what time your party may begin, but also when the caterer may be allowed to start setting up. If the caterer can't get in until 3 p.m., for example, he may not have enough time to have things ready for a five o'clock wedding.

➤ Is there ample parking nearby?

➤ Is there electricity?

➤ Can a caterer get food to the site?

➤ Is there level ground for tables and chairs?

➤ If the choice is a public park, do I need to apply for special permits? Are there restrictions on the type of party or music I can have?

➤ Is the area large enough (and wide-open enough) to accommodate a big tent?

➤ Is there backup in case of rain?

➤ Does the site match the formality of the wedding you're planning? (It can be hard to do anything formal on a beach, for example.)

Once you're sure that a particular setting will work for your ceremony or reception, get busy finding ways to make it happen.

*Get hitched at a down-home wedding.*
©Eric Sanford/
International Stock

# Making the Most of Mother Nature

Long ago, Adam and Eve met and fell in love in the Garden of Eden, surrounded by the splendors and pleasures of nature's bounty. Now you and your groom have chosen to recite your vows in your own Garden of Eden, wherever that is.

Begin by thinking about where you wish to recite your vows. Is there a natural spot for the ceremony? An opening in a long hedge, a fountain, or an overlook heading down to the water? There needs to be enough room (and flat ground) for chairs, if guests will be seated for the ceremony. Depending on the spot you choose, guests may have to stand for the ceremony—in which case, make sure you talk with your officiant about keeping the ceremony short. Other natural attractions you might consider: a ledge or large rock, the entrance to a formal garden area, a grape vine trellis, a gazebo, a foot bridge, a dock, a break in a stone wall. Perhaps a certain place has special meaning for you. If so, try to imagine your ceremony in that spot. Is the lighting right? Is it easy to get to? Is there room for everyone to gather comfortably?

Have the florist and caterer visit your outdoor site in advance to discuss ideas for bringing out its beauty. What can be done to set the ceremony area apart? Do you want to decorate a door or fence with beautiful garlands, tie a footbridge with white satin bows, string lights across the roofline of an old barn? How about filling stone urns with armloads of flowering branches or tying big white bows around the trunks of the tall trees lining the path to the "altar." Topiary trees can be rented for the day to create floral aisle markers. Rose petals can be strewn along a runner of grass, with chairs set up on either side for the guests. Or you might use long benches or even hay bales instead of chairs, adorning the ends of each with clusters of flowers and evergreens.

Other ideas: A large rock can host a basket of fresh-cut flowers. Stones marking the long gravel driveway can be painted white for the occasion. A wheelbarrow resting on the lawn can be heaped with flowers or pumpkins, depending on the season. Tie daisies to scrolled menus at the table; tuck lilies of the valley into napkins. Sunflowers make for a wonderful decoration at a country wedding.

Keep a sense of humor as you decorate the great outdoors. Stone figures at an entrance gate can sport big satin bows around their necks or crowns of flowers on their heads. At a recent country wedding, Meredith Waga Perez of Belle Fleur made necklaces for two lions flanking a doorway. She tied big yellow sunflowers around their necks with red satin ribbons. The bride and groom liked the look so much, they even posed for their wedding pictures riding on them! Statues can be similarly adorned with a bouquet placed in the statue's hand or a wreath of ivy or flowers crowning the statue's head.

Arrangements of food can sometimes rival the best floral arrangements. A bounty of fresh vegetables and fruits can be artfully arranged and displayed, still-life fashion, on banquet tables. Big red tomatoes, yellow peppers, dark green broccoli, orange oranges, shiny apples, yellow bananas can spill copiously out of baskets and bowls—a feast for the eyes as well as the stomach.

If your wedding party will watch day turn into evening, think about what kind of outdoor lighting is available to you. Does your site have enough electricity on hand to keep the party up and running past sundown? Will you be stringing lights or lanterns? How about torches or small votive candles in paper bags around a reflecting pool? One garden party I attended used hollowed-out artichokes as votive candleholders—as beautiful as it was original.

**Bridal Blunders**

Think about the timing of your day. At noon, the sun can be intense. You may have to change your time or find a more shady area. Likewise, think carefully about a late afternoon or evening wedding when mosquitoes may be out in force. Choose the gentlest season and kindest time of day. If possible, go spend a couple of hours at your wedding site at the same time of day and year you're planning to wed. You may be able to avoid some unpleasant surprises.

# Country Wedding Attire: Perfect for the Great Outdoors

If you're going to be walking down a grassy path in the open fields instead of a white runner indoors, you're going to need to choose a dress that fits in with the style of your day. Exclusives for the Bride in Chicago suggests no train and no beading. Beyond that, they stress the importance of the right fabric. Silk organzas, tulle, linens, and other lightweight fabrics work well for a garden party wedding.

Imagine how the dress will look and move on your day. Will there be a strong sea breeze? Do you need to climb steps or walk down a nature trail to arrive at your site? How comfortable will you be in the dress? Is heat and humidity an issue? If it is, think about the weight of the fabric; some of these dresses can get very heavy. Would a tea-length dress give you more freedom than floor length? Would a light pastel blend better with the dark-green fields behind you than a bright white? A slit up the side of a simple sheath can make movements free and easy.

For your hair, consider a wreath of fresh flowers for an air of simple country pleasure. Or opt for a light and airy fingertip veil—unless you're worried that a stiff breeze off the water will keep it in your face the whole time. If you take the whole scene into account when planning for your dress, it should be perfect.

For more country fun, consider adding a few funky touches:

➤ A cowboy hat for the groom

➤ White cowboy boots under the bride's dress

➤ A ruffled hem

➤ Lots of petticoats

➤ Calico bonnets for the bridesmaids and flower girls

➤ A bandana around the ring bearer's neck

➤ A white denim jacket to throw over the bride's shoulders as evening breezes pick up

## Rustling Up Plenty of Country Charm

Keep that country theme going throughout the wedding.

At a fall celebration, have a bonfire. Give children at the wedding little fishing poles to use at the creek. Have hayrides leaving every hour to tour the property. Set up games of horseshoes or bocce ball, badminton, or croquet, and let guests take a break from sitting at tables. Croquet is especially well suited to a formal occasion, because it can be played in a nice dress.

Release butterflies at the reception. Watch them wing their way to freedom—a moving sight. For companies that sell butterflies, check the appendix.

Cover picnic tables with red gingham or yellow-checked oilcloth. The bride and groom's picnic table can be set apart from the others with a white cloth tied down with beautiful red gingham bows. At a rustic country wedding, drape a family quilt over a fence or hang it on a wall in back of the head table. Place large rolls of hay around the site. To keep guests cool, lay pretty fans at each woman's place and a pair of sunglasses at each man's. Both items can be personalized with your wedding date.

Choose your wedding date to coincide with times of special natural beauty, such as the blooming of the cherry trees in Maryland or the bluebonnets in Texas. For a fall wedding, decorate with gourds and Indian corn. Colorful fall leaves can be strewn on a runner instead of flower petals. Mound pumpkins near the door to the house. Place an array of fall vegetables in a wheelbarrow. Hollow out a pumpkin and fill it with flowers.

Make your takeoff inventive, country-casual, and surprisingly sweet by riding off on the back of a tractor! Tie silver cans to the back so they can gleam in the late afternoon sunlight as you chug toward your first moments of privacy. You can always decorate the tractor with flowers or balloons for a final touch. Another fun getaway idea is to leave on a hayride. (The hayride is also a great way to get large numbers of guests from the ceremony to the reception site, if they aren't at the same place.) You can decorate the hay carts anyway you like, with flowers, ribbons, Just Married signs...For an old-fashioned touch, how about a horse and carriage? 'Or take your leave in a slightly more up-to-date country style by driving off in a cherry-red Chevy convertible from 1960.

## Toe-Tappin' Tunes

Hire a fiddler and a caller for a good old-fashioned square dance, or bring in a country-western band for line dancing and the two-step. If many of your guests are unfamiliar with this type of dancing, you might even hire a dance instructor duo to help out. Make sure the musicians you hire not only match your day but feel comfortable with the outdoor setting.

Consider a Dixieland band with trumpet and trombone players dressed in striped vests and rolled-up shirtsleeves. Or get funky by hiring a band with an accordion player and a Zydeco sound. Likewise, a great Cajun band can keep the joint jumping. Listen to the sound track from the Ellen Barkin movie *The Big Easy* for ideas. On the flip side, quiet jazz or classical music may best suit an elegant garden party wedding. No matter what type of music you choose, make sure the band has some protective covering over it.

## Preparing for Rain or Shine

Make a list of everything you'll need at your site. A tent is a good idea, especially if rain is a possibility (and it pretty much always is). Contact a tent rental company and have them come to the site to determine how large a tent you need and where it can be erected. If you've chosen a remote outdoor site for the ceremony, tenting may not be possible. In that case, you'll need a backup plan. Perhaps a nearby chapel, parish hall, or auditorium could accommodate you. Check on this first, then enclose a card with the invitation that says, "In the event of rain, the wedding ceremony will be held in the All Saints School auditorium at one o'clock." Be sure to give the address.

Another good "rainy day" idea: have plenty of big golf umbrellas on hand to get guests from car to chapel or tent to house. Station large receptacles at each location for depositing dripping-wet umbrellas.

Is hot sun likely to be a problem? Offer the women pretty parasols to keep the sun off. Have plenty of nonalcoholic drinks on hand, especially water.

Make sure there's ample parking near your site. Most guests will be arriving by car, unless this is a destination wedding and they are already with you at a campsite. You may have to ask neighbors about parking in front of their homes or even on their lawns. Let neighbors know, in any case, that an outdoor wedding will be held on your property. They'll need to be prepared for the traffic.

Set up ways to protect your food from spoiling in the hot sun. Refrigeration should be close by. Food should be kept under tents or in the shade so it doesn't spoil. Bugs can be a problem when you're outdoors, so spray in advance and talk to your caterer or wedding consultant about ways to keep ants and other uninvited pests away from your day.

If you think you'll need portable lavatories, arrange with a company to get the right number installed before your wedding day. Determine an appropriate and unobtrusive spot.

## Making Animals a Part of Your Day

As long as you're out in the country, you might wish to make friendly animals and pets a part of your day in creative ways.

If marrying on a farm, relax and enjoy the sights and sounds around you. Wouldn't it be great if a rooster crowed as you were announced man and wife, or when the call is made for dinner to be served? If there are other critters on the farm, think of ways to make them part of the complete wedding picture. Dress up the pigpen; put a straw hat with flowers on the cow. How about allowing a few lambs or sheep (in fluffy white, they already meet the dress code) to roam the fields behind your ceremony site? Tie satin ribbons around their necks to help them feel dressed for the occasion. Imagine the flower girls chasing lambs through the fields at the reception! In fact, if sheep are in evidence at your country site, you might want your flower girl to walk up the aisle carrying a Bo Peep staff tied with a pretty white or blue satin ribbon, instead of a basket of flowers.

**Consultants Say**

Many people no longer throw rice because it's dangerous for the birds. Consider having your guests throw birdseed or flower petals instead.

# Cooking Up a Country Wedding Feast

When you think country, do you think good, down-home country cooking? Of course, country cooking means one thing in Texas, another in Indiana, and something else entirely on Martha's Vineyard. Either way, you can have plenty of fun with an outdoor feast and a party under the open skies.

For a Southern or country-Western flavor, you might have an informal meal with ribs and corn bread and hot apple pie. How about a whole barbecued brisket and a smoked ham, complete with black-eyed peas, collard greens, and fried okra? Baskets of fresh-baked bread look, smell, and taste wonderful. Serve delicious, golden corn on the cob, and wonderful salads made of vegetables ripe from your garden. Keep plenty of warm, moist terrycloth towels on hand so guests can keep clean.

Look for ways to be original. One Texan restaurant uses horseshoe nails as corn on the cob holders—an unusual idea you may want to borrow. Provide each table with toothpicks (with your names and wedding date printed on them, if possible).

Of course, having your wedding on a ranch or farm doesn't mean you have to serve barbecue. If you want foie gras, salmon canapés and prime rib, go right ahead. Just remember that the menu should match the style and formality of your day.

**Bridal Blunders**

Don't forget that some guests these days don't eat meat. Be sure to have plenty of salad, pasta, and grilled vegetables for the herbivores in your group.

# The Elegant Country Wedding Meal

A far cry from the cozy comforts of the down-home country wedding, the more formal garden party takes place amid cultivated rose gardens and grape vineyards, with white runners on velvety green grass, silver candelabra on white table-clothed tables, and plenty of champagne.

Your reception tables and food can be every bit as elegant when served outdoors as when ordered from a traditional restaurant menu. Make sure, however, that the caterer you choose feels comfortable serving in this particular setting. Sit down with the caterer during the planning stages and discuss the assets and drawbacks of the site. Will a hot meal be too difficult to serve? Is it better to have a meal that can be served cold or room temperature?

At an elegant country-estate wedding, the bride and groom might serve local seafood specialties, roasted quail, a cold filet mignon with wild mushrooms. Graceful starters might include brandied peach soup, tomato bisque, or shrimp.

Even though you are seated out of doors, tables can be set as lavishly as indoors. White-skirted tables covered with china, stemware, and gleaming silver can make your outdoor reception site look elegant and glamorous. However, do be sure to go over all this with your caterer. How will they prevent tablecloths from flying up? The wind from knocking over floral arrangements or glasses? Are they prepared for rain or unseasonably cold or hot weather? Make sure you take appropriate steps to work *with* Mother Nature and not against her.

---

### The Least You Need to Know

➤ Choose a site that is beautiful and meaningful and also accessible to your guests.

➤ For optimal weather, schedule the wedding for the most comfortable season and best time of day for the location.

➤ Work with your florist to make the most of Mother Nature's beauty.

➤ Keep your country theme alive with the right decorations, music, and activities.

➤ Discuss with your caterer the best menu for your particular country theme— whether Southern home-style, country-western, or refined garden party.

---

# Chapter 10

# The Nautical Wedding

---

### In This Chapter

➤ Finding the right site by the sea

➤ Partying on a boat

➤ Decorating with a nautical theme

➤ Tying the knot on the beach

➤ Serving a seafood buffet

---

Do you and your groom love the water? Is being on or near the water the most romantic thing you can think of? Perhaps the man you love is an avid sports fisherman. Why not set off for a beautiful wedding at sea, or find a way to marry near the water, whether ocean, river, or lake? Or, if you're hopelessly landlocked and can't get to the water, then bring the water to you through color, foods, decorations, and attire that convey your love of sailing and the sea.

## Anchors Away! Getting Married on Board

Do you yearn to get married to the lapping of waves and the roll of the ship under your feet? Your choices are manifold. You could marry on a small sailing ship or on a large cruise ship. You could sail off on a raft like Huckleberry Finn, or rent a schooner large enough for half a dozen people. Or were you thinking a little bigger? Perhaps a luxury yacht or cruise boat? Some can accommodate up to 500 people. According to *Off the Beaten Aisle* (Citadel, 1998), a chronicle of real-life weddings in offbeat locations, it is even possible to rent a recreated pirate ship, complete with an appropriately costumed captain!

Of course, you don't have to be married on a boat in order to have the reception on a boat. The benefit of having both ceremony and reception on board, though, is that it eliminates transportation problems for guests. Everyone stays in one place—even if the scenery doesn't! When you're under sail, the views are ever changing, says John O'Mahoney, banquet manager at World Yachts in New York City. "If you pick a site on land, no matter how beautiful the views, it's the same view the whole time."

How long do you plan to be at sea? Most wedding cruises last about three or four hours, but depending on your situation, you may want to shorten the actual sailing time. Many couples choose to have the ceremony while still docked so that their officiant is free to leave after the vows are said. If guests are on call or have small children at home, you may also wish to bring the boat back early and serve dessert while docked.

If you don't have any timing concerns, then do whatever pleases you! Talk with your banquet manager and ship's captain about where the boat will be going and when and where you would like to put down anchor for the service. If you are circling New York City, for example, let the captain know that you hope to be married on deck with the Statue of Liberty lit up behind you. If you're taking a smaller boat onto the Essex River in Connecticut, do you want to pull into one of the little inlets and marry surrounded by the tall sea grass and the chirping of sea birds? Do you prefer to head straight out to sea instead? Just about anything you're imagining can be arranged, so long as the size of the boat and the number of guests coincide happily. Of course, depending on your boat, you'll need to stay a bit flexible, since wind, weather, and tides have a way of changing plans.

**Consultants Say**

Do sea captains really have the authority to perform weddings, as seen on TV? Sorry! Though some captains are certainly licensed to marry people, most aren't. (Maybe it's more important that the person sailing the boat be certified by the Coast Guard.) You'll probably need to find a licensed officiant to sail with you—preferably one who's not prone to seasickness.

# The *QE2* or a Small Canoe?

What kind of boat you choose will determine how many guests you can accommodate, what your wedding service and party will be like, and even where the boat can go. A boat that needs to be in at least 12 feet of water can't duck into some small tributary, no matter how enticing. You don't want to get stuck in the mud on your wedding day and have to be rescued by the Coast Guard!

When choosing your ship, think about the season and how much time you want to spend on deck. Some boats will be better laid out for your purposes than others will. No two yachts look exactly the same. The really big yachts are like floating ballrooms. Some have grand staircases; others may have balconies overlooking the dance floor. There may be an atrium effect for great views from the indoors, or the best views may be from outside on deck. Some will have a more casual feel, a top deck with relaxed canopy top and poles wrapped in rope. Go look at any boat you're planning to charter before signing a contract. Pictures don't always give an accurate portrayal. Make sure the contract specifies which boat you'll be renting.

Contact yacht charter companies and cruise ships to find out if they can accommodate your party. Many boat charters advertise in the yellow pages or through tourist agencies. Another good place to look is yachting, boating, and bridal magazines. Check out the ads. Call a few charter agencies. Pick up a local magazine that lists places for parties. Your wedding consultant or travel agent may also know of ways to book a party on board a boat.

Here are a few questions to ask when chartering a boat:

➤ How many passengers can the boat handle? Seated or standing? Indoors or outdoors?

➤ How large is the dance floor?

➤ Is there air conditioning?

➤ Can I bring on a live band?

➤ Can I use my own (off-premises) caterer?

➤ Is outdoor dancing under the stars available?

➤ Is there a bridal suite or cabin I can use for relaxing/changing?

➤ What sights will we cruise by?

➤ Do you have a built-in sound system?

➤ Does a bridal consultant or party planner come with the package?

➤ Do I have a choice of departure docks?

➤ Are there only certain times of the year when the boats run?

➤ How many restrooms are there?

If the boat is fairly small and you're a sailor yourself, you may wish to be actively involved in raising and lowering sails or hoisting anchors. Discuss this with the crew in advance and see if they can accommodate you. Wedding attire would have to be casually nautical in this case. When the ceremony takes place on board a small boat, ask your captain for the best place to stand for the vows. He may need to have you and your group be in a particular place on the boat.

Another nice touch: Perhaps you can arrange for a fireworks display to be a part of your nighttime wedding on board a boat. Some yacht charters will include this option with your wedding package. They would probably subcontract the fireworks display to another company, who would shoot off the fireworks from a barge. Fireworks cannot be shot off from the boat you're on.

**Bridal Blunders**

On a boat, even candles can be dangerous. With the unpredictable swells of the sea, something could tip over and start a fire. For this reason, only enclosed candles such as hurricane lamps are typically allowed.

Finally, a couple of cautionary notes. If you or your bridal party have any reason to be concerned about sea sickness, be sure to check with your pharmacist or doctor about remedies before you leave dry land. (Be careful not to mix liquor with any medications.) Alternatively, try to set sail in a larger boat or on the calmer waters of a bay or lake, instead of the open sea.

Equally obvious, but easy to forget until you're on board, is the muss factor. Simply put, the wind and sea air can make a frizzy mess of your hair on a day when you want to look your best. Be sure your hairdresser knows where you plan to marry so that the two of you can work out an appropriate hairdo for the day. She may want to use a lot more hairspray or gel than usual, and any veil or headdress needs to be well secured.

# Really Watery Weddings

Some brides and grooms take their love of the water seriously—so seriously they decide to get married in the water, even under the water, with scuba gear. The challenge here is finding an officiant who is willing and able to take the plunge with you. Ask at scuba centers or shops that sell and rent diving gear; they may have some names. Also check your favorite scuba publications for an article on underwater weddings, or for specialty ads. Local scuba diving groups may also know something.

Amore Dive Center in Key Largo (800-426-6729) can marry you near an eleven-foot underwater statue of Christ. Gloria Teague, a diving instructor and notary public with Lady Cyana in Islamorada, Florida, also marries couples underwater on beautiful fish-filled reefs. She has been what she calls "a justice of the Pisces" for years now and says, "I really enjoy it!" Teague can be reached at 800-221-8717 or **www.ladycyana.com**. The bridal couple typically wears bathing suits or wet suits, but occasionally a bride and groom have donned the traditional tux and gown and jumped overboard in full regalia. One bride wore a mermaid costume! Gloria Teague has the bride get in the pool for a "wet run" the day before the wedding if she's planning to wear a long gown. "They need to practice a different fin kick because the dress tends to wrap around the legs. Your weight in a wedding gown is different, too, so we need to adjust the weight belt to reflect that," she says. Whatever you decide to wear, make sure that your diving pro okays it for safety.

Who wants to get married under water? Apparently, couples who take their vows—but not themselves—too seriously. Also, according to Teague, "couples seeking adventure, couples who don't want a big wedding or who feel nervous walking down an aisle or saying 'I do' in front of a whole crowd."

Oh, in case you're wondering: Vows are written on slates. And when it comes time to say "I do"? Couples make the "okay" signal. The kiss we leave to your imagination.

**Consultants Say**

Parents and friends who aren't divers can snorkel above the couple while witnessing the ceremony. Instead of throwing rice, they can toss fish food!

# Staying Dry in Seafaring Style

For those couples who don't actually want to be in (or even on) the water, there are ways to be close to the water's edge without getting wet.

Even if you don't board a boat, you can still honor your love of the sea by hosting your reception at a yacht club, although you may have to be a member or know someone who is. It's worth a call to the club to find out how they handle private parties. At Bridgeview Yacht Club in Island Park, New York, guests often take a boat out for cocktails, then return to the yacht club for the dinner party. Some even arrive in their own launches (dockage is available).

*Why not take your wedding seaside? There's nothing like a celebration in the sand and surf.*
©Index Stock

The great feature of yacht clubs is the view—colorful sailboats bobbing in the water right outside the windows. If the club itself is bare bones on the inside, you can work with your florist and caterer to dress it up for the big day. One couple put sand in glass bowls and added votive candles. Another had the cake done in a light blue to express their love of the sea.

A marina restaurant overlooking the sea can also be a beautiful setting. Check out places near your favorite body of water and see whether any of them could accommodate your group. Would they be able to close the whole place down for your party? If not, how would they separate your group from the rest of the restaurant? Be sure to check out the food. Even if you love the view, if the food isn't wedding-day delicious, it may not be the right choice for you.

Aquariums offer spectacular views of fish in a dramatic and romantic setting. Patricia Bruneau, owner of L'Affaire Du Temps, a wedding consulting company in California, has done a number of weddings at the Monterey Bay Aquarium, where guests sit at tables near a floor-to-ceiling tank full of fabulous fish and a spectacular kelp forest. Invitations for one wedding were scrolled, attached with a ribbon to the cork top, and placed inside seven-inch bottles with an inch or so of sand and some little shells. At the reception, the tables were decorated with fish-shaped candles, and food stations were set up to encourage guests to wander through the aquarium's attractions. At dessert, along with the traditional cake, there were chocolate mousse truffles in the shape of seashells.

**Consultants Say**

Of course, if your family has a home right on the ocean, there's really no need to look any further. You can have a terrific seaside wedding on home turf. Make the most of the seafaring features of your home with striped awnings, a dinghy filled with flowers, or telescopes on the terrace for gazing out to sea.

A seaside resort is another popular option for couples who want a relaxed atmosphere by the sea. According to Judith Barry, catering manager for Castle Hill Inn, Newport, Rhode Island, some of their couples like the idea of marrying in front of a historic lighthouse on their property overlooking Block Island Sound. They can also arrange for such seaside fun as schooner trips for the bride and her maids the day before the wedding, clambakes on the beach complete with lobsters and steamers for the rehearsal dinner, beach bonfires, and more.

# Nautical Niceties

There are so many ways to slip the nautical theme into your day, whether you're on the water or not. Start with the invitations, which can depict a nautical scene or include wording that reflects your love of the water. Stationary can be decorated with tropical fish. A border of ship's knots can surround your announcement of the day when you intend to tie your own knot. Two crossed oars can signify your union. The wedding invitations can be delivered as a message in a bottle.

Make your own yachting flag and fly it high on your big day. Use fabric paints, a little imagination and some artistic talent to create your own family crest in your bridal colors, signifying your nautical union.

At the wedding, you and the groom can exit the chapel, church, synagogue, or other ceremony site under an arch of crossed fishing poles.

Clothes are another good way to express the seafaring theme. Think about a captain's jacket with gold buttons for the groom and something equally nautical for the ushers. The bridesmaids could wear straw boaters; the ring bearer would look adorable in a white sailor suit. Waiters can wear navy-blue shirts, white shorts, and white tennis sneakers. (Ask at the location is this is feasible.)

A sea whistle or hornpipe can call guests to dinner. After dinner, guests can dance to a love song from *The Little Mermaid* or *Titanic*. Have the band play "Anchors Away" as you and your groom speed off from the reception in a little motor boat.

## Decorating Ideas

At the reception, decorate the tables with a nautical theme. Here are a few suggestions (Pick and choose. Don't overdo your theme.):

➤ Fill wicker tackle boxes with flowers.

➤ Arrange flowers around a big conch shell or old buoy in the center of the table.

➤ Create a miniature lily pond centerpiece.

➤ String fisherman's nets across a buffet table; liven it up with an aquarium full of live tropical fish.

➤ Order a fabulous ice sculpture of a dolphin and display it at one of the food stations.

➤ Fill lobster traps with bunches of flowers.

➤ Decorate your wedding cake with seashells.

➤ Use ship's flags to spell out the bride's and groom's names.

➤ Decorate with blue and white or green and white stripes.

➤ Grace the head table with a replica of a lighthouse or boat.

➤ Make color copies of a sea chart and superimpose the words of the wedding program or menu.

➤ Place shell-shaped soaps in the rest rooms, along with framed photographs of the bride and groom on a recent fishing trip, in full scuba gear, or on board a sailing boat.

Use moderation, good sense, and good taste when incorporating creative theme ideas into your day. "When working with a theme, do it tastefully. If you have a program, explain the theme to guests so they will know why you're doing what you're doing," says Patricia Bruneau of L'Affaire Du Temps in Milpitas, California. She cautions against an overdone look. Over-the-top theme decorations can distract guests from the real purpose of the day. "You don't want to take attention away from the bride and groom," she says.

## Stars in Their Eyes

Being on a boat or by the sea at night naturally lends itself to star gazing. To make the most of the opportunity, at a recent party on board a World Yacht boat guests were given little maps of the stars. What better way to celebrate a marriage made in heaven! For added fun you can have an astrologist or tarot card reader on board. Plan your wedding for a night when there's a full moon. Wear moonstone earrings. Present guests with a beautifully decorated card listing all the full moons for the year of your wedding. (They are listed in many calendars.)

# Beach Party!

You can't get much closer to the water than when you're standing right on the beach. For some couples, like Cindy Crawford and Rande Gerber, there's no more romantic place to say their vows than with the sand between their toes and the surf crashing behind them.

One couple found a private setting on a private beach about a mile from the entrance. They made a path with seaweed and driftwood leading up to a circle of the same. The bride and groom and all their guests stood within this circle of natural items gathered from the sea. The bride carried a bouquet of tiny seashells instead of flowers. As they completed their vows, butterflies were released into the air.

### Something True

Moonstone was a popular gift for loved ones at the turn of the century. It was believed to bring good luck, especially in matters of the heart.

### Consultants Say

If you're planning to hold your ceremony or reception on a boat, beach, or dock, be sure to tell your guests so that they can wear the proper shoes. (Flat footwear is advisable.) As the bride, you may wish to change from high heels worn at a church ceremony to ballet slippers on board a boat.

A beach ceremony like this can be both magnificent and deeply moving, but remember that the setting may not be accessible to everyone. If you have any guests who are physically challenged, such a removed location may not work. You'll need to take your guest list into consideration when deciding where your beach wedding will take place.

If you're thinking about a reception on the beach, again you may face a number of logistical challenges. Will you be able to transport food, music, and whatever else you need onto the beach? Who will do the lugging? As darkness falls, will you be able to string lights or set up torches? Can guests get to the site easily? Is there any privacy, and if not, does that bother you? Talk to a DJ about the possibility of setting up on the beach, if there's any electricity available. If not, consider hiring a steel drum band to add a little island flavor to your day.

For some, the informality of a beach reception is exactly what they're looking for. After the ceremony, you might decide to change out of your wedding dress into white slacks and matching white lace T-shirt. With the sand between your toes and the sea stretching out in front of you, you can relax and have a great time. Dig a deep pit for a barbecue or clambake. Set up tables of food in a covered pavilion. Play volleyball, Frisbee, or touch football on the sand; challenge guests to a game of limbo. Fill colorful plastic sand buckets with flowers. Invite guests to bring bathing suits and have a swim. As night falls, get the bonfire roaring! At the end, hand out little red lobster-shaped lollipops.

# Fresh from the Sea Buffet

Do you and your groom love to fish? The day before (or day of) the wedding could be spent deep-sea fishing with close friends or family. At the reception, serve the "catch of the day." (Don't forget to alert caterers to the possible addition of fresh fish to their menus!) Of course, you'll have to have plenty of other food on hand as well, in case the bridal party returns with fish stories but no actual fish. If you do have a good catch, however, wouldn't it be fun to say that you and the groom actually caught what the guests are eating? It makes dining that much more intimate!

Serve up some goodies from the bounty of the sea—caviar, raw oysters, mussels, shrimp, lobster, and so on. Start with a raw bar including clams, shrimp, and oysters, and follow with a seafood buffet or sit-down menu. Red snapper is a particularly popular entrée choice. Watch out, though! Seafood buffets can get very pricey. Bill Hansen of Leading Caterers in Miami advises the bride who wants to serve shrimp or caviar to have the food passed by the catering staff rather than presented in a raw bar. "That way you can control the quality and the quantity," he says. "You won't have to buy as much, and you're less likely to run out."

Be sure to have plenty of hot, moist, terry cloth towels or towelettes on hand, and lobster bibs if you're serving lobsters. Personalize them with your names and wedding date written in calligraphy with felt-tip markers.

Serve tropical drinks like piña coladas, strawberry daiquiris and hurricanes. Or, make up your own names, reflecting your lives or wedding theme, for some unique tropical concoctions: Fiji fizz, Newport nightcap, sailor's delight, pirate punch or Ted's tropical toddy.

Menus can be printed on sea scrolls. Small ceramic lobsters or shells can be used as cake toppers.

**Bridal Blunders**

Some caviar is over $30 an ounce right now! Rather than allowing guests to help themselves to a couple of big tablespoons, have a server offer each person just a little.

# Nautical Party Favors

Send guests home with something to remember your nautically inspired day by. Some ideas for small keepsakes would be:

➤ A collection of pretty shells wrapped in white netting and tied with a bow

➤ A tiny boat filled with little chocolates

➤ Seashell-shaped chocolates

➤ A pair of binoculars (for the attendants)

➤ A silver sea whistle

➤ A sailor hat

➤ A little glass jar of pretty pink sand with a ribbon around it imprinted with your wedding date

➤ A sand dollar paperweight

➤ A little ceramic dolphin or other collectible sea creature

➤ A paperback book of nautical knots

➤ A lollipop shaped like a lobster or other sea creature

➤ A map of the stars

➤ A kaleidoscope

➤ A practical household object, such as a tray or trivet, hand painted with fish pictures

---

### The Least You Need to Know

➤ Before you charter a boat for your wedding or reception, inspect it, because every boat looks a little different. Confirm in writing which one you'll be renting.

➤ Make sure the boat you choose can comfortably accommodate your group and is suited to the season. (You may need air conditioning, for example.)

➤ Rethink your hair and dress if you're going to be on board a boat or on a beach for your vows or reception.

➤ You can bring a nautical theme indoors with a seafood buffet and nautically inspired decorations—but don't overdo it or attention may be drawn away from the bride and groom.

➤ For a beach wedding, think casual. Consider the accessibility of the site.

# Chapter 11

# Winter Holiday Weddings

## In This Chapter

➤ Planning a Christmas wedding

➤ Decking the halls

➤ Ringing in the New Year as husband and wife

➤ Shooting for a Valentine's Day union

➤ Wearing winter wonderland attire

➤ Serving up the right holiday food and music

I love the Christmas season, from Thanksgiving right through New Year's and beyond. It could be because my birthday is in December, as is my husband's. Perhaps it's just that I never grew out of that childlike feeling of wonderful expectation and delight at what might be under the Christmas tree. I love the smell of evergreens, the brightly colored lights, the music, the rich foods, the dark chocolates. It's no surprise that I chose to be married on January 2.

If you decide to marry during the winter months, what you give up in warmer temperatures you gain in an inner warmth that only this season can deliver. The festive atmosphere of December, January, and February lends itself perfectly to creative wedding planning.

## Deck the Halls: Creative Christmas Weddings

When you set your date for Christmas time, there's no need to think further about a theme. No matter where you turn, you are surrounded by the trimmings and trappings of Christmas. Most ceremony and reception sites are already decorated, and everyone's got the holidays on their minds. It can be a beautiful time of year for a wedding, with rich reds, vibrant evergreens, and thoughts of home, family, peace, love, and tradition.

**Bridal Blunders**

If you're counting on a decorated church or reception site, be sure to find out when the site will be decorated (and on what date their decorations come down). Some sites will have decorations up from Thanksgiving straight through to January 6. Others might not decorate until closer to Christmas, or take decorations away right after New Year's.

To add a little extra Christmas spirit to your wedding, you might wish to add some of your own yuletide touches. Christmas decorations don't have to be all commercial glitter: They can have a warm sophisticated feeling instead. Hang mistletoe in strategic locations around the reception site. Dress your tables with red tartan tablecloths, fill clear vases with pinecones (gilded or natural), use a wreath as a centerpiece, or place pinecone-shaped candles on the tables. For a sweet touch, display a beautiful gingerbread house or decorative Christmas cookies on the dessert table. Arrange golden Bosc pears and green apples intermingled with white candles down the center of your table.

Add a little winter cheer outside your reception site! Get some of your more talented elves to construct a wonderful snow-bride and snow-groom, complete with veil and top hat. If the weather is right, create ice sculptures for display inside or outside. At weekend weddings, ice sculpture or snowman-building competitions can be one of your featured events.

**Creative Corner**

Have some fun with the Christmas theme! What about naming tables after Santa's reindeer, instead of numbering them? Since this is a season of surprises, put a big present in the center of each table with a tag that reads, "Do Not Open 'Til Midnight" or other intriguing line. Inside, the guests will find their party favors, such as white candied almonds wrapped in tidy packages of white tulle and tied with fancy Christmas plaid ribbons.

## Spreading Christmas Cheer

For a warm glow at an evening Christmas ceremony, give each guest a slender lighted candle (fitted with a protective ring for dripping wax) as they enter. The effect is breathtaking.

Along with the traditional wedding music, it would be hard not to include a few favorite Christmas carols, such as "Silent Night" or "What Child Is This?" For a non-church setting, old favorites like "Walking in a Winter Wonderland" and "Chestnuts

Roasting on an Open Fire" are appropriate, too. Seasonal tunes are not only beautiful but familiar enough to invite guests to sing along. At a recent December wedding at the Carltun in East Meadow, New York, Christmas carolers were positioned at the entrance as guests arrived.

If the sites are not too far apart, a procession of carolers wending their way from your ceremony to the reception site would be equally striking, and if guests were to join in, this would give everyone a feeling of holiday spirit and togetherness. Make sure guests are aware of this plan in advance, however, so they can dress warmly. Prepare sheets with the words and the songs you plan to sing (in the order they will be sung). Bride and groom can lead the way or zoom past the carolers in a warm white limo decorated with ribbons and wreaths. If you decide to walk with the carolers from ceremony to reception site, you'll need, of course, to give some consideration to your footwear and a coat to match your wedding dress. White fake-fur boots and a warm stole or cape might serve the purpose well.

If the sites are more than walking distance from each other, one delightful alternative is to arrange for a children's choir to come to the reception and lead the guests in a holiday sing-along. Print words in programs placed on each plate.

### Creative Corner

For a special date, consider having your wedding on the winter solstice. This is a fabulous way to kick off the winter, since it is the first day of the season. Or maybe St. Patrick's Day is for you. Have a wonderful Irish wedding. Walk down the aisle accompanied by a harpist. Exchange claddagh rings. Serve corned beef and cabbage. But don't wear green, because it's considered unlucky at weddings.

## Winter Wonderland Touches

If you're marrying at a site that's a winter wonderland in its own right, make the most of the natural beauty of your location. Perhaps you have chosen to be married at a ski resort. Why not have your wedding party on the mountain itself? Most large resorts have very good restaurants in scenic spots high atop their mountains. Guests can be pulled up the mountain, hayride style, by the big "cats" that are used to groom the trails, or ride up to the reception in gondolas. Coming upon the warmth of a candlelit lodge in the cold, quiet darkness will be sure to take their breath away.

If your reception site has a fireplace, be sure to have a roaring blaze going. You might even add the decidedly Christmas smell of roasting chestnuts. They can be roasted on an open fire, just like in the song, but you'll need a chestnut skillet, available in specialty cookware shops. Roasting chestnuts takes about an hour. If you're having your wedding party in a lovely old country inn, the chef may already be familiar with this art.

If there's enough snow on the ground, consider leaving the reception by snowmobile—or, for a touch of old-world romance, make your getaway with horse and sleigh. Don't forget the bells on the harness!

### Consultants Say

For a wedding that falls over the holidays, send out invitations well in advance of the date. It's a good idea to send a save-the-date card as much as a year in advance. People make their holiday plans early.

Can Santa perform a wedding ceremony? Santa can do a lot of things, but marrying you is not one of them. Of course, for a secular wedding, you could ask your officiant—if he's an old family friend and has a good sense of humor—to dress in a red velvet costume and impersonate the jolly old gent. One bride had all the ushers dress as Santas. Such touches can, however, backfire, taking the guests' attention away from the bride and groom and the importance of what they're doing—so consider carefully before you start searching for a Santa suit that will fit your officiant or best man. A better option may be to allow Santa a brief visit to the reception to visit the kids' table and hand out favors to the guests as they leave.

## Visions of Sugarplums

When it comes to food, Christmas time seems to call out for traditional menus. Châteaubriand, crown roast of veal, lamb medallions served with a fine red wine, or perhaps quail or pheasant all fit the bill beautifully; so would a menu based on the holiday traditions of your ethnic or national heritage.

Have plenty of hot drinks on hand; mulled ciders or wines provide a wonderful glow. Cinnamon sticks or candy canes can serve as stirrers. Champagne can be kept cold in an ice bucket made out of ice, as it was at a recent December wedding at The Carltun.

For dessert, display a beautiful Bûche de Noël along with the traditional wedding cake. This traditional French holiday cake, sculpted to look like a yule log (complete with frosting mushrooms!) makes a wonderful presentation. If you're doing a full dessert table along with the wedding cake, this is the time of year when it can really shine—with ribbon candy, candy canes, gingerbread cookies, and fine chocolates. A wonderful book full of tabletop ideas, *The Perfect Setting* (Harry N. Abrams, 1985), suggests a delightful little fruit and nut dish for the holidays. To represent the twelve days of Christmas, fill twelve brown paper bags with dried fruits and nuts. Roll down the top of each bag to form a cuff; then tie a red or green ribbon around the bag beneath the cuff, just tight enough so the ribbon won't fall off; place the bags all together on a large round tray. Simple but festive, the bags can be refilled as the party goes on.

**Creative Corner**

The wedding cake itself could be designed to look like a stack of lovingly wrapped Christmas presents, complete with frosting ribbons and bows. Other ideas for a Christmas-theme cake might include a candy-cane motif, a cake topped with a gold star, or a cake that mimics the traditional gingerbread house. Talk with your baker about the feasibility of these ideas.

Some couples are now offering a cigar or "after party" hour accompanied by ports and cheeses. This touch is particularly warm and welcome at a December wedding. At The Carltun, banquet manager and owner John J. Tunney III says they threw big pillows down in front of the fire at the end of a recent wedding party. Glasses of port were served on gleaming silver trays, with strawberries and chocolate truffles completing the picture.

## My True Love Gave to Me

'Tis the season for giving; what better time to come up with creative favors for your guests? Pile them in tiers, making a Christmas tree shape, or wrap them inside Christmas presents at the center of each table. Here are some ideas you might want to try:

➤ Decorate plain Christmas tree balls as wedding favors. Hire someone to hand paint them with your names and wedding date (or perhaps a sketch of a bride and groom on skates). If you or a friend are artistic, this could be a do-it-yourself project.

➤ Give snow globes of your city, personalized with your names and wedding date, or create ones with your picture in them.

➤ For a simple treat, tie candy canes with a white ribbon bow printed with your names and wedding date.

➤ Give cellophane-wrapped gingerbread brides and grooms. (Frosting can be used to create a white dress on the gingerbread girl, a black or red bow tie on the gingerbread boy.)

➤ Tie a green and red ribbon around cranberry chutney in pretty jars. (The ribbon can be printed with your wedding date and names.)

➤ Give pretty candles—always a welcome gift during this season of lights. They can be wrapped in white tulle and tied with a Christmasy ribbon.

➤ Give a cassette tape of *The Nutcracker Suite,* or "Nutcracker"-themed ornaments.

# Ringing in the New Year as Husband and Wife

New Year's Eve has always been a popular time for celebrating, and many brides choose to combine it with a wedding party. As a time of new beginnings and new resolutions, it can be an especially meaningful time to tie the knot.

*Happy New Year! Ring in your next new year celebration with a matching set of rings, party hats, and noisemakers. (You can skip the Groucho glasses if you like!)*
©Joshua Ets-Hokin

If you decide on a New Year's Eve wedding, you will probably be partying late into the night, or even all night. Some couples begin the evening with cocktails and hors d'oeuvres at 11:00 p.m., followed by the wedding ceremony—timed so that the marriage vows are said at the stroke of midnight. However you do it, there's a good chance the party will last longer than the usual four or five hours, so you'll need to make some special arrangements for extra food service and music. If time (and budget) permits, consider hiring more than one band to get you through the night. You can use the switch to change the feeling of the evening—from quiet to raucous and back again. The party can end with breakfast at sunrise.

Here are a few other ideas for a New Year's Eve wedding:

### Something True

The pressure inside a bottle of champagne is 90 pounds per square inch, according to *Gourmet* magazine (December 1998). Champagne should be chilled for three hours prior to serving. When opening a bottle of bubbly, aim it away from people and breakables!

➤ Get people in the mood! Send invitations in plastic champagne bottles.

➤ Decorate individual slices of your wedding cake with festive sparklers or long slender candles. Sparklers or candles can even dress up something as simple as scoops of ice cream.

➤ Incorporate New Year's Eve traditions from your family cultures. In Spain, for example, it's the custom to eat twelve grapes at the stroke of midnight, one for each stroke of the clock, to ensure good luck in the New Year.

➤ Give out noisemakers and party hats—for good old American fun, they can't be beat. You might wait to hand them out close to midnight, especially if your reception decor is sophisticated.

➤ Arrange for a few special effects, including fog on the dance floor, strobe lights, balloons, and confetti.

➤ Celebrate past customs with a wassail bowl or the singing of "Auld Lang Syne." (If you're Scottish, this can be particularly appropriate: The Scots poet Robert Burns wrote the song back in 1788.) *Auld Lang Syne* means literally "old long since"—in other words, the good old days. A great way to say goodbye to the single life!

➤ Play a trivia game featuring facts about the past year. Write questions on cards and leave them on the various tables. Give out the answers later in the evening, with the grand prize going to the table that got the most answers right. Figuring out the answers can be a real icebreaker for people at the table who may not know each other.

➤ Ask guests for their New Year's resolutions and record them on video or in the guest book they're signing. These can provide amusing memories.

Brides lucky enough to marry at the turn of the millennium can have special fun with the New Year's theme. Consider naming the tables for centuries. Fill jars with 2,000 jellybeans or 2,000 pistachios.

If your wedding is an all-night affair, be sure that your caterer is prepared for a special sunrise breakfast of omelets, pancakes, croissants, and plenty of coffee and juice. Sunglasses can be handed out with breakfast to cover up that "I stayed up all night" look. The bride and groom can make their getaway after breakfast, riding off into the sunrise instead of the sunset.

And to remember the evening by? Wine stoppers make great favors for guests who shared New Year's Eve with you. Have them personalized with the bride's and groom's names and wedding date, says Patricia Bruneau of L'Affaire Du Temps.

**Something True**

Noise making dates back to ancient times and was originally intended to scare off evil spirits. A night of revelry before New Year's Day is supposed to symbolize the triumph of order over chaos.

**Consultants Say**

Planning on consuming buckets of bubbly as you combine your wedding reception with a New Year's Eve celebration? Borrow an old caterer's trick and serve the better (more expensive) champagne at the beginning of the evening. "The quality of the champagne is more noticeable at the beginning of a party when the guests haven't had anything to eat or drink yet," says Bill Hansen of Leading Caterers of America. Towards the end of the evening, you can serve cheaper champagne because people can no longer tell the difference.

# Valentine's Day

What better day than Cupid's own holiday to celebrate your love? Certainly you should have no difficulty coming up with ways to express the theme of the day. Some light touches in everything from the decorations to the food can make Valentine's Day an especially lovely choice.

The holiday season is past by Valentine's Day, of course, but in most places it's still the heart of winter. Take advantage of the frosty weather. Combine a celebration of Cupid with some winter wonderland magic in the form of sleigh rides and ice sculptures.

There are so many ways in which the heart theme or heart shape can be used in weddings—starting, of course, with the invitations. These could be heart-shaped, with an illustration of Cupid on the front and a verse or two of love poetry on the inside. Include a heart-shaped cookie cutter or charm, or enclose a tiny arrow along with some creative wording, like: "Cupid took his best shot, and it was straight through the heart."

For something special in the way of decorations, consider a marvelous ice sculpture of Cupid with his arrows.

Heart-shaped helium balloons can be tethered to columns or tables; heart-shaped pillows can be strewn on the floor in front of a roaring fire. The possibilities are endless. As you plan your wedding, keep your eyes open for heart-shaped items that could fit into your day or be given as gifts—everything from letter openers and cake knives to paperweights.

### Something True

According to one legend, Valentinus was a fourth century Roman priest. The Emperor at the time was Claudius. During times of war, Claudius forbade marriage because he believed it would weaken his soldiers. According to this legend, Valentinus secretly continued to marry couples in spite of the Emperor's edict. No one is sure if this legend is true, but this much we do know: Saint Valentine was canonized in the Middle Ages and is widely known and adored as the patron saint of lovers.

Be sure to tell your florist that you are playing up the Valentine's Day theme. Belle Fleur of New York City designed the flowers for a couple's February 14 ceremony with romance in mind. They used red anemones, red roses, red amaryllis, and red berries, lightened with softer greens and placed in silver containers. Votives were mummy-wrapped in red organza for a warm, shimmering effect. As a final touch, the petals from red Nicole roses were scattered on the tablecloths. Nicole roses have a variegated red and white color. "The look was very romantic, very passionate," says co-owner Meredith Waga Perez.

Although you may automatically think red for Valentine's Day, white can be just as striking. An all-white decor with white chair covers tied with gold bows, cream-colored tablecloths, white plates and white linen napkins can provide the wintry backdrop for a few well-placed dashes of color, such as bowls of deep red roses or dark green topiary trees in the shape of hearts. Or you can heat up the night with hot pink. Pinks can be fun and funky. Combine two different pinks with a lace overlay on your table—hot pink lace over soft pink works well.

Continue the theme with food! A dessert table can look delicious with red jelly beans in white ceramic bowls or, for a casual touch, white origami paper boxes. Butter and cheeses can be cut into heart shapes. For dessert, along with the traditional wedding cake, you could serve strawberries dipped in chocolate. The wedding cake could be in the shape of tiered hearts; cut into it with a knife that has a heart-shaped handle. Conversation hearts (those little candy hearts with sayings on them like "B-Mine 4-Ever") can work beautifully for weddings, especially if you have your own special sayings made up. Call The Wedding Company at 800-524-8523 for information on where to order conversation hearts that say special things like "Just Married" or "Always and 4Ever." The hearts are available from **www.bridalink.com**.

For favors, guests can leave with crystal heart shaped boxes, or a single red rose.

### Consultants Say

January and February are slower times of the year at many reception sites. For this reason, you may be able to save money on the reception hall; however, flowers are typically more expensive in the winter months. December can be pricey. Vendors of all types often charge a higher rate in December when there are lots of corporate and social functions being booked.

## Winter Wedding Attire

Something about winter lends itself to richness and elegance. At my January 2 wedding, I wore a long white velvet gown; my bridesmaids wore off-the-shoulder red velvet. Both the church and the reception site were still decorated for Christmas, so the look was well coordinated. Bridesmaids could also wear a dramatic black velvet or emerald green satin instead, or a long skirt in a Christmas plaid paired with a black, red, or green velvet top. The bride can carry a lush bouquet of red roses; red velvet ribbons could trail from the bridesmaids' bouquets. Or the bride or bridesmaids could forget bouquets altogether and carry cozy muffs in matching colors instead.

Depending on how you're getting from place to place, you might want to get a white silk overcoat or a real or faux fur coat. Fur trim on coat cuffs, collar, or headpiece can be the perfect way to fend off winter's chill.

Shiny, sparkling baubles, such as a well-placed necklace or drop earrings, can lighten winter's darker days as they catch and reflect the light. A tiara made with a snowflake design can make you feel like a winter queen. Shoes with a beaded snowflake design make a perfect accompaniment to your winter dress.

For a New Year's Eve wedding, consider how much dancing and late-night partying you're planning to participate in. You may want one look for the ceremony and another for the reception. Some wedding dresses have a detachable long skirt, revealing a sexy mini underneath. Or you might decide on a lacy overdress with a snappy little white shift underneath. Remove the lace and you're ready to get down to some serious dancing.

For a Valentine's Day wedding, consider pinks and reds for yourself and your maids. If you do choose a heart-stopping red color for your dress, have some fun with it. Play "Lady in Red" for your first dance together as husband and wife.

---

### The Least You Need to Know

➤ For a Christmas season wedding, coordinate your decorations with those already found on site. Depending on the timing, you may need to add very little.

➤ For a New Year's Eve wedding, be sure to find a reception site that allows late-night or all-night partying. Arrange with your banquet manager for extra food or a change in music if your party will last longer than four or five hours.

➤ At a Valentine's Day wedding, have fun with heart shapes and rich red colors. Since it's still the heart of winter, you can combine a celebration of Cupid with some winter wonderland magic in the form of sleigh rides and ice sculptures.

# Chapter 12

# A Wedding for All Seasons

---

### In This Chapter

➤ Getting a bang out of a Fourth-of-July wedding

➤ Hosting an all-American barbecue

➤ Treating guests to a Halloween bash

➤ Celebrating an Easter-season wedding

---

If you're planning to be married on or near a major seasonal holiday, such as Easter, the Fourth of July, or Halloween, why not make the most of it? You can choose to include just a few seasonal elements—or take the plunge by following a complete seasonal or holiday theme. Your decorations, dress, food, and music can all reflect the holiday spirit. It just takes a little creative thinking! Be sure that your wedding professionals, from the florist to the baker, know that you would like to have a holiday theme incorporated into your day.

## Celebrating the Red, White, and Blue on the Fourth of July

Did you experience fireworks the first time you saw each other? Feel that way again when you marry on the Fourth of July. You'll have the perfect combination of a glorious summer day, a built-in long weekend, a little history, and a cheerful theme with which to have some all-American fun. When you think of the Fourth of July, what are the first things that come to mind? Bright sunshine, fresh air, friends, picnics, fireworks? These are the essential components of the Fourth-of-July weekend wedding.

For an explosive Fourth-of-July wedding, begin the festivities with invitations that picture a fireworks display or include such creative wording as, "On Independence Day 2000, Janet Manne and Mark Roscoe will start their marriage with a bang at...."

Invitations can have a red-and-blue-striped border or star motif. Alternatively, you can send something elegantly plain and simple with an authentic colonial American look.

With a wedding held over the Fourth of July, your color scheme is pretty much laid out for you, right? Not necessarily. In fact, New York City floral designer Preston Bailey suggests that brides and grooms stay away from the red, white, and blue motif, and instead opt for a rustic early-American simplicity, using arrangements of field flowers and all-white linen tablecloths. "Keep the look understated and natural," he says. That can include metal lanterns, each containing a single taper, and pewter pots for vases.

Many couples, though, love the colors and spirit and good old-fashioned summertime fun of the Fourth of July. If that's your mood, by all means go with it, but don't go overboard. Cover each table with a red, blue, or white tablecloth—or make all tablecloths the same color with centerpieces of all red, all blue, or all white. Still another possibility: striped tablecloths and star-shaped votive candles. Hang an American flag from a tall flagpole or balcony. Early American quilts can provide the perfect backdrop for your reception site, if hung on walls or draped over tables or chairs. An antique early American weather vane can make a great focal point for a floral arrangement on the card table. Shiny silver and pewter pieces could be used where appropriate. Bowls of fuzzy peaches make lovely, simple centerpieces.

Flowers are a great way to decorate for the Fourth-of-July wedding. Fill a teapot with them in memory of the Boston Tea Party. Adorn each plate with a tiny cluster of blue and white flowers tucked neatly into a red cloth napkin. Pots of geraniums can sit on each table or at the food stations; a wooden wheelbarrow can be filled with potted flowers.

### Consultants Say

If you're planning a Fourth-of-July wedding, get started early. Send a "hold the date" card well in advance of the actual invitations, and book hotel rooms for guests at least six to 12 months ahead of time. Hotels will fill up quickly on this popular travel weekend, especially those near desirable destinations.

### Creative Corner

You'll probably want a great dance band for the party but consider throwing in a couple of nods to Independence Day. Ask the brass section to play a Sousa march as you enter the reception site, or see if the vocalist could lead the crowd in a patriotic song, such as "America the Beautiful" or "Yankee Doodle Dandy"! If you're worried that your guests can't carry a tune, consider a choir presentation of patriotic songs as part of the entertainment.

Is your ceremony planned for the outdoors? Have solid red, white, and blue parasols on hand to keep the noonday sun off everyone's heads. (Make sure your photographer has been alerted to this so he can get a shot of the whole gathering "in bloom"!) A funny banner could read: "Independence is not all it's cracked up to be, so we got hitched."

Old-fashioned fun is the name of the game on summer weekends, especially this one. Invite guests to play lawn games such as badminton and croquet—both of which can be played in ladylike fashion while wearing a dress. More active eighteenth-century games (sack races? three-legged races?) are perfect for the little ones, or if guests are dressed informally. At a weekend wedding, have guests compete in a mini-Olympics. Divide them into teams representing different countries and award chocolate "gold medals" to the winners.

### Creative Corner

If it's mind games you and your guests love, why not tease them with an old-fashioned American spelling bee? Include words near and dear to the bride and groom, such as the bride's mother's maiden name (Loiacono) and the name of the city in which the groom was born (Tallahassee)! You could also play a little Fourth-of-July trivia. Ask on what date in 1776 the declaration was signed. You might guess the Fourth of July, but you would be wrong; the official signing was on August 2, 1776. We celebrate Independence Day on July 4 because that's when it was ratified by the Continental Congress. Here's another one: What great American novelist and short story writer was born on July 4? Answer: Nathaniel Hawthorne.

Favors for guests can include baskets of fresh blueberries, little American flags, star-shaped paperweights, bandanas with a stars-and-stripes pattern, red and blue candles, quill pens, and tea bags (in honor of the Boston Tea Party). Drive off in a red convertible, or leave the reception in a hot air balloon. Some couples even choose to marry in one! Balloon Adventures of South Dartmouth, Massachusetts, has flown couples over Rhode Island and Massachusetts, allowing them to say their vows up in the clouds. You can meet guests later for an after-party.

## The All-American Barbecue

At a Fourth-of-July wedding, great food usually stars. You may opt for an elegant sit-down supper; breeze through the day with an informal barbecue; or try to include elements of both—baby back ribs, hamburgers, and fried chicken at one food station, grilled fish, beef kabobs, grilled shrimp, and roast lamb at another. Serve it all up with plenty of barbecue sauces, salsas, and flavored butters. Add baskets of fresh corn, red potato salads, and fresh tomatoes.

For a great all-American barbecue, have your caterer cook up some classic char-grilled vegetables, including tomatoes, zucchini, squash, corn, artichokes, and asparagus. Enhance the flavor of your barbecued foods by asking your chef to add some fresh herbs to the fire. Fennel, sage, thyme, and rosemary can be placed on the coals for a fragrantly delicious flavor! If you don't want to be grilling, cold, sliced filet mignon can be the perfect buffet picnic item.

**Bridal Blunders**

Cooking out? Don't place the barbecue near trees or hedges. Be sure the barbecue is on level ground so it won't topple over.

**Bridal Blunders**

Do-it-yourself fireworks are illegal in most states and dangerous in all of them. If you're interested in enjoying fireworks on your wedding day, either coordinate your wedding and reception times with a scheduled civic display or contract with a licensed company. Ask your caterer or wedding consultant for suggestions.

Frosty glass pitchers of lemonade and ice tea are the perfect accompaniments. Sliced oranges and lemons look delicious floating in the pitcher.

For a picnic-style reception, fill large wicker baskets with paper plates, forks, and napkins. You can even buy disposable champagne glasses in gold, silver, or clear plastic. Set up sturdy tables that can stand on uneven ground and cover with fabric wrapped neatly around the top and secured underneath to prevent "fly-away" syndrome. Red and blue bandanas make spirited napkins and basket liners. Decorate basket handles with ivy vines. Champagne bottles can sit in an old-fashioned wash tub full of ice.

Since it's the Fourth of July, you may not be able to resist having ice cream sundaes or cherry pie along with your traditional wedding cake. Pop some sparklers into the sweet treats you're serving for a sizzling summer presentation. The wedding cake, of course, can have a Stars-and-Stripes theme or be decorated with lots of fresh flowers in red, white, and blue. Or, the tiers themselves can be star-shaped. What a grand finale!

If yours is a long-weekend wedding, consider hosting an old-fashioned pie bake-off one afternoon. If it's too difficult to arrange for guests to bring pies, you could provide an assortment for a pie-tasting afternoon or pie-eating contest! Think of red, white, and blue food, such as blueberries and strawberries with whipped cream. Watermelon is the perfect end-of-day treat.

## Revolutionary Attire

For those who are really in the Spirit of '76, there's always the fun of period dress. This can be a particularly playful theme if one of you is American and the other British.

Why not search for a dress with eighteenth-century styling? Look for a gown with a tiny waist and a fitted bodice with a low-cut, square neckline. Sleeves stop at the elbow, where they are met by a bow and a ruffle. Check out a few pictures of Martha Washington for the general idea. If you like, top it off with an authentic frilled cap. A simple velvet or pearl choker may be all the jewelry you'll need. Wear simple button shoes or lace-up ankle boots. Consider carrying a fan in place of flowers.

Groomsmen, bridesmaids, ushers, waiters, and waitresses can all be in traditional colonial costume as well. Men can wear knee breeches and waistcoat, a shirt ruffled at the neck, white socks, and big black buckle shoes. And don't forget the tricorn hat!

Of course, you can also pay tribute to the Fourth-of-July holiday without actually being historically accurate. Bridesmaids can dress in crisp red, white, or blue summer cottons, and straw hats decorated with daisies and trailing white ribbons. If you happen to have three ushers, ask each one to wear a different color cummerbund: one red, one white, and one blue. These little color touches show a sense of humor and can look bold and beautiful.

As the bride, you might want to appear in historic, dramatic red, the "color of defiance" sported by many brides who married during the Revolutionary War. You should be able to find a red bridal gown in one of the larger bridal salons.

> **Something True**
>
> To ensure adequate food, clothes, shelter, and money for the new couple, a Colonial custom involved putting a small piece of bread, a piece of fabric, a splinter of wood, and a coin in a small pouch, which the bride wore pinned to her petticoat. You can replicate this custom or even give each guest his or her own little pouch for good luck.

## Finding Historic Sites

What better place to celebrate a Fourth-of-July wedding than with a weekend wedding at a location with true revolutionary war history? Historic towns you might want to consider for a weekend wedding are Concord and Lenox, both in Massachusetts and, of course, Williamsburg, Virginia. Colonial Williamsburg boasts more than 120 eighteenth-century buildings, including the state capitol building and Governor's Palace. Street characters wander about in eighteenth-century dress; horse-drawn carriages can take you to and from your ceremony or reception site. You can dine in a pre-Revolutionary war home, see a mock Revolutionary War battle, and attend a silversmithing demonstration.

In Williamsburg, authentic colonial cooking is at its best. Invite guests to join you for a "Baron's Feast." Begin with oxtail soup; continue with seared fillet of flounder, whipped sweet potatoes and plum pudding with brandied hard sauce, washed down with pitchers of ale. Hire a fife and drum corps to help you celebrate, or have madrigal singers or balladeers to serenade you. After-dinner entertainment might include colonial jugglers. According to Naomi Flythe, banquet manager at Colonial

Williamsburg, one couple rented colonial costumes for all the guests to wear at the party. Even if you don't go quite this far, you could certainly arrange for the wait staff to be in authentic colonial clothing. Put out a guest book and ask your Fourth-of-July guests for their best "John Hancock." Have a quill pen available for signing.

Another fabulous place to celebrate our nation's history is, of course, Washington, D.C., where there are parades past the historic monuments every Fourth of July and a terrific fireworks display over the Washington Monument.

Look around for other historic colonial sites. At the Mystic Seaport in Mystic, Connecticut, costumed characters wander the streets. Old Sturbridge Village in Worcester, Massachusetts, recreates an eighteenth-century New England village. There's also Greenfield Village in Dearborn, Michigan. Ask your travel agent for suggestions.

# Turning a Halloween Wedding into a Treat

Is Halloween your favorite day of the year? Celebrate with a wedding on October 31, or on the closest weekend. An evening commonly associated with witches, ghosts, and devils, the Halloween wedding can be full of spirit and fun. Getting married can be scary enough: The Halloween theme can cut through the tension with a little laughter.

As with other holidays, you can borrow an element here and there or give the whole wedding a Halloween theme. Whether you're looking for spirited fun or something more ghoulishly glamorous, you can create the right atmosphere with a few creative touches. Make sure your wedding professionals are aware of the look and style you are trying to achieve.

You can opt for the traditional orange and black color scheme or decorate with a lighter touch, using golds and light oranges. New York City floral designer Preston Bailey says, "For something really dramatic, go with a totally black background—black tablecloths, black plates and black napkins." Turn to your flowers to provide the color, such as orange catalea orchids and rose of Leonides. Burgundies, roses, reds, oranges, and yellows keep the fall color theme going. At one party, each table had its own haunted house centerpiece! You might prefer to place just one on the table displaying the seating cards or another strategic location. Lighting is especially important for an All Hallow's Eve celebration. For an inexpensive but hauntingly beautiful decorative idea, arrange numbers of candles of all heights and widths. Light them before the guests arrive and let them melt down and drip wax. At each plate, tuck an orange catalea orchid into a black napkin.

Bridesmaids can be dressed all in black or in gauzy white. Depending on the look you want to achieve, you might ask guests to come in costume. (No bride costumes, please!) Alternatively, you might arrange for the wait staff to be in costume for a little extra Halloween spirit! For a more elegant formal wedding, have guests come in black tie but place sophisticated Mardi-Gras style, hand-held masks at each plate.

Choosing a Halloween reception site can give great scope to creativity. Are there any old castles in your neighborhood that you could rent and decorate like a haunted house? How about an old underground wine cellar? A museum of ancient history with its mummies and stone temples could be the perfect spot for a frightfully glamorous reception. To complete the picture, hire fortune-tellers or palm readers. Let guests look into a crystal ball.

Commemorate the anniversary of Harry Houdini's death (October 31, 1926) by hiring a magician to entertain. He'll be sure to include some spine-tingling tricks! Just don't let him make the groom disappear. On the other hand, what would Halloween be without a few harmless pranks?

### Creative Corner

Pumpkins, with their fabulous colors and shapes, can make wonderful centerpieces. With candles inside, they can also provide a warm glow at the wedding. Find someone talented enough to do some creative carving for you. Pumpkins don't have to be carved into the traditional jack-o'-lantern look. You might cut out your initials, an outline of wedding bells, or a church and steeple instead. The pumpkin can look sophisticated carved in the style of a cameo ring, with portraiture of the bride on one pumpkin and the groom on another. Hollowed out, pumpkins make creative vases for seasonal flowers.

To please the kid in you, don't forget traditional Halloween sweet treats, starting with bowls of candy corn on each of the tables. Serve a wedding cake decorated with black spiders, or opt for a more traditional cake but with lots of autumnal flavor—a carrot cake perhaps, decorated with deep greens and pale oranges. Decorate the cake table with Halloween lights. Talk to your caterer about throwing a little dry ice into a punch bowl for a foggy "witches brew" look.

Why not borrow a theme from *The Phantom of the Opera*? It's both a deeply romantic theme and spooky at the same time. Consider having the party in a wine cellar for an intimate, romantic feel of being cloistered away from the real world. Patricia Bruneau, a California bridal consultant who put together a Phantom-of-the-Opera wedding for a client had the engraver do a Phantom mask on the program. In the reception location, tall candelabra were draped in black and white fabric and tied with gold ropes. Different sizes of pillar candles lit the tables. On each plate, guests found a white chocolate mask and a little card decorated with the Phantom mask that said, "Thank you for being part of our day." Underneath the mask was a long-stemmed peach rose. *Phantom* music was played at the reception.

Assuming there are no werewolves in attendance, plan your wedding to coincide with a full moon—or a total eclipse. Check the calendars. Ask the band to play a little mood music to match:

➤ "Moondance" (Van Morrison)

➤ Songs from the *Moonstruck* movie soundtrack

➤ "Blue Moon"

➤ "Moon Over Miami"

➤ "Monster Mash"

# Celebrating an Easter-Season Wedding

Skip April Fool's Day (who would believe the vows?) and head straight for a springtime ritual. Planning a wedding around a time of rebirth and renewal can lend a freshness to your celebration. After all, you and you your groom are making a new start, leaving behind your old single lives and reinventing yourselves as a couple. The Easter or springtime theme can be full of wonderful meaning.

Spring is a beautiful time of year. Emphasize its romantic beauty with invitations decorated with pearl-embossed calla lilies. For a fresh look, print the invitation on a translucent-white overlay and place it on top of a card depicting springtime flowers. For a card that calls upon religious inspiration, embossed candles, roses, an open bible, or a cross are sentimental reminders of the Holy Season in which you plan to marry.

**Something True**

Easter is a Christian holiday, of course, but some of its traditions have their origins in pagan celebrations. Eastre, the ancient goddess of spring and fertility, was honored in April. Celebrations included the painting of eggs with bright colors. The rabbit was another symbol of fertility for these ancient people, which is how we ended up with the Easter Bunny and his famous basket of eggs.

At the reception, be sure to introduce all sorts of soft pastel colors and other signs of spring into your decorations. Peach napkins, lavender tablecloths, lemon-colored candles, pale blue plates can all harmonize together into a riot of springtime colors. A basket of dyed eggs can serve as a centerpiece. A beautiful array of colorful straw, wicker or even ceramic baskets can hold Easter surprises for all. Eggs can also be hung from tree branches like Christmas ornaments. New York City floral designer Preston Bailey suggests arranging a profusion of springtime branches in earthy looking pottery vases. "It's very dramatic to display branches of dogwood, quince, cherry blossoms, or forsythia, especially when they are used alone and not mixed with flowers in the same arrangement," he says.

Two stuffed bunnies dressed as a bride and groom can grace a separate table near the entrance to the reception hall. Ceramic rabbits could make sentimental little cake toppers. Have some fun with figurines of chicks, piglets, ducks, and other farm animals. Host an egg roll on the front lawn.

*If you both love being near the sea, have your wedding on a boat or close to the water.* Top photo©Joshua Ets-Hokin. Bottom photo©Eleanor P. Labrozzi Photography, Shelter Island, NY

*Are you and your fiancé big kids at heart? Do both of you claim that recess was your favorite class? Have your photo taken on a playground!* ©Joshua Ets-Hokin

*These nature-lovers tied the knot in the middle of a beautiful forest. If you have a favorite spot or park, call your local Department of Parks and Recreation to see if you can arrange for Mother Nature to be at your wedding.* ©Joshua Ets-Hokin

*There's nothing like a good escort: This bride had a cowboy* and *a Mountie walk her down the aisle.* ©Index Stock/Wilson Goodrich

*Make the most of your setting. If you live in a rural area, you have the perfect setting for a country wedding at your disposal.* ©Joshua Ets-Hokin

*Viva Las Vegas!* ©Mike Lichter/International Stock

*This couple wed at the eight mile marker of the New York City marathon. Who says wedding dresses and tuxedos can't be practical?* ©Richard B. Levine

*Uh…er…well, you know, whatever floats your tub.* ©Richard B. Levine

*Love crowds? Get married in one.* ©Richard B. Levine

*Your photos don't have to be stiff and posed. If you feel like jumping for joy, go ahead—just make sure your photographer is nearby!* ©Joshua Ets-Hokin

*You can creatively incorporate your theme into your photos in lots of ways. Here, a wedding's beach theme was even incorporated into a shot of the invitation.* ©Eleanor P. Labrozzi Photography, Shelter Island, NY

*There are lots of ways to incorporate your heritage and culture into your wedding.* Top left photo©Joshua Ets-Hokin, top right photo ©Joshua Ets-Hokin, bottom photo©Meredith Waga Pérez/flowers by Belle Fleur, NYC

Celebrate spring with a menu including rack of lamb, fresh baby green beans, and a carrot mousse. Instead of giving away white sugared almonds, offer multicolored ones, or wrap colorful jellybeans in white tulle instead. Scatter colorful jellybeans decoratively around the wedding cake table or display them in pretty glass bowls.

This is the perfect season for a romantic pastel gown. There are many from which to choose these days. Crystal butterfly barrettes in your hair would be a perfect accompaniment.

The Easter hat and the Easter parade have always held a special place in people's hearts. If a lot of children will be attending your service, a parade of kids in outlandish hats around the reception tables can be adorably funny.

---

### The Least You Need to Know

➤ Be sure to give guests plenty of advance notice for a Fourth-of-July wedding. Fold in a little Americana for a summer celebration that sizzles. Concentrate on food and decorations.

➤ Check books out of the library and contact historic towns and museums if you want your wedding to be authentically "colonial" or representative of Revolutionary times.

➤ Add a little Halloween spirit for a wedding day that's all treats and no tricks. Spend a little extra time to find an appropriately "frightful" reception site.

➤ Celebrate a time of new beginnings by hosting a springtime-rites wedding. Bring on the bunnies and bonnets!

# Chapter 13

# History in the Making

## In This Chapter

➤ Researching an historic time period wedding

➤ Planning a medieval wedding

➤ Following a Victorian theme

➤ Going back to the antebellum South

➤ Partying in the roaring twenties

➤ Throwing a fifties-sock hop, sixties-love-in, or seventies-disco wedding

Were you born in the right century? The right decade? Some people feel a decided pull to another time. What would it be like to be a medieval maiden? Are you a Victorian girl at heart? Maybe the Jazz Age is your thing, or the swinging forties. You can party in the decade you like best just by arranging the food and ambiance to match. If you're drawn to an era that's not your own, you might want to consider building your wedding day around it.

## Finding Your Place in Time

Many couples are opting for historical themes that help them focus all their creativity in one place. You may want a total period-style event, right down to costumes for yourselves and your guests, or you may prefer to simply borrow elements of style from a particular era. To determine which era is for you, look at historical books that focus on a particular period, or even a book of costumes through the ages. While you peruse the pages, ask yourself some questions: Are you immediately drawn to a certain look? Is there a dress you're just dying to see yourself in? Do you imagine yourself as some-one who would have fit in during that time?

And don't just stop at the clothing. Check out the modes of transportation as well. Were horse-drawn carriages the way to get around back then? Were there automobiles? If so, what were they like? What do you see yourself leaving the reception in? You should also pay close attention to the music and dance that was popular back then. Were minuets the sounds of the time? Maybe it was the roar of the Twenties and everyone was doing the Charleston. Or was swing the thing?

Once you pinpoint an historical period of interest, delve a little deeper. Read up on the era's traditions, styles, customs, literature, and architecture. What aspects of the era are you drawn to? Which of these could work for your wedding day? (the dress? the music?) What's not appealing to you? (the corset? the whole roasted pig?) For now, I'm going to give you a closer look at a few of the most popular period themes.

# Go Medieval!

Do you dream of being married in a castle? Are you and your groom happiest when treated like royalty? Is pomp and circumstance the type of circumstance you want to find yourself in? During the Middle Ages, marriages among the royalty and nobility were often the reason for great weeklong celebrations, with feasting, jousting, and plenty of entertainment. Although the marriages were usually arranged, and real romance was at a minimum, the pageantry was played out to the max.

## Finding Your Castle

If this sounds like your kind of celebration, start by finding a site that matches the mood. There are seven popular medieval locations across the nation where you can marry with all the style and trappings of a bygone era. Medieval Times, a themed dinner theater, can help you arrange weddings at any of these various castles around the country.

- ➤ Medieval Times in Buena Park, California 1-800-899-6600
- ➤ Medieval Ties in Kissimmee, Florida 1-800-229-8300
- ➤ Medieval Times in Chicago, IL 1-800-544-2001
- ➤ Medieval Times in Dallas, TX, 1-800-229-9900
- ➤ Medieval Times in Lyndhurst, NJ 1-800-828-2945
- ➤ Medieval Times in Myrtle Beach, SC 1-800-436-4386
- ➤ Medieval Times in Toronto, Ontario, Canada 1-800-563-1190.

Any of these sites can help you travel back to the days of yore through jousting, feasting, and pageantry. Picture the following scene:

The couple might decide to say their vows in the Hall of Arms, a large room with a high vaulted ceiling decorated by flags, medieval murals, and armored knights. After the ceremony, the bridal couple and guests might move into a private room for cocktails. A surprise trumpeter enters and gets everyone's attention. The Lord Mayor makes the announcement: The King is entering. As the bride stands alongside her groom, the groom kneels down on a pillow and the King ceremoniously knights him and places a cape around his shoulders. After the knighting, the couple and their party are taken to the arena for dinner and a show. As they feast on soups, breads, roast chicken and spare ribs (eaten with the hands of course), they are entertained by knights on Andalusian horses. The tournament of games has begun! The show lasts about two hours and includes jousting, horsemanship, falconry, and fighting.

If one of the sites named above is too far for you to travel, check with your state's Chamber of Commerce to see if there is Renaissance fair in your area or nearby. These events appear annually throughout the country in various places. Your wedding date might coincide with the date of a Renaissance fair near you. With food, music, and entertainment already built in to the day, you can enjoy the fun and romance of an historic marriage without a lot of the legwork.

You can also pick a reception site on your own that seems to fit the bill. Look for a castle setting with a grand staircase and stone walls. Surround yourself with decorations including suits of armor, tapestries, and crossed swords. Trumpeters with long silver trumpets can sound your arrival and departure; a white knight can guard the entrance. Waiters can dress to look like serfs and wenches.

If the castle setting you find isn't already set up to look like a medieval castle, you may have some extra leg work to do. Contact the props department at a local theater, tell them what you're looking for and ask if you can borrow or rent from them. Also, try **www.footlite.com** to rent everything from court jester outfits to knights' costumes to a Robin Hood-style bow. For other unusual props, try Design Toscano at 1-800-525-1233 or The Weapons Emporium at 1-800-932-7660. They can even sell you a suit of armor—but the cost of that alone could use up a good chunk of your wedding budget.

## My Cup Runneth Over

The banquet should be hearty and the food abundant. (Some may even choose to eat with their fingers.) Think of drumsticks and large platters of meat, such as roasted pig served on trenchers (big plates meant to hold the meat and the juice).

For a true Medieval touch, roast a piece of pork, beef, mutton or poultry on a spit where guests can see it. Serve soup from a great iron cauldron. Consider asking your caterer to experiment with a typical Medieval meal such as "blankmanger," a pounded chicken paste mixed with rice, milk, and sugar, and garnished with almonds. Fish was also a popular Medieval entrée. Shad, sole, flounder, trout, herring all would have been caught fresh and served to guests. Common vegetables of the time included peas and beans and onions. It was the custom to put dishes of salt on the table. Mustard was always available and used in great quantities. Serve any of the above meals with thick slices of bread. (The bread itself was often used as a plate for the meat.)

Large trestle tables should be set with cloths. Ample silver cups for drinking are a nice touch. Steel knives and silver spoons would have been used at the time. (Medieval and

Renaissance-style goblets and other items are available from **www.ffoundry.com** or by calling Fellowship Foundry Pewtersmiths at 1-510-352-0935.) Stews and soups were drunk out of "mazers," shallow wooden bowls. Meat was eaten with the fingers. Typically, two people shared one dish (a romantic tradition, at least for the bride and groom to consider). For dessert, cheese, nuts, fruit and spiced wine were popular.

For more information on Medieval life read, *Life In A Medieval Castle* by Joseph and Frances Gies (Perennial, 1974). It will give you lots of good ideas for Medieval customs to include at your wedding. Or, you could always subscribe to *Renaissance Magazine* by calling 1-508-325-0411 or by going direct to their Web site at **www.renaissancemagazine.com**. A one-year subscription (4 issues) costs $17.00. They recently published a Special Edition on Medieval and Renaissance Weddings (issue #9) which you can order from them for $6.00. It includes information on everything from wedding cakes to appropriate Renaissance music and readings.

### Something True

Medieval wedding guests had hearty appetites. Sixty cattle were gobbled up at the wedding of Henry III's daughter to the King of Scotland on Christmas Day, 1252.

### Something True

In medieval times, the couple did not need a priest or minister to get married. As long as their vows were made before a witness, they were legally married. When clergy were present, it was only to bless the couple. Since you're marrying in the twenty-first century however, and not the thirteenth, you'll have to find a legal officiant!

## Getting Ye Olde Word Out

To set the stage for your medieval match, send invitations on parchment scrolls. Use Old English wording. Tie the scrolls with a pretty ribbon or—better yet—use a seal with your two initials intertwined and mail in tubes. The bride and groom could even use their last names to create regal wording on their invitation, referring to the wedding as the marriage of "The House of Smythe with the House of Connor." For a medieval look, suggest the following fonts to your printer: Percival, Cloister, Block (BT) or Old English Text. Instead of being pronounced husband and wife you can be pronounced Lord and Lady, Prince and Princess, or King and Queen. It's a fairytale come true.

## I Take Thee, Grizelda...

You also should give some thought as to where—and how—you would actually like to tie the knot. In later medieval times, the bride and groom often married outside the church door so that everyone in town could see. After the ceremony, they went inside the church for Mass. Later, musicians accompanied the couple and their guests as they walked from church to a feast at the bride's house. You, too, can have strolling musicians; or perhaps mandolins, lutes, and woodwinds could play during your ceremony or reception. Jesters and jugglers could provide the entertainment. In Medieval times, there was often dancing after dinner. A circle dance in which participants all joined hands, known as a "carole" was popular. You may be able to work out a variation on this theme. Parlor games were also played, from chess to a type of blind man's bluff. The cake could be a replica of a castle.

For information on medieval costumes, manners, and history, try history books and the Internet. When thinking about vows or readings, peruse medieval love poetry and stories such as *Tristan and Iseult* or the tales of King Arthur. Or, if your vision is flexible enough to incorporate the Renaissance, check out the works of William Shakespeare. Re-read some love sonnets or favorite plays for ideas on everything from your wedding dress to music to invitations.

## *Medieval Attire*

Think of brocade fabrics, rich velvets, royal golds and blues. An overdress with slits revealing a long, tight underdress gives a medieval look, as do draped sleeves. For a headpiece, choose between a simple wreath of greens or flowers, and a tall cone-shaped hat with a veil attached to the back, such as you often see in pictures. When model Kirsty Hume got married in a medieval-style dress, she put her long blonde hair in two braids, then capped off the look with a Celtic veil and crown. Read *Fashion In Costume 1200–1980* by Joan Nunn (New Amsterdam, 1998, 1999) for accurate illustrations of clothing from this period and others.

Brides and grooms often wear velvet; the groom, if he wishes, can even rent a costume that makes him look like Henry VIII (although, Henry didn't exactly have the best track record in the realm of marriage). Crowns are optional but popular. For more fun and a more authentic feel to the event, ask guests to come in costume as well.

Feathered masks at each place setting can make fun favors for reception guests. If you choose to marry at one of the Medieval Times theme locations, they can help you get outfitted for your day. Nearby costume companies will rent you the perfect medieval attire. "Usually about half the guests come in medieval garb," says Joann Ciancitto of Lyndhurst Castle in New Jersey. Or you can look for your own costumes on the Internet, (see index for sites). Suggest that your guests all get into the spirit of your day by dressing in costume. Give names of stores and Web sites so they can comply. Not everyone will, of course, but those who do will make your day that much more festive.

### Something True

Fickle Henry VIII racked up six marriages in his lifetime. How did he keep track of them all? Well, somebody made up the following rhyme to keep at least the outcome of each marriage straight: "Divorced, beheaded, died. Divorced, be–headed, survived!"

# Victorian Themes

What era can equal the Victorian for classic romance and femininity! This is a very popular time period around which to build a wedding theme. To get ideas for having your wedding with this theme, search for historical information within the years 1837 through 1901. The Victorian Society in Philadelphia can give general information, as well as answer specific questions. You can reach them at (212) 627-4252 or visit their Web site at **www.libertynet.org/vicsoc**. The National Register of Historic Places might also be able to suggest appropriate Victorian locations.

Magazines such as *Victorian Homes* and *Victoria* are also good sources for Victorian ideas, photos, and information. If you have the time, why not read some of the literature of the time? Pick up novels by Charles Dickens, Thackeray, the Brontës, George Eliot, and Anthony Trollope.

## *Lace and Flowers in Her Hair*

When searching for the right clothes for your bridal attire, look no further than the queen herself. Queen Victoria popularized the white lace gown and veil adorned with orange blossoms, a simple choice for her time but one that looks romantic and rich to us now.

For a Victorian gown, look for a fitted bodice, small waist, and high neck trimmed with lace, possibly with a cameo brooch at the throat. This very romantic look makes the most of the female form. Although Queen Victoria wore white, blue was also a popular color for wedding dresses. Dresses often had a V-shaped ruffle that ran from the shoulders down to the bust line. The Victorians also favored a blouson-style blouse, nipped in tightly at the waist. Finish the look with a wide satin bow tied around the waist. For Victorian-style details, opt for tiny buttons down the back and a bustle behind. Lace gloves are a wonderful finishing touch, and Victorian high shoes (boots) are definitely a "step" in the right direction. Large brimmed hats can be trimmed with fresh or silk flowers and worn in place of a wreath and veil. For more ideas, read Alison Gernsheim's *Victoriam and Edwardian Fashion* (Dover, 1981) or *Wedding Fashions 1862–1912* edited by JoAnne Oliam (Dover, 1984).

Carry a Victorian posy or tussy mussy. A tussy mussy is a cone-shaped holder containing a tight round bouquet.

Actress Kate Winslet's groom looked dashing in a Victorian-style suit with a knee-length black frock coat. Search flea markets and vintage clothing shops for authentic clothing ideas. Amazon Drygoods, a catalog company, is a good source for authentic Victorian hats, corsets, fans, shoes, snoods, toys, and more. They even

### Something True

A blouson-style has a puffed-out fullness from shoulders to waist, but then is drawn in at the waist with a belt or other closure.

have dress patterns, if you're making your own Victorian gown. Carry a beaded Victorian style bag, or provide them for your bridesmaids. You can contact Amazon Drygoods by phone at (800)798-7979 or visit their Web site at **www.amazondrygoods.com.**

You may wish to have your bridesmaids dress all in white. During Victorian times, this would have been common, because one of the attendants' main duties was to confuse evil spirits by dressing like the bride and groom. (Notice that this practice is still with us, though without the superstitious associations.)

Ring bearers will look adorable in velvet knickers and short jackets. Flower girls can wear lacy dresses with matching white Victorian ankle boots. For an extra touch, add a big satin bow to a little girl's hair.

**Something True**

Over 100 women worked to create Queen Victoria's wedding dress.

**Creative Corner**

Sentimental brides might enjoy the Victorian custom of using gems or flowers that spell out words of love. During the Victorian period, it was especially popular to have the flowers in the bride's bouquet literally spell out her groom's name or other message. For example: Carnation, Anemone, Rose, Lilly spells CARL. Lilac, Orchid, Violet, Evergreen spells LOVE. See what message you can come up with. Make sure your florist feels the blooms in your alphabetical arrangement would be appropriate together.

## A Word from the Queen

Set the theme for your day by enticing guests with a romantic Victorian invitation. Include a love poem on the inside flap. To get ideas for this (and for readings at your ceremony, as well), check out the romantic words of Victorian poets Robert Browning, Elizabeth Barret Browning, and Alfred, Lord Tennyson.

Tell your stationer about your theme so he can show you some appropriate designs. Use hand-made paper and a graceful, stylized font. A Roman-style print or flowering script are good choices. Convey Old World

**Something True**

A deckle edge is an irregular, untrimmed edge on handmade paper. For ornamental reasons, the deckle edge can today be reproduced on machine made paper.

**151**

elegance and charm by ordering a feathery deckle edge on the paper. Romantic raised roses or bells on the invitation can complement the Victorian mood of your day. A scroll design or lace design can be embossed around the edge for a border. Seal the envelope with a foil seal.

For favors or programs, print a few words of thanks on parchment or vellum paper, roll into a scroll, and close with a little silver or gold band.

## A Place in Time

Consider having your wedding on a day that would have had a special place on the Victorian calendar. Invite guests to a marriage on Twelfth Night (January 5) or to a Candlemas celebration (February 2). According to *What Jane Austen Ate and Charles Dickens Knew* by Daniel Pool (Touchstone, 1993), nineteenth century law demanded that marriages take place in the morning. The reception afterwards would then have been a wedding breakfast. By the 1880s however, couples were allowed to be married as late as 3 p.m. If you wish to be authentically Victorian, you may decide to take these time guidelines into consideration.

### Creative Corner

According to a delightful little book called, *What Jane Austen Ate and Charles Dickens Knew* by Daniel Pool (Touchstone, 1993), there were scores of societal rules that polite men and women simply had to abide by. Why not neatly print out some of the more amusing Victorian rules of etiquette and frame them? Place one in the Ladies' Room and another in the Men's room for a laugh:

For The Gentleman:

1. A Victorian gentleman does not speak to a lady he meets on the street unless she speaks to him first.

2. A Victorian gentleman does not smoke in front of a lady.

3. A Victorian gentleman should precede a lady up the stairs, but follow her down them.

For The Lady:

1. A well-bred Victorian lady does not wear pearls or diamonds before noon.

2. A well-bred lady does not dance more than three times with the same person.

3. A well-bred Victorian lady under the age of 30 must always have a chaperone with her, unless she's just walking to church.

For the reception site, look for a Victorian mansion. If you're lucky, the mansion will have a romantic, Victorian name like Thrushfield Manor or Wildwood Hall which you can put on the wedding reception invitation. If the fireplaces work, ask that a fire be lit in each of the rooms you are using. Serve cocktails in the drawing room, dinner in the dining room. Gentlemen should be encouraged to "take the ladies in" to dinner. Retire after dinner to the billiards room or the smoking room (historically for gentlemen only…but as a millenium bride, you can bend the rules).

Beeswax candles, gas lights or lamps lit with paraffin oil can throw a romantic Victorian glow throughout the room.

Leave the reception in a horse-drawn carriage, the cars of the nineteenth century.

## Mutton, Anyone?

If you care to serve a typical Victorian holiday meal, ask your caterer about goose or mutton, two popular entrees. Fish, lamb cutlets, roast fowl and a sweetbread au jus might also be on the menu. Fancy dinners could be as many as 10 courses long. Potatoes and cooked vegetables were almost always served alongside the meat. Peas and asparagus were favorites. Be ready, of course, to pour plenty of beer and ale. And what would a Victorian meal be without one of the popular puddings of the day: plum pudding (the "plums" were usually raisins), roly-poly pudding (pastry roll with jam inside) black pudding (a sausage made with blood) or bread and butter pudding?

## Sing a Song of Sixpence

A string quartet can accompany your walk down the aisle. An orchestra at the reception can play a minuet, waltz or quadrille at the reception. A quadrille was a dance which involved four couples at a time, as they walked through 5 prescribed figures (similar to square dancing).

Popular drawing room games of the time could be set up on tables, or perhaps played during one afternoon of a long weekend Victorian wedding. Card games such as Whist, Beggar-my-neighbor, Cribbage and Speculation were especially well-liked. You can find out how to play these games and more in the book, *What Jane Austen Ate and Charles Dickens Knew* by Daniel Pool (Touchstone, 1993)

**Something True**

A deckle edge is an irregular, untrimmed edge on handmade paper. For ornamental reasons, the deckle edge can today be reproduced on machine made paper.

# Antebellum South

Have you read *Gone With the Wind* more than once? Is it your favorite movie to cry over? Move over, Scarlett! There's a new bride in town. The Civil War period lasted from 1861–1865. Do a little research on the years leading up to the war and the war itself, so you'll better understand the period — its customs, costumes, and culture.

Lincoln was elected president in 1860. By the time he took the oath of office in 1861, seven southern states had already seceded from the Union. Mark Twain is another good source, as he describes southern life from the 1860s to the 1880s in books like *Life on the Mississippi* and *The Adventures of Tom Sawyer*.

*Make history at your wedding in full period regalia. This couple went back to their Southern roots and donned Civil War era outfits.*
©N.E. Stock Photo

## The Belle of the Ball

If you're drawn to the days of Scarlett O'Hara, you may want to host a wedding that has all the trimmings and trappings of a lavish Southern plantation affair. Luckily, you don't have to make your dress out of the curtains in your home. You can buy a beautiful Southern-style wedding gown. Tell the bridal salon about your theme so they can help you pick a ball gown that reflects the Civil War period. Look for a big hoop skirt and lots and lots of ruffles. Lace gloves, a large hat, and a parasol can complete the picture. Encourage your groom to rent an outfit befitting a Southern gentleman. Arrange costumes for the wait staff. The bartender could be encouraged to wear sleeve garters. For more ideas, read *Costume and Fashion* by James Laver (Thames and Hudson, 1982) or *The Chronicle of Western Fashion from Ancient Times to the Present Day* by John Peacock (Harry Abrams, 1991).

## Take Me Back to Tara

To find a plantation for the wedding ceremony or reception, check listings of locations near you that allow parties. Plantation homes can be wonderful for parties indoors or out. They simply exude Southern hospitality! Exchange vows outside or on a wide veranda, with the smell of magnolia blossoms in the air. Come and go in a horse and carriage. Create the right antebellum atmosphere by boarding an historic, restored riverboat with your guests. Chug off under steam with a paddleboat. Play music from the musical *Showboat*. Other nice touches: Hire a drummer boy to lead the bridal party from the church to the reception site. Or if you don't mind fast-forwarding to the turn of the century, you can opt for a Dixieland band to play at the reception. Rent a player piano for fun in an anteroom, or simply hire a banjo player.

## Southern Hospitality

Serve mint juleps! Mint juleps sound relatively harmless, but they are actually straight bourbon with a little bit of sugar and a lot of fresh mint. Other popular Southern drinks to serve: old-fashioned lemonade, cinnamon water, and ice-tea with lemon or mint.

Prepare enough food to feed an army! An ample Southern spread might include such items as: country fried steak, fricasseed rabbit, fried chicken, chicken and sausage gumbo, hush puppies (cornmeal balls), sweet potatoes, boiled turnip greens, fried okra, collards, black eyed peas and watermelon rind pickles. For those along the coast, blackened catfish, fried oysters and boiled shrimp are naturals.

Don't forget the breads: buttermilk biscuits served soft and hot or grit biscuits, made with leftover grits. Cornbread is, of course, always popular.

For dessert, make sure no lover of Southern cooking goes home hungry. A wedding cake can be displayed on one table, and an array of sweets on another. Guests will be tempted by any of the following: ambrosia (a sweet fruit salad), syllabub (whiskey mixed with heavy cream and sugar), chocolate pralines, old fashioned peanut brittle, pecan pie, shoo-fly pie, blueberry crumb cobbler, peach cake, bourbon fruitcake, strawberry shortcake or stack cake (layers of molasses-soaked biscuit-like cakes with a rich apple puree).

For more ideas and recipes to match, check out *Shuck Beans, Stack Cakes and Honest Fried Chicken* by Ronni Lundy (The Atlantic Monthly Press, 1991) and *Mr. Food's Simple Southern Favorites* (William Morrow, 1997).

### Something True

According to *Mr. Food's Simple Southern Favorites* (William Morrow, 1997), hush puppies were originally cooked up so that Civil War Southerners would have something to throw to their hounds to keep them quiet as Yankee soldiers approached. Thus, the name "Hush Puppies."

# The Roaring Twenties

Take a trip to the twenties. Warren Harding was president in 1920, followed by Calvin Coolidge in 1924. It was a time of unusual prosperity. The crash would not occur until 1929. Known as the Jazz Age, the 1920s were a decade of flappers and youthful fun. Get in the mood with a little D.H. Lawrence, F. Scott Fitzgerald, and Virginia Woolf. Listen to some early jazz tunes. Ask great-grandparents about what life was like for them in the twenties; look at photos of family members who married during that time. Go on the Internet and search for information on the twenties. Some keywords to try are : Prohibition and Roaring Twenties.

## A Dress Fit for a Flapper

A twenties wedding dress was either calf or ankle length, but the veil was extra long. In true flapper style, the dress should have a drop waist and be belted around the hips. Add satin shoes with crossover straps. A silk organdie cloche hat trimmed with a flower could be perfect for the bridesmaids. You may be able to find the right dress in your own family attic. (Your great-grandmother's dress could fit to a Model T!) Huge bouquets were common place, with long-stemmed orchids and lilies the most popular. Choose flapper-style dresses for the bridesmaids, and add a long string of beads. A traditional flapper headband with a feather in it enhances the effect. (Rent some old movies, such as *Thoroughly Modern Millie*, *The Great Gatsby* and *The Sting* for more costume ideas.) Read *Fashion Sourcebooks: The 1920's* by John Peacock (Thames and Hudson, 1997) for lots of fashion illustrations.

### Something True

Art Deco is the term used to describe a popular design style from the 1920s and early 30s. The term was first used in 1925 after a Paris exhibition entitled, "Exposition Internationale des Artes Decoratifs et Industriels Modernes." Art deco style is characterized by clean lines, elegant sleekness, and symmetry. Two well-known examples of art deco interior design and architecture are: The Chrysler Building and Radio City Music Hall in New York City.

## The Grandness of Gatsby

Marry at a grand mansion for a Great Gatsby effect or on board a cruise ship. (See Chapter 13 for more on weddings at sea). In planning an art deco party, floral designer Preston Bailey suggests couples stick with a sophisticated look in silver, white, and black. That could mean silver tablecloths, clean white plates, and fluted vases with white, long-stemmed cala lilies. At one wedding silver trumpet vases were filled with white ostrich feathers. Elegant sophistication is the name of the game.

Have fun dancing the Charleston to an old-time jazz band sound. The Charleston was based on black folk dances from Charleston, South Carolina and became a craze in the 1920s. (If you take lessons before the wedding, you'll really wow your guests.) Give guests feather boas for fun photos and dancing. Keep bottles of champagne on ice in wash tubs, as a wink at the bathtub gin of the twenties. If you have a printed menu, refer to the drinks as "hooch, bootleg, or moonshine." Offer after-dinner brandies and cigars. Leave the reception in a 1920 Packard or Studebaker car. Twenty-three Skidoo!

# The Height of Swing

Dating from the 1930s and early 40s, swing music is as fashionable these days as it is fun. The Big Band era was led by Duke Ellington and Fletcher Henderson. Movie goers were treated to Busby Berkley musicals. Fred Astaire and Ginger Rogers were busy dancing their way into the hearts of millions. The Great Depression had a stranglehold on the country from 1929–1940.

## Take the A Train

Invite guests to a 40s style swing soiree by sending invitations that look like old advertisements for The Cotton Club. Use an illustration that's evocative of the era, picturing trumpets, for example, or an old fashioned radio microphone, or two sophisticated looking cocktail glasses. Superimpose your invitation wording over the sheet music for A Sophisticated Lady or In A Sentimental Mood, two of Duke Ellington's greatest hits.

## A Jumpin' Joint

If you're into swing, why not get your guests to jump and jive along with you at your reception?

Popular dances of the 1930s and 1940s were the jitterbug, the black bottom and the lindyhop. The rumba, mambo and chacha arrived in the early 40s. Get the moves down in a dance class prior to your big day. Grab your Daddy-O and head out to look at some reception sites that might fit the bill. You want a club feel. Rent out a supper club, light up the dance floor, and get twirling. Read about The Cotton Club in New York City's Harlem, where Duke Ellington played, for atmosphere ideas.

Since music is the name of the game at this party, make sure you hire a terrific swing band. Listen to lots of different tapes. Or preferably, go and see the orchestra play live. Do they make the crowd want to get up and boogie? Since swing is so popular now, you probably won't have to look to far to find the right musicians. Before you begin your search, get into the mood by listening to recordings by Cab Calloway, Count Bassie, Ella Fitzgerald and Billie Holiday. The 40s were dominated by the likes of Charlie Parker, whose bebop style started a revolution in the jazz world. The big band era was winding to a close by the end of the war in 1945.

## That's One Fine Dame!

A bride in the 1930s might have worn a sleek satin floor length dress with a bias-cut skirt gathered from a low hip yoke. The groom would have looked dashing in a dark grey morningsuit with a light grey top hat and black shoes with grey spats. Bridesmaids might have sported hats with shallow crowns and wide brims. You could instead choose a more informal forties-style dress—one that will allow you to be out there on the dance floor doing the jitterbug or jumping and jiving with the rest of the guests. The groom could wear a zoot suit.

# Fifties Sock Hop

The nifty fifties will never go out of fashion. Think how long *Happy Days* stayed on the air (you can still watch it on Nick at Nite!). Rent movies! There are soooo many to watch—*Rebel Without a Cause, Beach Blanket Bingo,* and anything with Elvis, Sandra Dee or Annette Funicello. You'll find a lot to work with here. Elvis starred in four movies between 1956 and 1958, including *Love Me Tender* and *Jailhouse Rock.*

## Rock Around the Clock

At the reception, have a "swell time" dancing to irresistible hits from the fifties, such as Little Richard's "Tutti Frutti" or "Good Golly Miss Molly." Consider hiring a DJ for a 50s party instead of a band. Think of your party as your own private American Bandstand show. A DJ spinning records is really the perfect fit for this, and it will probably cost you less than a live band. Ask the DJ to play music by Otis Redding, Booker T., Bill Haley and the Comets, Chuck Berry, Elvis Presley, Jerry Lee Lewis and Buddy Holiday. If you do opt for a live band, find one which replicates the 50s in both its style and its dress.

Consider sending invitations that have a 50s rock 'n' roll feel. If this is too casual for the wedding, you might want to use the idea for a pre-wedding party or rehearsal dinner. The invitation could be designed to look like a 45 RPM record with your names on the label. Or, a cartoon likeness of the two of you in penny loafers, jeans and leather jackets could grace the cover. You could have fun with the language, inviting guests to "Rock Around The Clock" with you. Or, use a picture of a frothy chocolate shake complete with two straws and a proclamation that love has you "All Shook Up."

For 50s memorabilia, contact Back To The 50s at 702-361-1950.

Instead of using table numbers, name tables after hits or entertainers from the era. Decorate the card table with old 45s; pass out bubble gum and hold a bubble-blowing contest. Ask the DJ to get people up and hula hooping to a bee-bop tune; give a prize to the person who lasts the longest. Serve cherry cokes. For the bride and groom, order one ice cream soda with two straws! Leave the reception in a 1950s fin-tailed Cadillac.

## What to Wear to the Soda Shop

Encourage guests to come in fifties attire: penny loafers, poodle skirts, saddle shoes, and letterman sweaters. Waiters can wear rolled-up jeans and tight white T-shirts. (Rent *Grease* if you need ideas for costumes.) For more formal 50s attire, the bride could wear a satin dress with fitted bodice and a chiffon cummerbund. A deep V-shaped neckline framed by a high satin collar could complete the picture. Veils were often waist length in the 50s. Bolero style jackets were popular over strapless dresses. Strapless, prom-style dress with lots and lots of crinoline are a stand-out.

A groom in the fifties might have worn an evening suit with a double breasted jacket with padded shoulders and a wide satin shawl collar. A more formal 50's groom might have chosen a dark grey wool tail coat with grey and black striped trousers, a white shirt with wing collar, and grey striped cravat with pin. To complete the picture: in his lapel, a small flower and in his breast pocket, a handkerchief.

Put the flower girl in a short skirt, bobby socks and saddle shoes. Put her hair in a pony tail. Dress bridesmaids to look like the pink ladies from *Grease*.

For more ideas and illustrations so good you could take them straight to your dressmaker, get a copy of *Fashion Sourcebooks: The 1950's by John Peacock* (Thames and Hudson, 1997)

# Sixties Love-In

For groovy couples who want the time to be a changin' right back to the sixties, there are plenty of ways to bring the hippie generation to life at your wedding. Before you begin, try to recall a little 60s history. Martin Luther King made his famous "I Had A Dream" speech in 1963. John F. Kennedy was president from 1961–1963, followed by Lyndon Johnson from 1963–1969.

The sixties celebrated youthfulness. Twiggy was the ideal fashion female—super skinny with big fake eyelashes shading her doe like eyes. Joan Baez sang folk songs. Anti war protests were everywhere. Beatlemania was sweeping the nation. In 1967 the Beatles' Sergeant Pepper's Lonely Heart Clubs Band was released. In 1969 Woodstock became a touchstone for the 60s generation—three days of rock bands, and an estimated 400,000 spectators, all groovin' to the same music. *Hair* was playing on Broadway in New York.

For tons of information on this time period, check out a copy of *The Sixties* by Arthur Marwick (Oxford, 1998).

## *Groovy Clothes*

There are really several directions you can go in when deciding on the appropriate 60s fashion for your wedding. There's the Jackie Kennedy look – suit and pill box hat from the early sixties. Imagine a straight and simple floor length dress with a high-waisted wide belt closed with a bow. A high neckline with a center split adds a small touch of 60s drama. Tease the hair and add a large bow on the top of the head from which the veil poufs out and you're all set. There are also the styles made popular by the 60s designer, Mary Quant with her trademark short skirts and bright colors. This decade saw pantsuits, cat suits, mini skirts, maxi skirts, and hot pants. Bridesmaids could all dress in pantsuits or in mini skirts with tall white boots. Groomsmen can sport ruffled shirts and blue velvet tuxes.

For a more relaxed "flower child" look, think of flowing white shifts, headbands, beads, and leather accessories. You could wear your hair straight and loose, carry a simple arrangement of fresh wildflowers such as daisies, and wear a wreath of flowers in your hair. Go barefoot or wear leather sandals! The groom can wear a nehru jacket over a white turtleneck. For a bold 60's look for the daring male: loud checked and flared pants with a wide belt at the hips and white moccasin shoes would certainly command attention, or at the very least the comment, "Can you believe people actually wore outfits like that back then?"

At the rehearsal dinner the night before, ask guests to come wearing their best 60s style hats such as wide-brimmed, floppy velvet numbers.

Since the 60s weren't so long ago, you may find some great fashion ideas right under your own nose: Look in your old family photo albums or even in your Mom's closet. Check it out!

## Come Together...Right Now!

Invitations can also have a sixties flair, if you (and perhaps your consultant) put your minds to it! The card might have a Peter Max or Roy Lichtenstein look. Consider an invitation shaped like a Campbells's Soup Can, with your names on the label. Or look into doing a tie dyed or splotchy psychedelic background. You could instead include a peace symbol or have a host of daisies decorating the borders.

Wording for the invitation could include typical 60s phrases like "groovy" "outta sight" and "far-out." Or, you could draw on lyrics or song titles from the 60s, such as The Beatles' "All You Need Is Love" or Bob Dylan's "Blowin In The Wind."

## Far Out Weddings

Get a guitarist to play folk music at the ceremony. Choose a reading from the words of Martin Luther King or the lyrics of Bob Dylan. At the reception, hang beads from doorways and cover the tables with tie-dyed tablecloths. Burn a little incense. Use lots of candles on the tables for atmosphere. Have the cake designed with peace symbols on it. As favors, give out peace and love decals or little packages of incense.

At the reception play music that represents the 60s – everything from Joan Baez and The Beatles to Jimi Hendrix and The Grateful Dead. Play songs made popular by the musical, *Hair*. Don't forget other popular musicians of the day: Crosby, Stills, Nash and Young; Sly and the Family Stone; Richie Havens; Janis Joplin; The Who; and The Jefferson Airplane. Lead your guests in some popular sixties dances such as the fish, the hitch-hiker, the frug and the jerk.

After the reception, drive off in a VW bug, or a van with a bumper sticker that says, "Keep on Truckin'."

Need even more ideas? It wouldn't hurt to rent the movie, *Woodstock*...and of course, who could resist watching *Austin Powers* one more time?

# Disco Daze

Does something about your groom remind you of John Travolta as Tony Manero in *Saturday Night Fever?* Let seventies fever take over your wedding reception! Let's take a trip back in time: Richard Nixon was president from 1969 until he resigned in 1974. Gerald Ford stepped in from 1974–1977 and Jimmy Carter finished out the decade as president. *The Tonight Show* starring Johnny Carson was on TV. The Wiz was on Broadway. Oscar winners of the 70s included such films as *The Godfather*, *Rocky* and *Annie Hall.* People were reading such bestsellers as *Jonathan Livingston Seagull* by Richard Bach, *Once is Not Enough* by Jacqueline Susann and *Breakfast of Champions* by Kurt Vonnegut.

## Won't You Take Me to Funky Town?

A great dance floor with a swirling disco ball is at the heart of a good seventies party. Light up the floor with colored strobes and let the disco inferno begin! A DJ is the perfect solution for your dancing needs. Ask the DJ to play tunes like Alicia Bridges', "I Love the Nightlife" Diana Ross' Love Hangover" and Donna Summers' "Hot Stuff." The Bee Gees on the *Saturday Night Fever* soundtrack will bring the room alive.

The 70s wasn't only about disco, however, and you may want to play some other hits from that era. Don't overlook songs by The Doors, The Rolling Stones, The Eagles, Fleetwood Mac, Chicago, Stevie Wonder, Elton John, and David Bowie. Throw in a little folk (James Taylor and Carole King) and a little reggae (Bob Marley and Jimmy Cliff) for good measure.

## Disco Dress

Family photo albums should be loaded with ideas for 70s attire. Men's pants were still flared. Corduroy jackets with patch pockets and half-belts were popular. Leather boots with platform heels made men look taller. Women, too, loved the height and style of the platform shoe. For the famous *Saturday Night Fever* disco scene, John Travolta wore a white suit with matching vest. For the bride who intends to dance the night away, comfort and style should be a major consideration. A knee-length white dress would be dynamite. The dress should move and twirl with the bride. Since bridal fashions haven't changed so dramatically since the 70s, the bride and groom can really wear whatever they like and still be in keeping with a 70s theme.

**Bridal Blunders**

Strobe lights can cause seizures in people who suffer from epilepsy. To play it safe, let guests know in advance that your disco dance party will include a strobe light.

**The Least You Need to Know**

➤ Use the library and the Internet to find information on the time period you love the most. Search for information on music and costumes; read up on the history of the period.

➤ Contact historic agencies or organizations that can help give you more information on how people dressed, entertained, or married back then.

➤ Don't worry too much about historical accuracy. Borrow elements you like, drop or change ones you don't. This is a wedding, not a term paper.

➤ Make the food, music, and decorations reflect your historic theme.

# Chapter 14

# Ethnic Touches and Traditions

> ## In This Chapter
>
> ➤ Turning a blast from your past into a breath of fresh air
>
> ➤ Researching your background
>
> ➤ Mixing everything together in the marriage melting pot
>
> ➤ Finding foods that say who you are
>
> ➤ Discovering specific ethnic traditions

When one person marries another, two worlds collide. Each person arrives at the altar with years of family history behind him or her. The generations that have gone before are reflected in everything that the bride or groom is today. "I always encourage couples to include ethnic traditions, because our country is so ethnically mixed these days," says Elaine Parker, wedding consultant in Nashville, Tennessee. To honor the roots that have helped each person to grow, many brides and grooms today want to include ethnic and cultural customs in their wedding day. A little music here, a little food there, a special prayer, a second language, and suddenly your union is a multicultural celebration. The ceremony and reception become like a tapestry of your past lives, richly supporting your desire to make a new life together.

## Digging for Roots

Perhaps you want to incorporate some multicultural traditions but are unsure of where to begin. The best (and most convenient) place is at home. Your parents, grandparents, great aunts and uncles may be storing a wealth of information about your heritage and the way "things used to be done." Ask about their own weddings. What did they wear? What kind of vows did they recite? What music did they dance to? Where was the ceremony held? Ask about favorite foods and recipes. If any of your relatives lived in another country, take them out to lunch and listen to their stories about that land. You may get some creative ideas.

Remember, the point is to find out how *your* family celebrates. It's okay if that's not exactly what the books describe. Customs vary from region to region and from family to family. Talk with your parents and future in-laws about your desire to include elements of your family and cultural history in your wedding day. Help them to understand why these gestures are important to you.

You can also get lots of information on line. Just type in a key word for the country that interests you. Or go to **www.askjeeves.com** and ask a question such as "Tell me about Italian wedding customs." Click on "ask" and you'll be on your way to the answer. Another approach is to contact the embassy or consulate of the country you are interested in. They'll probably be more than happy to give you information about wedding customs. You may even get lucky and find someone there who can speak from recent experience!

# The Marriage Melting Pot

There's no such thing as too many different elements. Elaine Parker of Weddings with Elan in Nashville, Tennessee, has counseled brides as they put together a wedding to reflect such separate backgrounds as Cherokee Indian, Mexican, British, Jewish, Italian, and Spanish heritage all in one day! A challenge, certainly, but one Parker handles routinely. One couple whom Parker is working with is planning to release butterflies, an Indian symbol of freedom. An ivory lace favor bag will be filled with Mexican wedding cookies, Jewish rugala, Italian Jordan almonds, and chocolate gold coins (another Indian tradition). They may be only small touches in a larger picture, but gestures like these make every family member feel welcome and included. If you are Chinese, for example, but you are having a Jewish ceremony, you can still honor your Chinese heritage. One bride's mother hand-made large red Chinese symbols of love and happiness for display at the reception site.

My husband grew up speaking Dutch. At our New York City ceremony, which was in English, we asked the father of the groom to give a reading in Dutch. Even though most of the guests could not understand what he was saying, we thought it was important for the Dutch language and heritage to be recognized. Hearing the sounds of another language floating out over the congregation provided a sense of the diversity of our group and, simultaneously, a feeling of togetherness. I'm sure it also made those relatives who made the trip from The Netherlands to be with us that day feel even more welcome and comfortable.

At another wedding the bride's grandfather read a T'ang dynasty love poem, first in Chinese and then in English. It was a high point of the day. Many couples choose to use a second language on their wedding invitations for this same reason. English can appear on one side and the other language on a facing page. If you are not

**Consultants Say**

"Find out what grandma and grandpa's special song is. Have the band play it as they take a special dance together," suggests wedding consultant Bev Dembo of Northbrook, Illinois.

entirely fluent in the language in question yourself, make sure a native speaker checks your spelling and grammar before you head off to the printer.

# Ethnic Customs

Not only each country but often each region of the country will have its own unique wedding customs. The discussion of traditions that follows is not intended to be exhaustive. Needless to say, that is beyond the scope of this book. Rather it is intended to get you thinking and asking questions about your heritage. Included are some Old-World and some contemporary rituals. If you don't find your ethnic background represented here, it doesn't mean you have no wedding traditions. Keep on searching.

It bears repeating: The best place to start looking for wedding customs is within your own family. If your grandmother or grandfather believe a certain custom is appropriate, consider including that one, no matter what the books tell you. Here, then, in this chapter are some ideas that have been associated with the wedding folklore of several countries throughout the world.

## African Traditions

Africa is a large continent of many countries and customs, making marriage customs far too numerous and complicated to list in any one book. Here, then, are just a few ethnic customs you can think about including in your day.

Kente cloth, a woven red, gold, and green design, is often used in African-American weddings. The colors in the cloth are highly symbolic. Red represents the bloodshed of slavery, gold represents prosperity, and green represents the fertile homeland. Another important African color is purple, the symbol of royalty. The invitations, dress, and decorations can all reflect a Kente cloth motif.

The bride may wish to wear a traditional headpiece and a loose-fitting skirt and blouse. Traditional for the groom is a long pullover tunic top and a box-like hat; or he might wear a tuxedo, turban, and chest banner. Wearing cowrie shells by the bride was at one time believed to encourage fertility.

One African-American tradition that has been gaining in popularity is called "jumping the broom." It began among black American slaves, who, because they were regarded as property, could not enter into legal marriage contracts. The broom had long been a symbol of marriage in Africa, because the bride used a broom to sweep out her mother-in-law's house prior to the wedding. In the United States, the practice of jumping over a broom became a way for couples to sanction their own unions. It symbolizes new beginnings—sweeping away the old and welcoming the new.

The ritual itself is simple. Guests form a circle around the couple as they stand in front of the broom on the floor. The officiant should say a few words about how the broom symbolizes the joining of the couple and the combining of two families, and about the need for the community to support the couple. The bride and groom then join hands, and everyone counts: One, two, three...Jump!

**165**

Broom jumping can take place at the ceremony or the reception, depending on how the couple and officiant wish to handle it. If done at the ceremony, it usually happens just before the recessional. The broom, decorated with flowers, ribbons, bows, or cloth, can be placed by a member of the wedding party or another person of significance to the couple. Sometimes drummers and dancers bring the broom up the aisle and place it before the couple.

If you and your officiant feel that this custom would be better observed at the reception, you can introduce it at the beginning of the reception or just before you and your groom take your first dance.

As you leave, guests might throw corn (for fertility) instead of rice. Gospel music, folk songs, and spirituals can be moving additions to the ceremony.

## Argentinean Traditions

At Argentine weddings, dulce de leche wedding cakes are baked with trinkets or favors hidden inside. Each favor is attached to a string. Single women at the party each get to pull one string. If you get the ring, it means you'll be the next to marry!

## Chinese Traditions

Red is the color of joy, so invitations and even the bride's dress are usually red. Numbers are to be taken into consideration for everything from picking the date, to determining how many tiers are in the wedding cake or how many courses to serve. According to the Chinese Historical and Cultural Project, special wedding foods include such items as jellyfish, lobster (called dragon shrimp), chicken feet (known as phoenix feet), shark's fin soup, roast suckling pig, Peking duck, sea cucumber, fish, and noodles. Each food has special significance or brings luck. Large Chinese characters are often placed on the wall behind the head table to signify double happiness. For more information on Chinese wedding traditions, go to the Chinese Historical and Cultural Project Web site at **www.chcp.org**.

## English Traditions

In England, the bride, the groom, and their wedding party often walk together to the church. Orange blossoms may be sprinkled on the ground in front of the bride, who might carry or wear a small horseshoe for good luck. According to *Ethnic and Specialty Wedding Guide* by Lois Pearce (published by the Association of Bridal Consultants), a square of cloth called the "care cloth" was historically held over the heads of the bride and groom during the benediction. Church bells are rung to scare off evil spirits as the couple enters and leaves the church.

The wedding cake is often a rich fruitcake decorated with marzipan. The top layer is known as the "christening cake." It is saved and served at the baptism of the first child. In the seventeenth century, wheat was thrown at the couple. Instead of a bachelor and bachelorette party, they have stag parties and hen nights.

Although I have not read about its significance in any other book, one British wedding I attended incorporated an amusing custom at the reception. The groom was blindfolded. All the women at the party were asked to line up and extend a hand. The groom's job was to walk down the line, feeling each hand until he found his bride by touch! Luckily for him, the groom at this wedding managed to pick out his beloved from a rather long lineup. (Perhaps he peeked). Is this a true British tradition or just a fun game this couple made up? I'm not sure, but it was fun.

**Something True**

In Britain it's good luck to be kissed by a chimney sweep on your wedding day.

## French Traditions

In France the bride and groom and their wedding party walk to the church together. Children run to stand in front of the entrance with white ribbons that the bride must cut in order to enter the church. During the ceremony, a silk wedding canopy is held over the couple to protect them from evil spirits. Laurel leaves line the bride's path as she exits the church.

At the reception, a two-handled cup known as the *coup de mariage* is used by the couple for toasts. In times past, biscuits or cakes used to be crumbled over the head of the bride. For a uniquely French wedding cake, the bride and groom can order a croquembouche, a seventeenth-century tower of cream puffs glazed with caramel. It is customary to throw wheat rather than rice as the couple leaves.

## German Traditions

In Germany a *Polterabend* is a dinner party the night before the wedding. Traditionally, the couple is "roasted" and plates are broken.

On the morning of the wedding, a "bridal soup," or breakfast, is held for guests at the bride's house. In Old Germany, after the vows, the couple would stage a playful thumb war to see who will get the "upper hand" in the marriage. The German bride might also try to step on her new husband's foot. In Old Germany, this little love match would determine who will rule the roost.

Another playful exchange occurs at the end of the ceremony, when guests "rope" the couple in with a barricade of ribbons and garlands of flowers. To get out, the couple has to promise the guests a party. Naturally, schnapps will be served.

## Greek Traditions

The couple may wear crowns attached by ribbons. In the Greek Orthodox service, the couple takes three sips of wine from a cup. A lump of sugar tucked into the bride's glove will supposedly ensure sweetness in marriage. Nuts and dates might be thrown instead of rice.

# *Hispanic American Traditions*

Some Hispanic customs come from Spain, others from Mexico. Find the ones that suit your style.

In prewedding rituals, the godparents present the couple with a kneeling pillow, often lavishly embroidered, for the ceremony. The groom gives 13 gold coins to the bride (the number signifies Christ and his 12 apostles) as a way of saying, "I trust you with all my worldly goods." Sometimes a rosary or decorative cord of orange blossoms is hung around the bride's and groom's necks, binding them together in a loose figure eight.

For the first dance, guests form a heart-shaped circle around the couple. The Spanish-American bride may choose to wear a mantilla and a flamenco-style dress with ruffled hem. Some Spanish brides wear black, symbolizing their commitment until "death do us part." The bride might carry a fan instead of flowers. The groom might wear tight pants and a bolero jacket for a matador style. It is traditional for one of the attendants to carry flowers for the Virgin Mary.

Traditional foods might include tapas (hors d'oeuvres), paella (a rice and seafood dish), and sangria. Wedding cookies known as "pastelitos de boda" can be served with dessert or given as favors.

### Creative Corner

At the reception it might be fun to ask some of your guests to give their toasts in Spanish. From *A Treasury of Spanish Love Poems, Quotations and Proverbs* edited by Juan and Susan Serrano (Hippocrene Books, 1995) you can find such wonderful sayings as this one by Marques de Santillana, "Ama y seras amado y podras hacer lo que no haras desamado." (Translation: "Love and you will be loved, and you will be able to do all that you could not do unloved.") Other books in the same series include collections of poetry and quotations in Arabic, Czech, Finnish, French, German, Hungarian, Italian, Polish, Russian, Ukrainian, and more.

# *Indian Traditions*

The Hindu bride usually wears a red and gold sari with lots of jewelry and a veil that covers her head. An orange powder (sendhu) is put on the bride's forehead. The wedding may last up to several days.

Prior to an Indian wedding, the bride hennas her hands and feet, a practice known as *mehandi*. The groom often rides to the wedding on horseback; his arrival can be heralded by the beating of drums. After the ceremony, men and women are sometimes served dinner separately.

## Irish Traditions

The Irish wedding ring is called a claddagh ring, which depicts two hands holding a heart. Fruitcake is a traditional wedding cake. Everyone loves the Irish Wedding Blessing: "May the road rise to meet you./ May the wind always be at your back,/ May the sun shine warm upon your face/ The rains fall soft upon the fields…." You can also check out the love poetry of Irish poets W.B. Yeats or Thomas Moore to see if anything catches your fancy. The Irish often ring bells, rather than throw rice, as the couple leaves the church. The bride might carry a small horseshoe for good luck. For invitations, favors, claddagh rings, wedding programs and more, contact The Irish Tinker in Keyport, New Jersey at 732-335-1999 or on the Web at **www.irishtinker.com**. You can get cake-toppers, cake knives, and claddagh wedding candles, from **www.celticart.com**. .

## Italian Traditions

Wedding knots, or "farfallette dolci" made of twisted dough are popular wedding treats in Italy. Sugared almonds, called confetti, are given as favors. The tarantella, a traditional circle dance, is danced at the wedding.

## Jamaican Traditions

In Jamaica the whole village usually turns out to see the bride on her wedding day. Traditional foods include curried goat and rice. To drink: rum punch. The cake is a dark fruit cake full of raisins and other dried fruit soaked in rum. The party often lasts all night.

## Japanese Traditions

In choosing a wedding date, a Japanese couple looks for an auspicious day of good fortune. The ceremony usually takes place in a Shinto shrine or Buddhist temple, where offerings of rice water, salt, fruit, and sake are given at the altar. The ceremony is presided over by a Shinto priest and miko (serving girls) dressed in red and white dresses. (Red is a color of happiness. As part of the ceremony, the bride and groom are served sake in three cups. They each take three sips from each cup, repeating this process three times, to complete what is known as the three-times-three ceremony (San-San Kudo).

The bride wears a traditional quilted robe over a white kimono. A special sash (obi), representing female virtue, is tied around her waist. In times past she would also wear an elaborate wig. The groom wears a black kimono.

Today, Japanese brides often change several times during the wedding—from white kimono to a white Western-style wedding gown to a colorful kimono to a ball gown. At the reception, guests might be served red rice, kelp, and fish. Candies in the shape of flowers are also popular at wedding celebrations, as are origami (folded paper) cranes. The cranes are a symbol of fidelity.

## Jewish Traditions

Jewish wedding traditions and customs will differ depending on the rabbi and the congregation and depending on whether the service is Orthodox, Conservative, or Reform. Customs include a huppah (canopy held over the bridal couple's head,), the seven wedding blessings, and the breaking of a glass by the groom. Weddings may not be held between sundown on Friday and sundown on Saturday.

### Something True

Sometimes a *badekan* ceremony precedes a Jewish wedding. This custom, which originated in biblical times, allows the groom to see the bride and place the veil over her with his own hands—thereby insuring that no one could switch the bride, causing the groom to marry the wrong woman.

Before the wedding, the Orthodox or Conservative bride has a ritual bath (mikvah). The bride wears white at the wedding, while the groom often wears a short white robe called a kittel over his suit. A marriage contract in Hebrew outlining the groom's responsibilities to his wife is called a ketuba. (Today it might also include the bride's responsibilities to her husband as well.) Many couples engage an artist to create their ketubas, which they then hang in their home.

The bride is escorted up the aisle by both her parents. She takes the last few steps alone, however, to signify her willingness to enter into this marriage. During the ceremony, which takes place under a huppah, the rabbi or cantor presiding might wrap the couple in a prayer shawl, known as a talis, to signify their unity. Traditionally the Orthodox bride circles the groom seven times. Some see this as a symbol of the creation of a new family circle.

After the ceremony comes the traditional breaking of the glass. The best man places a drinking glass (wrapped in cloth) under the groom's right foot. As the groom smashes the glass, the congregation shouts "Mazel Tov" (Congratulations!) and applauds. There are many different ideas about the meaning behind the breaking of the glass. Some say it symbolizes the breaking of the hymen; others that it stands for the sorrow and death that are also a part of life, or that it pays homage to the destruction of the Jerusalem Temple in 70 A.D.

After the recessional, the bride and groom enjoy a *yichud*—and have a few moments alone before greeting their guests. At the reception, before the meal is served, the wedding challah (braided bread) is blessed. Israeli folk music may be played, including the hora, a traditional dance of celebration. The guests link arms and dance in a circle around the couple. The groom and bride might be hoisted in chairs by their guests and danced around. At the end of the party, a booklet of songs and readings is distributed to the guests. Called "benchers," these booklets can make lovely favors as well.

## Moroccan Traditions

There may be as many as eight days of festivities surrounding a Moroccan wedding. Two days before the actual wedding ceremony, for example, a henna service takes place. The bride's hands and feet are painted with beautiful designs. Often the bride undergoes a ritual purification bath in a pool.

As a sign of fertility, the bride and groom may be showered with dates and figs. Dates, figs, and sweet teas are also commonly offered at wedding parties.

## Native American Traditions

According to *Ethnic and Specialty Wedding Guide* by Lois Pearce (published by the Association of Bridal Consultants, 1998), in many Native American traditions the bride and groom say their vows while facing to the east, considered to be the direction of the future. Drumming and stories set to music are usually popular elements of the celebration. Both bride and groom undergo a ritual hand-washing ceremony representing their washing away of past loves and past evils. White and yellow cornmeal are mixed into a mush and shared by the couple during the ceremony to symbolize their union. Of course, there can be great variations in wedding customs from tribe to tribe and state to state.

## Russian Traditions

A gleaming silver tea urn known as a "samovar" is the centerpiece of a bride's trousseau. In Russian orthodox services, crowns are held over the heads of the bride and groom to symbolize their roles as a king and queen of creation. To rid their new home of evil spirits lurking in the chimney, a fire of straw would be started in the fireplace.

## Scottish Traditions

In Scotland the first item to be brought into a new home should be salt, to scare off bad spirits. The cake is often a layered fruitcake, one layer of which is eaten at the wedding while the other is saved for the birth of the first baby. Kilts may be worn by the men. The bride might wear a tartan sash over her gown in a matching plaid. Bagpipers may play at the wedding or reception. The Highland fling is a traditional dance. In the old days the groom would purchase a silver teaspoon and have it engraved with the couple's initials and wedding date. This was called the "wedding spune."

## Swedish Traditions

An old adage suggests that the bride leave her shoes untied. A fertility symbol, it brings good luck and means you will have children early.

# You Are What You Eat

One of the nicest (and often easiest) ways to pay homage to a particular ethnic background is through food. With today's trend toward food stations at wedding receptions, it's easier than ever to include food from many different cultures. If you like, each nationality could have its own table, appropriately decorated. Guests can wander from "country" to "country" sampling the delicious varieties of foods. If you prefer a sit-down affair, a skilled caterer can help you to plan the menu.

**Consultants Say**

Actress Kathy Najimy chose to honor her Lebanese ancestry by serving Middle-Eastern appetizers at the wedding reception. British actress Kate Winslet served up traditional English fare at her party: bangers and mash with turnips, red onion gravy, and English mustard.

**Bridal Blunders**

Although it may seem like a great idea to ask grandma to whip up her famous stuffed grape leaves, your reception site may not allow it. The caterer and the facility worry about their liability and who would be responsible in case anyone becomes sick from the food. Ask grandma if she would be willing to share her recipe with the caterer.

Alternatively, couples who decide to marry in two separate ceremonies can honor both halves of this union by having two different meals! One bride married in a Hindu service in the morning, followed by a luncheon of delicious Indian food. Later that day the couple remarried in a Methodist church, followed by an all-American dinner. The same guests attended both functions for a full day of wedding festivities.

List your wedding specialties on a beautifully presented menu. Take the time to explain why each of the dishes is special to your family. This little touch helps guests to understand the ethnic touches, and provides a lovely little keepsake as well. More ambitious would be to create a little booklet for the reception menu and recipes to match. This can make a useful and charming wedding favor for your guests.

Bridal consultant Elaine Parker can help you plan your menu. For a fee, she will research the culinary background of each country in question and create a seamless menu that reflects the various regions or nationalities you specify. For an additional fee, she will research and provide you with the recipes for the dishes. Contact Parker at 615-292-7433 or e-mail her at **elanconsultants@juno.com.**

The wedding cake offers another opportunity to honor one's national or ethnic heritage(s). Fancy gum paste designs are replacing fresh flowers on many wedding cakes. Why not consider a design that reflects a particular nationality—such as something inspired by Islamic art. A cake designed by The Cake Gallery of Atlanta, Georgia, made use of a pale blue and white Delft pattern for a touch of the Netherlands.

For that matter, why fight over one flavor? Some couples are asking for a different flavor on every tier, so every person at the party can have their cake and eat it too! Cream cheese cakes, carrot cakes, chocolate cakes are all alternatives to the standard white cake.

# Moving to the Beat of a Different Drummer

Everyone dances to the beat of a different drummer. Let your rhythm be heard at your wedding or reception. Actress Kathy Najimy treated her guests to the sounds of an Arabic band. You could honor Indian ancestry with sitar music, Scottish ancestry by walking to the altar or from the ceremony to the reception accompanied by bagpipes. At the reception, Scottish country dances can be fun for all, as can the traditional jigs and reels of an Irish folk band. Liven up the place with Brazilian dance music. Argentinean? Practice the tango for a hot, romantic number!

### Consultants Say

If you and your groom are unfamiliar with some of the ethnic dances you are trying to incorporate, it's a good idea take dance lessons prior to the wedding. Dancing can be a fun tension reliever during the wedding planning process, and you'll really look great during the first dance together if you know the steps.

### The Least You Need to Know

➤ Talk with your relatives about the foods and traditions that are important to them.

➤ Research a country's traditions at the library or on the Internet.

➤ Pick and choose the traditions that you like. Borrow from many cultures if you wish.

➤ It's okay to take a little creative license and make the tradition what you want it to be. This is a party, not a social studies report.

➤ Work on the look, feel, taste, and sounds of the country in question.

# Part 4
# Making It Your Own

*Seize the day! This is your wedding and it should reflect who you are as a couple. Personal touches are what it's all about. Have your wedding your way.*

*Consider writing your own vows. Weave some new declarations into the traditional ones. Choose some original readings to share with your guests. The ceremony should be a personal and intimate expression of your love for one another.*

*Discover the most creative ways to use flowers and music at your ceremony and reception. Make a dramatic exit. This section covers everything from the cake to the favors for your guests, with lots of ideas on every aspect of your wedding day. There's something here for everyone!*

# Chapter 15

# Creative Attire

---

## In This Chapter

➤ Choosing a wedding gown

➤ Matching your gown to your wedding theme

➤ Recycling mom's or grandma's dress

➤ Dressing the groom with creative flair

➤ Outfitting children

---

The music begins to play, all eyes turn, and Here Comes the Bride! Everyone is craning to get a look at you in your wedding attire. How will you choose to appear? In a cloud of tulle? As a vision in lace? In a whirl of white? From sleek lines of simplicity to the extravagant fantasy, the choice is yours. This is your day to shine.

## Wedding Gown Traditions

Before 1800, couples in the U.S. just put on their "Sunday best" and went to meet the preacher. In other countries they may have worn traditional costume. Up until fairly recently, what the bride wore on her wedding day often wasn't specifically wedding attire and could certainly be worn again on many other special occasions. Although we can all agree that this is a practical approach, many brides would miss the romance and extravagance of what we have come to know and love as the wedding gown.

The idea of a white dress for a wedding is relatively new, and many cultures continue to honor other colors at their marriage ceremonies. Historically, the first white wedding dress was worn in 1498 by the wife of Louis XII of France, but her choice did not appear to set a trend. Brides continued to wear many other colors over the next 300 years.

Brides have worn veils since ancient times. Veils were believed to protect a bride from evil spirits on her wedding day. In some cultures the veil covers the entire head and face, making it impossible to see the bride's face. In an arranged marriage, the groom's

first look at his wife might have been when that veil was lifted at the ceremony. The veil is also a symbol of virginity.

In the last 200 years of American weddings, bridal gowns have gone through many transformations. We've had big hoops and moderate hoops. We've had Civil-war-era tiny, tiny waists with big skirts and big mutton sleeves. We've seen the sleek, drop-waisted, ankle-length dresses of the twenties with their fabulous long veils.

Who knows where bridal fashion will take us in the coming century? Maybe your choice will set the next trend. For now, though, there are plenty of styles to choose from that both borrow from the past and look to the future.

## Choosing a Wedding Gown

This is the one and only rule: Start your quest well in advance—some gowns take six months to order! So give yourself plenty of time to choose a gown, have it made or altered, and find the right undergarments, shoes, head piece, veil (if you're wearing one) and other accessories to go with it.

There's so much to look at and try! With hundreds of styles represented in the larger salons, you should have no trouble finding the perfect gown for your day. Different looks will flatter different figures, heights, bust sizes, and personalities. Strapless and backless or high-necked and long-sleeved—whatever you're looking for, it's probably out there. You can go for the demure, the dramatic, or the divine. Sleek sheaths with a tank-top effect are as popular today as the more traditional ball gown. Your gown can be as traditional, contemporary, or just plain different as you want it to be. Creative looks abound—both in bridal shops and beyond.

Although occasionally a bride will fall in love with a particular look and build her day around that look, most choose a wedding location and settle on a style or theme before beginning to shop for a dress. If you know how formal your wedding is going to be, you'll have an easier time. The formality of the wedding attire is typically determined by a) the kind of wedding you are having and b) what time of day you are having it. After six o'clock, for example, white tie is the traditionally "correct" choice.

"No one should tell the bride what she should and should not wear," counsels Cetta Fessett, manager of Exclusives for the Bride in Chicago. "There are no rules." When you arrive at a bridal salon, describe what you want. Give the person helping you some idea of the type of dress you have in mind. "Tell us your dream, your fantasy. I don't care if you're an attorney if what you want to look like is a princess!" she says.

*No matter what your personal style is, there's bound to be a way to incorporate it into your wedding attire.*
©Index Stock

If you have a wedding theme, be sure to tell the bridal salon. They may have just the thing. If you have a particular fashion style in mind, describe it. Are you the kind of bride who would feel comfortable only in a short skirt? An ankle-length dress? Something that just sweeps the floor? If you can imagine it, it's out there—cathedral, chapel, and sweep trains, handkerchief hems and bustles. There are even dresses with removable skirts so you can go long and traditional at the ceremony, short and modern at the reception. What's your style?

A small addition can playfully tweak the traditional and make it into something truly special. An otherwise traditional dress might have cutouts at the midriff for a daring peak at a toned and sun-tanned bride. A white leather motorcycle jacket thrown over a strapless ball gown will be sure to

### Consultants Say

Need more information? Check out *The Bridal Gown Guide* by Denise and Alan Fields ($11.99). It describes about 1,000 gowns, with their style numbers and prices, and reviews bridal shops and designers, and lists Web sites of interest. Call 800–888–0385 or go to **www.windsorpeak.com** to find out how to order a copy.

### Consultants Say

Since you're looking for something really special, you'll want to take your time. Call to make an appointment in advance at a bridal salon so you have the attention of one consultant. Shop on a weekday if possible for a less crowded experience.

### Bridal Blunders

Don't try to buy your dress a size too small because you're planning to lose weight before the wedding. It's a lot easier to take in a dress than it is to let it out.

### Consultants Say

Check out **www.ModernBride.com** and log onto their fashion center for a look at what's hot, what's happening. The program will even let you check out bridesmaid's dresses in dozens of different shades.

get attention. A sudden surprising addition like this can balance your frilly feminine side with a tougher dare-devil side. A crown of crystals in your hair could be a bright spot. A faux white rabbit evening purse can get your makeup and comb from ceremony to reception in style. A pair of sexy sandals, cowboy boots, or even bare feet can peak out from underneath your hemline. More than any other aspect of your wedding, your gown is about you. This is the one area where compromise is unnecessary. After all, many people have to eat the food and dance to the music, but only you have to wear the gown!

Of course, if your wedding day looks to be really out of the ordinary, a bridal shop may not have what you want. Their stock of medieval costumes, shorts and tank tops, and white bikinis could be limited. Thinking of getting married while skydiving? You'd better stick with a jumpsuit. (You can always change into more down-to-earth bridal attire for the reception.) Couples who marry underwater face similar fashion constraints—although some have been known to wear tux and gown.

## If the Shoe Fits...

Shoes, though they may barely peek from beneath a hemline, should be chosen with care. Comfort is the first consideration. You'll need to be able to walk, dance, maybe even stand on your tiptoes to kiss that tall groom of yours. Every child who has ever heard the story of Cinderella understands that the right footwear is the straightest path to living happily ever after with your prince. The lesson of that story? You get to wear the shoe only if it *fits*. Cheat on this and your feet will never forgive you. (Plus, you don't want Uncle Maury to be able to say he lasted longer than you did out on the dance floor.)

Don't pass on style, though, just because this is a "wedding shoe." A satin band, a rhinestone buckle, or a chiffon bow can give a shoe that certain something and complete your fairy-tale look. you can even buy clear shoes for the "glass slipper" look. The pump is a classic, but brides can also choose a stiletto heel for something a little sexier, a little more daring. An open toe or strappy sandal can be perfect for a breezy summer wedding. (Remember, this means no stockings—and a pedicure becomes a must.)

Make sure the height of the heel works with your dress and style. How high you go also depends on how tall you want to be and how comfortable you are walking in a heel. You're going to be standing all day; if the ceremony or reception is outdoors, you may be running around on uneven ground. Make sure your shoes are comfortable and that you can walk with confidence. Wear the shoes around the house prior to the ceremony in order to break them in without dirtying them.

## Creative Colors

The tradition of wearing white to a wedding doesn't go back very far—only to the mid 1800s. Nor is white the worldwide choice. In China and Islamic cultures, for example, the bride wears red. In Korea, ceremonial robes of red and yellow mark the day; in Russia, blue is favored. Although we may think of white as the symbol of virginity, blue has historically been the color of purity. In ancient times, Hebrew brides wore blue ribbons on their gowns at wedding ceremonies as a sign of chastity. Green, however, has been seen as unlucky by many cultures, perhaps because of its association with jealousy, or fairies and their tricks (according to *Wedding Album: Customs and Lore Through the Ages* by Alice Lea Mast Tasman [Walker Publishing, 1982]).

Wedding gowns today are blooming with color all across America. Recording artist Tori Amos wore an ice-blue dress for her wedding. Pastels are particularly popular. Bridal magazines are highlighting gowns of peach and ivory, bustled in the back with pale flowers to reveal layers of dreamy, peach-colored tulle. Gowns in subtle palettes of golds and yellows are walking down runways. Soft greens, icy lemons, sheer lavenders, and powdery pinks are popping up all over. Even the beading has gotten bolder. Pink, purple, and blue beads adorn the bodice of a pale-green dress that's all romance and whimsy.

Be brave. Be creative. Add a splash of color, if that's what you want.

**Something True**

An ancient Greek custom called for guests to throw shoes at the newly-wed couple, believing it would ward off evil spirits and bring good luck. If you weren't hit, *that* would be luck! Apparently the state of Colorado prefers not to leave this to chance. According to *Loony Laws and Silly Statutes* (Sterling, 1994) this state passed a law making it illegal to throw shoes at the bride and groom.

**Something True**

The white wedding dress was originally a symbol of wealth, not purity. A bride who could afford to wear such an impractical color was obviously in a position to be extravagant. The fact that the dress was created for just one day added to the impression of luxury.

# The Second Time Around

Bridal suits are perfect for the less formal or second-time wedding. Suits can be very dressy—with linen, satin, or lace. Other dressy touches include rhinestone buttons, ruffles, and gold embroidery.

Of course, there's no need for second-time brides to feel wedded to the bridal suit. Cetta Fessett, manager of Exclusives for the Bride in Chicago, says she has seen second-time brides choose everything from an all-out traditional gown with all the trimmings to a beautiful suit. "It's really up to you!"

# Grandma's Gown

What better way to honor the women in your family than by wearing your mother's or your grandmother's gown? Grandma's gown can be particularly appropriate if you are looking for a style that's a little retro. You may have to go all the way back to great grandma before you can find anything truly historic, however.

If you do decide to wear a family heirloom, you'll probably need to make some changes to it. The fit may or may not be perfect. The fabric may need some cleaning, repairs, or updating.

Take the gown to a dressmaker or restoration specialist. Discuss how you want the gown to look and fit, and how much the work will cost. Depending on the fit and condition of the gown, using grandma's dress may not be that much of a cost saver.

# Theme Wedding Dresses

If you're going to carry out a particular theme at the wedding, why not start the ceremony with the right attire? A nautical look for you and your bridesmaids might be perfect for a wedding on board a yacht, or even on dry land back at the yacht club. The groom might choose to dress like a ship's captain. The bridesmaids can wear sailor dresses and straw boaters.

A plantation wedding calls for a frilly Southern belle gown, possibly with parasol. A Christmas gown makes a warm yet elegant statement in soft white velvet. Fur or faux fur trim can be a winter wonderland touch for a seasonal wedding.

Some themes revolve around a particular time period. For a romantically old-fashioned look at a French country wedding, one bride wore an ivory dress with a gold and bronze brocade bodice. The groom, an actor, wore a Versace three-quarter-length frock over a cotton shirt trimmed with lace cuffs. To complete the picture, the reception was held in a seventeenth-century French chateau. To match your dress to a specific era, you'll need to do a little costume research. A number of museums have collections of wedding gowns on display. Costume exhibits are a lot of fun, if you have access to one, and might provide some inspiration. And don't forget to check your local library for books of dress fashions through the ages. Whether you're buying from a designer or having your own dress made, you may get some good ideas from the past.

# United Nations of Dresses: Different Styles to Celebrate Different Cultures

Many couples choose to honor their culture with traditional dress. An Indian couple might opt for a sari and a Nehru jacket; a Spanish wedding gown in gold or red with a matching mantilla can be dramatic. For an Asian wedding, the bride might choose to wear three different gowns: changing from a bridal gown to a ball gown, to an evening gown.

*It's not* all *about the bride—even the groom's attire can express his personal style or cultural background.*
©New England Stock/ Bill Bachmann

Chinese wedding custom calls for red clothing symbolizing joy. Red shoes and red veils are part of the look. Until recently, Icelandic brides wore black velvet on their wedding days—often embroidered with gold and silver.

Consultant Elaine Parker of Weddings With Elan in Nashville, Tennessee, has attended weddings in more than 34 different countries and has been helping brides put together multicultural weddings for years. At a recent mixed-marriage wedding Parker attended, the bride wore a red sari for her wedding in a Hindu temple, then changed into a white wedding dress and was remarried in a Methodist church. At another wedding, Parker helped arrange a Shinto/Jewish ceremony. The bride, the bride's mother, and even the groom's mother wore kimonos.

### Creative Corner

Consider asking your guests to dress according to your theme or wedding style—hats for a garden party; all white for an ethereal summer wedding; stylized masks for a carnival night of revelry; rock-and-roll attire for a fifties period wedding. Make up your request in clear language on a insert in your wedding invitation. If you're hoping that guests will come in period costume, include the names and telephone numbers of local costume shops where such outfits are available. Remember, though, not all guests will oblige. Be flexible.

An American bride who was married in Morocco honored her hundreds of guests by appearing in the various costumes of every region represented. She changed five times at a special dinner reception held two days before the actual wedding. "Four women helped to dress her. All of the costumes were rented and represented different provinces. They were loaded with pearls and other jewels. One headdress weighed 55 pounds," says Elaine Parker, who went dressed in a fabulous caftan of royal blue, gold, and silver.

## To Buy or Not to Buy? That Is the Question

The traditional bridal gown can be a very expensive proposition, averaging about $900. Designer gowns have price tags in the thousands.

### Consultants Say

To keep costs down, remember: The veil can be borrowed. After all, this is a one-size-fits-all item.

Is it worth it? Brides commonly buy their gowns, wear them once, and then keep them in the attic for the next 30 years. A few more pragmatic types prefer to rent the gown, just as the groom usually rents rather than buys his tux. Just so you know, however, there are creative alternatives.

One bride took one look at the hefty prices in the bridal salons and headed over to a department store, where she purchased a white prom dress. "It was only $140, and if I didn't tell you it was a prom dress, you wouldn't know," she says. A friend of hers did the same thing, then took the dress to a tailor for a few additions, like a lace hem.

# Hair and Now

You've chosen the gown—now you want to get a headpiece to go with it, like icing on the cake.

A floral wreath can be simple and beautiful. Actress Joely Fisher wore her hair in curls, pinned up in a chignon and wreathed with roses for her New Year's Eve wedding. After the ceremony she let her hair down. Actress Jennifer Lopez pulled her locks straight back and up into a ponytail. Ten sections were then pin-curled into place and decorated with stephanotis flowers. A waist-length white veil was the finishing touch. You may not be a star yourself, but there's no reason you can't look like one on your wedding day!

Flowers are great, but some prefer jewels! A crystal tiara can lend a princess-like quality to the outfit. Headbands are also popular in metal, enamel, or crystal. A headband with gold and silver flowers is a keeper. Even crowns are being put into service. Many brides are putting crystal butterfly barrettes in their hair. This can be a great way to dress up very short hair.

Veils come in all colors and lengths, some of them decorated with a tiny rosebud design. The fingertip veil just reaches the shoulders; the elbow-length veil, true to its name, stops at the elbows. A chapel-length veil heads all the way down to the floor and beyond, measuring nine feet. The cathedral length is the longest—12 feet of veil! After the veil comes off at the reception, you can dress your hair up with a pearl-studded hair pin, plain white silk headband, or floral comb.

According to Exclusives for the Bride in Chicago, veils are very much in fashion right now, as are tiaras. You can find tiaras in many styles—with colored stones, gold or silver leaf, or a tiered effect. Try some different styles to see what flatters your face and matches your dress. Maybe you'll settle on an Indian-style forehead pendant, as actress Kate Winslet did at her wedding.

### Something True

Braiding your hair (or a piece of it) was believed by the Irish to bring good luck and power to the bride. Caribbean and African brides also braided their hair and put cowrie shells in their hair to ensure fertility.

### Consultants Say

Consider a veil that is attached to the head piece with Velcro. You can remove it easily at the reception without having to redo your hair.

# Pretty Maids All in a Row

Bridesmaids, too, can dare to be different. In times past, maids all wore identical dresses, usually one that repeated an element of the bride's dress. This custom is no longer de rigueur. Think of Julia Roberts in *My Best Friend's Wedding*. If Julia doesn't have to dress like everybody else, why should your maids? There are lots of ways to go. Some brides say "Wear whatever makes you feel beautiful." Others set a few guidelines and then let their maids pick out their own outfits. You might ask bridesmaids to find any long black skirt and jewel-colored top. You might ask them to dress in all white, or all black, or you might choose a variety of styles to suit their individuality, but all within the same color palette. Bridesmaids will certainly appreciate being able to wear a dress that not only fits but flatters.

**Consultants Say**

Choose your own gown first. Once your style is set, begin to look for complementary styles for your attendants.

If you have a specific theme, the bridesmaids' attire can certainly help complete the big picture. At a Renaissance wedding, the more people in costume, the more fun. At a Fourth-of-July wedding, one bridesmaid could wear red and the other blue, while you stand out in white. For a Christmas wedding, bridesmaids can all wear velvets. Think your theme through. You can really be creative with bridesmaids' outfits—and make them a standout. Take the wedding of actress Thandie Newton. She designed her own bridesmaids' dresses—embroidered white shifts paired with red Chinese flip-flops. A bridal shop or bridal consultant will have plenty of ideas, if you need them. Tell them about your theme, your taste, and your vision, and see what they show you.

# Grooming for Groomsmen

Are the men's fashions at your wedding an afterthought? Put the spotlight on them. You can have a lot more fun these days with the groom's attire. Hot looks now include the single breasted four-button jacket. With shiny metal buttons, the look can be almost military—close-fitting and sexy. Paired with a black shirt, on the right guy, it'll take your breath away!

If he's planning to go for the traditional tux, liven it up with some color. Cuff links and studs can be shiny or colorful; and how about a snazzy silk bow tie in the shade of your choice? Vests with seven buttons or more can give a long, lean look to a trim, fit groom.

The groom, ushers, and father of the bride traditionally dress alike. The father of the groom might want to go along with the crowd, too. Your groom can dare to be different, however, if he likes. For example, he could wear tails when the rest of the men in the wedding party are in tuxedos, or stand out from the crowd with a carefully chosen accessory such as colorful suspenders, a different color cummerbund, a boutonniere, or a silk cravat.

## *Fit to Be Tied*

For the rehearsal dinner or even for the actual wedding, have some fun with ties. One groom wore a navy necktie decorated with gold wedding bands to honor the occasion. The tie might also reflect the wedding theme or a particular hobby or interest the two of you have. Was your first date at a museum? Get him a Jackson Pollak or Picasso tie from a museum shop catalog.

## *Body Builders*

Just as you want for yourself, you want your groom to go in a style that fits and flatters his personality and physique. Just between the two of us, is there something about your guy that should be, er, minimized on the wedding day? Check out this list to find out what to get and what to avoid:

➤ *Beer belly?* Try a double-breasted jacket to cover up.

➤ *Tall and thin?* Go for the single-breasted look, just two buttons.

➤ *Short?* Try a cutaway to create a look of height. Consider peaked tuxedo labels to draw the eye up and out.

➤ *Long legs?* Go for tails, of course!

➤ *Thick neck?* Stay away from winged or banded collars. Choose a collar that lays down flat.

# Child's Play

Dressing the little ones for a part in your wedding can be particularly fun and rewarding. They look charming as ring bearers, flower girls, junior bridesmaids, and pages. A ring bearer can be a boy or a girl. Be creative. At one wedding, the flower girl wore Chinese pajamas (white with red trim) and went barefoot. My young daughter wore an antique Dutch costume and painted wooden shoes at the wedding of her American babysitter to a Dutchman. There are so many styles to choose from:

➤ White linen sailor suits

➤ White shorts paired with a blue blazer and knee socks

➤ Youthful tuxedo

➤ Child-size bridesmaid's dresses

➤ An ethnic or historical costume

➤ A white ballerina gown

*Why not add some flowers to your flower girl's hair? These little charmers each had a band of rosebuds for that extra special touch.*
©Joshua Ets-Hokin

## The Least You Need to Know

➤ Tell the bridal shop exactly what you want. Let them know about the theme of the wedding, if you have one—even if you're not sure you want your dress to match the theme.

➤ Consider the date, time of day, and location of the wedding when making your choice. Don't forget to think about weather as well.

➤ Feel free to let your dress say something unique about you—through the color, the style, the headpiece, or a dramatic and daring style.

➤ Enjoy the new freedom of bridesmaids' dresses that don't all have to be identical.

➤ Get the groom groomed!

# Chapter 16

# The Sound of Music

---

### In This Chapter

➤ Choosing music for the ceremony

➤ Honoring your background and beliefs

➤ Hiring a DJ, interviewing bands

➤ Choosing dance music

➤ Arranging the hit list

---

"Without music," remarked Friederich Nietzsche, "life would be a mistake." Make no mistake—music can be one of the most important elements of your wedding day. From the opening strains of the processional to the last dance at the reception, music can say a lot about you, your groom, and the type of wedding you're having. There are so many different ways you can play it—from the elegantly quiet notes of a single harp to the raucous beat of a rock band. When vows have said all that they can say, music takes over and says all the rest.

You can incorporate music into your day in so many creative ways, simply by listening to your heart. Whether you're having a cousin sing "Ave Maria" in the church, inviting the a cappella group from your college alma mater to serenade you, or dancing to "your song" at the reception, you can have some fun with your musical choices. Be funny! Be wild! Be jazzy! Be sentimental! Be classical! Be punky! It's up to you. The melodies from your day will live on in the hearts and minds of your guests.

## Choosing Music for the Ceremony

You're ready to walk up the aisle. Nervously you try to put one foot forward, but you freeze. Just then the regal strains of your processional begin. Without thinking, you are propelled forward by the music and the moment. If not for the music, you might not have had the courage to move.

### Something True

According to *A Bride's Book of Wedding Traditions* by Arlene Hamilton Stewart (Hearst Books, 1995), a piece written back in 1826 is still probably the most popular wedding processional played: Mendelssohn's "A Midsummer Night's Dream," first played at the 1858 wedding of a daughter of Queen Victoria. Prince Edward propelled another piece to popularity when he had Handel's Processional in G Major played at his 1863 wedding. Wagner's "Here Comes the Bride" was first played in 1860 at the New York wedding of an American bride and a European groom.

Needless to say, where you choose to get married will influence your choice of music. Some churches, for example, request that only religious music be used. When you meet with your officiant, talk about what kind of music you would like to play at your wedding and which instruments you are thinking of having. Some may sound better than others, given the size and acoustics of the space. A guitar melody might be lost in a soaring cathedral; a brass quintet might be way too much for a little country church. If a church has an organ, it usually has a select list of acceptable organists to play at weddings. You would contact and choose among them.

You may also be able to bring in some outside instrumentalists, such as a trumpet player or chamber group. A children's choir could be magnificent. Hand bells give a beautiful and unusual touch. A simple harp can sound heavenly.

If you hire an organist, he or she will probably wish to meet with you sometime before the big day to discuss music and make selections. The organist can be extremely helpful in guiding your choices and helping you set the right tone. If you plan to bring in outside instrumentalists for part of the service, be sure to share your plans with the organist to make sure everyone is on the same page.

### Creative Corner

Do you have a friend or relative who is a talented musician? It can lend a personal and unique touch to the ceremony to have a sister or cousin sing or play an instrument. At my wedding ceremony we hired an organist and a single trumpet player. They sounded beautifully elegant, even regal, the notes wafting up to the vaulted ceilings of St. Patrick's Cathedral. Along with traditional voluntaries such as "Jesu, Joy of Man's Desiring," they played an original piece for trumpet and organ written expressly for our wedding by a composer/uncle of my husband's who lived in France and could not attend in person. His music certainly made his presence felt, and it was very special to have a piece written in our honor.

Sometimes the minister or priest will keep a list of hymns and voluntaries (instrumental pieces) suitable for weddings. If you are unfamiliar with them, you may be able to borrow CDs of wedding music or classical music from the library to help you make your selections.

For the ceremony, you will need to pick about 20 minutes worth of introductory music to be played as guests are being seated, and separate pieces for the family's entrance, bridal party's entrance, bride's entrance, and recessional (the exit of the bridal party). In most cases, you will also choose something to be played or sung during the service. Make sure your selections are in keeping with the type of ceremony you are planning. The formality or informality of the pieces should reflect your ceremony style.

Whatever you choose, it's a safe prediction that the minute they start playing it at your ceremony, you will be moved by music as never before.

## Incorporating Your Ethnic Background

Many couples want to find joyous ways to announce and celebrate their cultural diversity. One particularly rich way of honoring your past is through music. An African-American heritage, for example, can be celebrated through gospel music, folksongs, and/or African drumming. Mariachi music or flamenco music can be played at a Hispanic-American celebration. Traditional dances, from a Celtic jig to an Italian tarantella to a Brazilian samba, can be a part of your reception party. Whatever instruments and styles are associated with your cultural heritage, whether banjos or bagpipes, they can be incorporated to add life and beauty to your special day.

Talk to parents and grandparents about the music and dances that have meant something to their lives and heritage. With the help of your bridal consultant, band, or DJ, try to track some of this music down. The library should have several useful books on the ethnic group or culture whose customs you are most interested in.

### Creative Corner

Getting married at an early American historical site, such as Williamsburg, Virginia? Why not have a fife and drum corps accompany you as you walk from the ceremony to the reception site? Do you or your groom have Scottish ancestry? Bring on the bagpipes! Is this a Christmas wedding? Call in the carolers! Whatever your theme, choose music that fits the spirit of the day.

# Rockin' at the Reception

At the reception there will probably be fewer restrictions on the music played than at the ceremony. The size or layout of the room, however, may lend itself more easily to one type of music than another. The 20-piece band you imagined might not even fit in the room you have chosen. The swing band may fit, but if there's no dance floor for the guests to swing on, what would be the point? Consider also the volume of the music. You might want to hire one group of musicians for entertainment during dinner when guests are trying to talk, and then follow with a louder dance band after dinner. Think about the mood of your day and match the sounds to your theme:

➤ A jazz band for swing dancing

➤ A country western band for line dancing and the two-step

➤ A big-band sound for a forties swing wedding

➤ A rock band

➤ A top-forties group

➤ A bluegrass band for an informal Southern wedding in the country

➤ A Cajun band for a Louisiana wedding

➤ A classical quartet for a small, formal buffet

➤ A steel-drum band for some island flavor

➤ A fiddler and caller for a square dance at a country wedding

➤ A mellow band specializing in Gershwin and Cole Porter tunes

➤ A woodwind ensemble

➤ A single harpist

➤ Chamber music

➤ A Brazilian band

### Something True

According to *Instyle* (February, 1999), the most popular first-dance numbers are "Someone to Watch Over Me," "You Are So Beautiful," "The Way You Look Tonight," "It Had to Be You," and "Somewhere Out There."

There are also other variables to take into consideration. How loud will the music be? Do you want gentle background music so that you and your guests can talk? Choose a string quartet or a bass player and piano. Do you want to dance? Choose a band that makes you want to jump out of your seat and boogie. Should you segue from one type of music to another? Some couples hire two bands, one to play during cocktails and dinner and another to play at the after-dinner reception. An all-night party might go through a few different bands to keep the joint jumping.

Make sure you spell out your likes and dislikes to the band ahead of time. If you really want some form of circle dance or line dance, such as the hora, let the band know in advance. If you really hate circle dances and line dances, let them know that, too. Make it absolutely clear to them and your immediate family that you don't want to hear the "Hokey Pokey" or the "Bunny Hop" played.

Check with your reception site manager to make sure the facility has the space and electrical capabilities to accommodate the band you've chosen.

### Creative Corner

Singing can be a wonderful way to draw people together. Depending on the style of the reception, you may well want to invite guests to sing along to well-known tunes. Sing Christmas carols at a December wedding, or start up an impromptu round of tried-and-true school songs if a large number of graduates from the couple's alma mater are present. Print the words if you think guests will have trouble remembering them, or if you've used creative license to make the words of a well-known number reflect your own names and circumstances. At my mother's wedding, for instance, her grown children and her new husband's five children all came together to serenade them with a song about their lives together. We wrote our own funny lyrics and had the pianist accompany us to the tune of "Hello, Dolly."

Get ready for your first dance as a married couple by alerting your DJ or band leader to the song of your choice. You two may have a special song you consider to be "your song." If not, you can ask your band or DJ for some nice first-dance suggestions and choose among them. If you wish to stun guests with your fancy footwork, consider taking dance lessons with your groom in advance of the big day. Learn to waltz, fox trot, cha-cha, or tango. Or, jump on the latest retro bandwagon and learn to jitterbug, do the lindy, and swing! After the first dance you can relax and just have fun.

Is a special guest celebrating a birthday or anniversary? Request a special song, or invite them up to dance to something they love.

## Hiring the Band

The fun of choosing a band is often in the listening. It gives you and your fiancé a great excuse to go out to clubs and listen to different bands! Circumstances permitting, it's always nicer if you can pick them from a live performance rather than a tape. That way you can see how they dress and behave, and how a live crowd reacts to their music. If you like what you hear, set up a time to talk with the bandleader.

## Bridal Blunders

No matter what band you end up hiring, think about the noise level in the room. You don't want the music at your party to be so loud as to be annoying. Many guests would rather talk than dance, and no one likes to have to shout to be heard. Ask the band or DJ to be sensitive to this. If possible, position the dance floor a respectable distance from the tables where people are sitting and talking. Also, be sure to check with your location—there may be restrictions on sound levels and playing times.

Make sure you know exactly whom you are hiring. Sometimes bands switch musicians, playing with a different drummer one night or an additional saxophone player another. It's a good idea to talk to the bandleader before you sign a contract and clarify what is being agreed to. There were two trumpets in the band you saw; will there still be two at your wedding, or only one? Some bandleaders have a number of different bands all working under the same name. If you want the bandleader himself at your wedding, you'll need to specify that and be willing to pay a higher price. Will there be a singer? Make sure the band who is coming is the same one you heard.

It's important to always have a contract with the band, specifying the players, the date of your wedding, the amount of time they'll be playing, and how much it will cost. Agree in advance how much they will be paid up front and how much they will be paid at the end of the gig. You should also find out how many breaks they plan to take. There's nothing more annoying than a band that takes breaks every 20 minutes, just as the guests start to come alive.

## Creative Corner

Ask for songs that have meaning for both of you, whether they're school or camp songs or the number-one hit from the year you met. A song that includes the bride's or groom's name in it can be both humorous and special: the Fifth Dimension's "Wedding Bell Blues" ("Marry Me, Bill") or the Beatles' "Lovely Rita" or "Lucy in the Sky with Diamonds." At my cousin's wedding, the band played "Once in Love with Amy," which the crowd loved since her name is—guess what—Amy. Maybe the band knows some other fitting songs you've never heard.

You can also match a song to a theme. Is it a rooftop reception? Play Carole King's "Up on the Roof." Did you meet at the beach? Play "Under the Boardwalk." Are you both theater lovers? Serve up some Broadway show tunes, like "People Will Say We're in Love" from *Oklahoma* or "On the Street Where You Live" from *My Fair Lady*.

Finally, you need to discuss with them how much talking and announcing they usually do. (If you have seen a live performance, you'll have a pretty good idea of how the band handles the room.) If you would like to have the band announce some specific things such as the first dance or the cutting of the cake, be sure you tell the band in advance and specify when and what you want them to say and play.

If you have specific requests, check with the band to make sure that they know how to play those numbers. If not, are they willing to find the music and practice it for your wedding? If you check out the band in person, you'll know how they dress for a gig. If not, ask for a picture of the group or a description of their attire.

Don't be afraid to prompt or guide the band in the course of the evening. Things come up. Parties tend to take on their own unpredictable personalities. It's perfectly acceptable to ask for one more line dance because they're so popular, or to suggest that the band slow things down a bit for the older relatives.

## Hiring a DJ

Sometimes live music just doesn't fit the program. Perhaps it's not allowed at your reception site, or maybe you just prefer the kind of atmosphere a good DJ is able to create. Another possibility: Start with a live band and then go to a DJ later on. This works especially well if you want nonstop music or are hosting a really long reception, such as an all-night party.

A DJ can really transform a party and make it swing—or fizzle. Interview some potential DJs to make sure your DJ's personality matches your own. Ask:

> ➤ What type of experience have you had?

> ➤ How many weddings have you done?

> ➤ May I have names of recent clients as references?

> ➤ What mix of music do you usually play at weddings?

> ➤ Can you accommodate specific requests by the couple, even if they're obscure recordings? (Give the DJ a few specific song titles you would want played.)

> ➤ How do you handle requests by guests?

> ➤ Do you plan to talk between songs?

> ➤ What kinds of things do you do to get people dancing?

**Something True**

The ten most popular songs requested at weddings, according to *The Top 10 of Everything 1998* by Russell Ash (DK Publishing, 1997), are: 1) "Endless Love" (Diana Ross and Lionel Richie); 2) "Your Song" (Elton John); 3) "Everything I Do" (Bryan Adams); 4) "The Best" (Tina Turner); 5) "Crazy for You" (Madonna); 6) "Love Story" (Andy Williams); 7) "I Will Always Love You" (Whitney Houston); 8) "Love Me Tender" (Elvis Presley); 9) "I Just Can't Stop Loving You" (Michael Jackson); 10) "Unchained Melody" (Righteous Brothers)

➤ What does your setup look like?

➤ What do you usually wear?

---

### The Least You Need to Know

➤ Choose music that fits the space and style of your ceremony site. Whether you have trumpets and an organ, two guitars, or a full choir, the music should complement, not overwhelm, your space.

➤ Include music that reflects your heritage, either at the ceremony itself or during the reception. Find the right tunes by talking to relatives or reading books on your cultural heritage. Music can provide a bridge between generations and families.

➤ Be sure to listen to your band and feel comfortable with their musical style before signing a contract with them.

➤ Find creative ways to bring people together through your musical selections—either by inviting guests to sing along or by choosing numbers that have special meaning for a large number of participants.

---

# Chapter 17

# Flower Power

---

### In This Chapter

➤ Finding a creative florist

➤ Making your wishes and dreams known

➤ Choosing bouquets and boutonnieres with flair

➤ Creating fun, fabulous centerpieces

---

The poet William Carlos Williams said, "It is at the edge of a petal that love waits." Flowers are an indispensable addition to any wedding. At a creative wedding you don't want just any flowers—you want something creative, something memorable. Your theme cries out for something more than the standard bouquet of roses—your historic period wedding dress needs a bouquet to match—perhaps when you close your eyes and imagine your reception site, you see something unusual in place of the average centerpiece. It may not be more elaborate or expensive, but it's unique. It says something special about the two of you as a couple.

## Finding a Florist

For the couple on the lookout for creative decorations, the right florist is a must. Where can you find a florist who knows just how many roses you'll need to cover a 30-foot red runner with pink rose petals? What kind of florist would know just the right way to decorate the two powerful stone urns at the entrance to the country chapel where you plan to wed? (Hydrangeas? Mountain laurel?) Who can coordinate flowers that match a nautical theme for your yacht-club wedding?

Begin looking for a florist about six months before your wedding date. That should give you plenty of time to find the right person for your day. If you are trying to book a popular florist for a popular weekend, you may need to start even sooner. The summer season is the most popular time for weddings, but you can expect the same level of activity around Valentine's Day, Christmas, and Mother's Day. My florist surprised me by alerting me to a possible rose shortage as soon as I told him the date of my wedding. We were married the day after New Year's Day when Pasadena's annual Tournament of Roses parade uses just about every available rose bud in the country!

Ask for references from friends, or contact a florist you have worked with before. Have you been to a wedding recently where the flowers were fabulous? Ask the bride for the name of the floral designer she used. (Even if you don't end up using that designer, borrow some ideas!) If you don't know any florists, ask the manager of your reception site. He or she will be able to give you the names of florists who have decorated that space before. Similarly, if you're being married in a religious setting, it might be worth asking the officiant or wedding coordinator whether he or she can recommend a florist based on past experience. If you are using a wedding consultant, she'll be able to direct you to the right person for your needs and taste.

The society pages of local magazines and newspapers are another good resource. If you like the floral arrangements in a particular photo, find out who the floral designer was and begin your search there. As a last resort, you can check the yellow pages and begin the search on your own—a more time-consuming approach, but one that is likely to succeed if you are persistent and thorough.

Make an appointment to see a couple of florists. You want to find someone who understands your theme and style and can make creative suggestions for enhancing the beauty of the ceremony and reception. Look around the person's retail shop to get an idea of how he or she does business and what his or her style is. Is the shop beautifully decorated? Do the flowers in the display cases look fresh? Is the florist a good listener? It's okay for you not to know exactly what you want. A good florist should be able to come up with workable ideas that fit your site, your style, and your budget. Ask:

➤ Have you worked at my ceremony site before? If not, would you feel comfortable decorating that space?

➤ Have you seen the reception site or decorated it before? How often have you worked there? Do you expect to face any particular challenges there?

➤ Do you charge by the item or do you offer a package?

➤ Is there an extra labor charge for setting up on site? For delivery or pickup of rental item?

➤ Can you handle some special extras that I'm interested in (silver and white helium balloons attached to each centerpiece, feathers mixed in with flowers, ornamental columns....)

➤ Do you have references from other wedding parties?

➤ Can you get any unusual blooms? (Our florist heard we would be headed to Hawaii for a honeymoon immediately after the reception, so even though it was January, he incorporated some bird of paradise blooms into the floral arrangements at the head table. It was a nice touch, and one I wouldn't have thought of myself.)

**198**

➤ May I see samples of your work? The designer may have photos—or she may invite you to visit a site when she's there setting up for an event.

➤ How much of your business is devoted to weddings?

➤ What suggestions do you have for a bridal bouquet to go with my dress? (Bring a picture of your dress or a piece of the fabric if possible.)

After your meeting, think about how it felt dealing with this designer. Were you happy with the way the shop looked? Did you feel that the designer understood your style? Did he or she have creative suggestions that you liked? Was he responsive to your suggestions? Did she seem sensitive to your budget?

### Creative Corner

Don't overlook opportunities to add a decorative touch to interesting spots. Flowers need not be confined to the centerpieces on tables. If you have a wooden swing hanging from an old oak tree, festoon the hanging ropes with white flowers. Tie white satin ribbons on an old wooden fence. Hang garlands of variegated ivy in an outdoor tent. Tie a spray of flowers to the prow of an old rowboat at the dock. If you see a spot for a floral decoration, point it out to your florist and exchange ideas.

## Getting What You Want

As with any other aspect of your wedding, good communication is the key to success. The florist may have lots of suggestions and ideas of her own, but she needs to hear from you too. Show her pictures of arrangements and bouquets. It doesn't matter if you don't know the names of flowers. Bring in books that have the style you're looking for. Show the florist pictures of bouquets you found in bridal magazines. Bring a sketch of your dress or a photo of you in it. Tell the florist what flowers you like—or, just as importantly, don't like. If anyone in the bridal party has allergies, describe the situation to the florist. Point out particular fragrances that you love. If you're good with pen and paper, make a sketch of the bouquet you have in mind or the centerpieces you envision. Ask what flowers could be used to make your vision a reality.

Make sure the designer knows which aspects of the arrangements are most important to you—the fragrance, the meaning behind the bloom, the shape of the arrangement, the size of the flower, the colors used, its relevance to your theme, or the longevity of the flowers. All of these instructions will help your designer deliver the flowers that will make you happiest.

## Creating the Right Effect

If you have any interesting floral "leads," share them. For example, if your husband is Dutch, you may want to feature tulips. If you gravitate toward bright colors, let your floral designer know that you're not afraid to make a strong color statement. "The petals covering the aisle up to your wedding could be hot orange instead of white," says Meredith Waga Perez of Belle Fleur in New York City, citing one example. If your garden wedding will have the feel of Elizabethan England, a nosegay of rosemary may be just the thing. If you're planning a wedding with a nautical theme, the designer might wish to make a point of florally adorning the large anchor that sits on your property.

### Bridal Blunders

With a creative wedding there's a bit more room for miscommunication. You're saying peach, the florist is thinking pink. You're talking about a cluster and the florist thinks you mean a bunch. To make sure you get exactly what you want on your wedding day, have the florist create a sample bouquet a few days before the wedding. You'll have to pay extra, but it may be worth it—especially if you are ordering something to match a precise color, theme, or style.

Certainly your designer should have a very clear idea of what you're wearing. Satin ball gown? White miniskirt? Fancy pantsuit? Lots of tulle? If you're wearing a Victorian wedding dress, your designer may suggest a reproduction of a Victorian posy holder, with tiny pansies. If you're wearing a big dress with a big train, he may advise something grander.

The more aspects of your day the floral designer knows about and understands, the better she will be able to accommodate your desires and provide you with the bouquets, centerpieces, and decorations of your dreams. Creative touches involve a little inspiration. That's what you provide. The designer's job is to put it all together.

## Florally Challenged?

Are you one of those people who can't tell a daisy from a freesia or a bouquet from a boutonniere? You're not the only one. Lots of brides have the same problem. Take this quick crash course:

➤ *Biedermeier:* concentric rings of flowers, each circle in a different color, tightly pulled together in a holder with wire.

➤ *Pomander:* a "ball" of flowers hanging from a ribbon (often carried by the children in the bridal party.

➤ *Nosegay or posy:* a small bouquet.

➤ *Tussy mussy:* a Victorian-inspired, slightly larger version of the nosegay, in a horn-shaped holder.

➤ *Pageant bouquet:* what Miss America carries—long-stemmed flowers held in the crook of your arm.

➤ *Cascade:* what Princess Di carried at her wedding to Prince Charles. Many flowers tied together in a waterfall effect.

Even if the language of flowers is difficult for you or you're not sure about what you want, you can describe the feel of it to the designer. For example, do you envision masses of blooms? A simple hand-tied bouquet of fresh-cut flowers? A deliberately unstructured armload of long-stemmed flowers? Something antique looking? Try to think of a word to describe the bouquet of your dreams: Opulent? Elegant? Dramatic? Colorful? Fresh? Flirty? Controlled? Radical? Imaginative? Tidy? Lavish? Your designer can use some of these words as a springboard for his or her selections.

# Bouquets That Take Your Breath Away

The flowers carried by the bridal party require careful thought. These include the bride's and bridesmaids' bouquets, the basket of blooms held by the flower girl, and the groomsmen's boutonnieres. The flowers can range from the simple to the dramatic; the most important thing is to make sure they fit the setting and the bridal party attire. Whether you hold them, pin them in your hair, or clip them to the tips of your shoes, personal flowers can be highly creative.

**Something True**

Since Early Greek times brides have relied on herbs to help celebrate and enhance the marriage ritual. Each herb had a particular meaning and role to play. Mint and marigold were considered to be aphrodisiacs, sesame and poppy symbolized fertility, garlic could ward off evil spirits, rosemary symbolized faithfulness.

## *The Bridal Bouquet*

Bouquets have changed in size and shape over the years, but they have never gone out of fashion. From the voluptuous and lavish shower bouquets of gardenias, lilies, and roses carried by brides at the turn of the nineteenth century to the smaller nosegays of the twenties and thirties to the simple, hand-tied wildflowers of the sixties, bridal bouquets have reflected the times in which we lived. Feel free to draw from the wealth of designs and styles used by brides over this past century, or make up your own mix.

Consider what various flowers stand for. Red roses represent love, lilies are associated with purity, violets are a sign of modesty, ivy signifies fidelity, honeysuckle represents faithfulness, and orange blossoms stand for happiness and fertility.

Make sure your bouquet complements your dress and the bouquets of your maids do the same. Your bouquet should reflect the formality or informality of your day, as well as the style and proportion of your dress. The florist should be able to help you choose a bouquet that nicely balances your look. If you're wearing a big dress with a cathedral-length train, for example, you'll want a lavish bouquet to match. If you're marrying in your backyard wearing a simple slip dress, something as simple as a bouquet of daisies might be exactly what you need.

Your size is also an important factor in a bouquet choice. Are you tall? Petite? Your bouquet should match your proportions in a way that's comfortable for you. A petite bride holding an enormous bouquet can look unbalanced; a tall bride with a tiny nosegay can look awkward.

As with other aspects of your wedding, you can be clever and creative with a bouquet, matching it to your mood as well as to your dress. Princess Di's romantic and extravagant, not to mention enormous, cascade of white roses was absolutely the perfect choice for her. That doesn't mean it would be the perfect choice for you. The flowers, the size of the bouquet, the style of the arrangement, and even the fragrance of your buds should suit who you are—not what's fashionable, traditional, or expected. The classic bridal bouquet, of course, is a rounded bouquet of white roses, white stephanotis, and white carnations. But roses and stephanotis are not the only flowers to consider, and a structured, hand-held bouquet is not the only way to go. Here are some creative, less traditional choices:

➤ A tiny nosegay of little pansies

➤ A spray of wheat or oats

➤ Bunches of red berries (especially wonderful at Christmas time)

➤ An armload of evergreens with gilded pine cones

➤ A garland of flowers hung around your neck (perfect for a Hawaiian destination wedding)

➤ A wicker basket full of flowers

➤ A boa of white roses and other flowers draped elegantly around you like a stole

➤ A cluster of flowers pinned along the neckline of your dress

➤ A line of flowers pinned along the edge of your gloves

➤ A necklace of delicate flowers tied with a ribbon around your neck

➤ A hat brimming with blooms

➤ A bouquet of dried flowers

➤ A beautiful blend of high-quality silk flowers (this bouquet can be treasured forever as a wedding keepsake)

➤ An unusual ribbon, cord, or tie to hold the flowers together

➤ A sentimental piece of antique lace or ribbon (perhaps from a grandmother's wedding gown or veil) worked into the bouquet

➤ Tiny buds dotted through your upswept hair

➤ Flowers attached to hair combs

➤ A crown of delicate flowers encircling your head

➤ A halo of orange blossoms

➤ A tiny spray of cheerful flowers tucked into a chignon

➤ A single long-stemmed rose

➤ A single giant white calla lily

➤ A single white orchid

➤ A dozen or so of long-stemmed tulips (in one or two colors) loosely tied with pretty ribbons

➤ A branch of flowering quince or forsythia

➤ A loose armful of favorite flowers from your garden

➤ A bright-red or deep-pink bouquet

➤ Gilded or silver-sprayed branches within a bouquet of flowers

➤ A wreath of myrtle leaves (for a medieval look) instead of flowers

➤ A bouquet of Austrian crystals, tied together with wire and ribbon

One of the hottest trends in bouquets is creative ribboning. Ask your florist about some fun ways to use ribbons and streamers in your bouquet. Floral stems can be wrapped in a French-braid ribbon. Ribbons with stripes, plaids, and even polka dots are being used, as is sheer organza and lace. Most bouquets are handheld, the stems wrapped together. Plastic holders are out of favor.

Whatever you decide on, your bouquet can be pretty and feminine while still having some creative touches. The unexpected addition of berries, grape hyacinths, or a little lime-green Lady's Mantle can make all the difference in your bouquet.

## *Move Over White!*

White is fabulous and always appropriate, but bridal trends are pointing to bigger, bolder bouquets. You no longer have to feel like a maverick if you decide to carry a bountiful bouquet of red, red roses. Vivid picks are very popular right now.

**Something True**

In ancient times, quince (a kind of fruit) was believed to enhance a couple's love for one another.

**Something True**

Flora, the goddess of flowers, was honored by Romans in the month of April. As the season of new beginnings, springtime was a popular and auspicious time to marry, just as it is today.

Says Meredith Waga Perez of Belle Fleur, "Fun candy colors are in right now—hot pinks, hot oranges, vibrant purples and deep reds." She has also seen a trend toward soft springtime colors, including yellows, soft tangerine, lavender, and lime green. Jewel tones, she says, are less popular, and she's not asked to do many all white or baby-pink bouquets anymore.

For the bride who wants a bouquet done all in one color, there are many ways to go. A bouquet of rich red anemones or 100 sweet pea stems can be fabulous. A bouquet containing a gradation of color—from the softest lavender to the deepest purple—sparks interest while remaining soft and feminine. The one-color bouquet allows you plenty of room to play with ribbon colors, as well.

## Bridesmaids' Bouquets

Your attendants will each be carrying their own bouquets, and these can complement your bouquet as well as their outfits. The focus should be on the bride's bouquet, but even if you are carrying a traditional all-white bouquet, you can have a little fun with the bridesmaids' blossoms. They could go for the all-white approach—or each could carry a bouquet in a different color. At a Fourth-of-July wedding the maids could carry red, white, and blue flowers. At a Christmas wedding the maids could carry red roses while you carry white—or holly, evergreen, and red berries could be mixed into their white bouquets.

Sometimes the challenge of the bridesmaids' bouquets is to find a suitable color to match their dresses. Be sure to bring a fabric sample and a photo of the bridesmaids' gowns to your florist so the match can be made. The florist should know what the bridesmaids are wearing so that the color scheme and size and style of the bouquet will match.

**Bridal Blunders**

The pomander, which is so beautiful for a flower girl to carry, is also very delicate when constructed of fresh flowers. If children are swinging it around by its ribbon, the flowers are likely to come off. A heartier choice with the same look would be a pomander of silk roses or silk gardenias. It will withstand a child's exuberance, and can remain with your flower girl as a lovely keepsake.

## Flower-Girl Power

Flower girls have been part of wedding celebrations since ancient Greek times. The presence of children at a wedding is a visual wish for fertility. Early flower girls often carried wheat (either fresh or gilded)—another sign of fertility. Sometimes they would toss wheat on the floor for the bride to walk on, often with sweet-smelling herbs mixed in. Any of these ancient customs can be creatively incorporated into your modern-day wedding.

The flower girl (or girls) can play different roles. The most common role is that of preceding the bride down the aisle, sprinkling her way with petals from a basket. (Check with your church first to find out if there are rules about using petals.) Another is to carry small bouquets for the mothers of the bride and groom. Some brides like to ask two children to walk down the aisle with a garland that they then drape on an altar rail at the front of the church. These roles take courage, of course, especially if a crowd is present, so be careful who you ask to take part. If children are young or nervous, you should be happy if they can simply walk down the aisle without dropping whatever flowers they have in their hands or tripping over the runner. (Come to think of it, that may be about all you can hope for from yourself!)

Flowers, of course, look darling in a little girl's hair, whether as a crown of flowers or a single bud fastened to a hair band, barrette, or bow. The flower girl can carry a basket of flowers, small bouquet, or pomander (increasingly popular). In lieu of a basket, you could fill a small watering can or teapot with blooms or have her carry a straw hat full of flowers. Something new which Belle Fleur in New York City has been using (and which they say brides love) is a small lightweight silver metal basket, in lieu of the traditional wicker flower basket.

You can have some fun with a child's bouquet, weaving a small teddy bear or brightly colored lollipops into the design. If you've always loved the children's story of *The Red Balloon*, you could get your flower girl to carry a single red globe-shaped helium balloon. (Check with the church or other ceremony site to make sure this is allowed.) Be liberal with satin streamers, ribbons, and ruffles, and make sure that whatever you give a child to handle is manageable in little hands and not terribly fragile.

**Bridal Blunders**

Children can easily get into squabbles when they perceive an unfairness. Think twice before you provide different bouquets to different children. A quarrel may break out (complete with tears) about who got the bigger or better bouquet to carry. The more similar they are, the better.

**Creative Corner**

Is there a very special dog in your life? If he's going to be at (or even in) the wedding, have the florist make a modest floral dog collar, or attach a couple of small flowers to your dog's regular collar yourself. Either way, make sure the flowers are securely attached, so that they don't fall off Fido partway through the ceremony. Won't your pooch be proud to walk down the aisle with you in his necklace of blossoms! (Avoid making them too fragrant. Remember, a dog's sense of smell is very acute.) Silk flowers may be preferable to fresh ones.

For an evening wedding, weave a string of battery-operated lights through the doggy garland. If you dare, your dog could even be your ring bearer and carry the ring in a pouch on his collar.

The ring bearer's pillow can be pinned with a carpet of flowers, the ring (or, better yet, a facsimile thereof) nestled amid the blossoms. The ring bearer could also walk down the aisle carrying a large stuffed teddy bear, with the ring tied around the bear's neck with a big satin bow.

## Boutonnieres

The groom and ushers have comparatively fewer floral needs, but the right choice of boutonniere can say a lot of about your wedding style. Men usually sport just a single flower pinned to their lapel—traditionally a single red or white rose or white carnation. Other options might include grape hyacinth, orchids, or a trio of little tea roses backed with ivy. "It has to be a hearty flower," points out Perez of Belle Fleur, "since a pin goes through it and it rests on fabric."

The groom should stand out from his groomsmen with a different bud. It could be a flower that appears in your bouquet, but it doesn't have to be. Dark green leaves, a little ivy, or a tiny spray of evergreen can provide the perfect background to set off the boutonniere. Fathers need their own signature flowers, as well, to make them easy to identify.

Of course, if the gentlemen in your party prefer not to wear flowers, that's fine, too. A dashing silk handkerchief placed in the breast pockets of their suits may provide more than enough color and panache.

## Creative Centerpieces

The ceremony is over! Now you can really have fun! The flowers at the reception can reflect that feeling of celebration and festivity. Table decorations can be beautiful, whimsical, dramatic, or elegant. They can underline the wedding theme or celebrate the season. The right flowers can turn an ordinary room into something spectacular.

### Creative Corner

Let guests take the floral theme home with them. Packets of seeds can be given out as favors, wrapped in white tissue paper and tied with a ribbon printed with your names and wedding date. Or place the seed packets in beautiful envelopes, printed with your wedding date. For another beautiful (albeit pricier) idea, put an individual floral arrangement at each place—a little cup of flowers or a miniature topiary tree in a clay pot—for guests to take home after the party.

Think about height when you're planning table arrangements. Will they be tall or short? Will guests be able to see around them to talk to other guests across the table?

Make some notes on the décor of the room, including the color of the walls, carpeting, and chair cushions. You don't want your centerpieces to clash. Chairs can be slipcovered or exchanged for rentals in a different color, but there is little you can do about carpeting and wall color.

For a simple and elegant look, arrange white tulips in clear globe-shaped vases, or choose a different single color for a dramatically different look on each table. Get creative with containers. Cast-iron urns, silver trumpet vases, and plain plastic containers covered with moss or leaves make for striking centerpieces.

Flowers are not the only things that can adorn your tables. Consider incorporating candles into a table display, or small silver picture frames with pictures of the bride and groom as children. Feathers are the newest "nonflower" addition to the party scene—very popular, according to Belle Fleur of New York City, either mixed with flowers or on their own. At a recent wedding, white ostrich feathers were placed in silver trumpet vases. As a favor the wedding couple gave the female guests feather boas, while the gentlemen received sunglasses, to match the swing band, supper-club-style atmosphere at their reception.

If you have a long rectangular table, consider skipping the traditional centerpiece and instead assemble an array of votive candles, flowers, spilling grapes, ribbons, and pillar candles running the length of the table. In the fall, little artichokes or other vegetables could be worked into the lineup as well. According to Perez of Belle Fleur, "It looks like a beautiful landscape."

Entry tables can play host to more daring arrangements, such as dogwood branches hung with glass-enclosed votive candles or a birdcage filled with flowers.

Even the cake can be decorated with flowers, a popular alternative to the plastic bride and groom cake toppers. Decorated with ranunculas, sweet peas and hyacinths, your cake will look almost too good to eat.

---

### The Least You Need to Know

➤ Begin looking for a florist about six months before your wedding.

➤ Make sure the florist you choose is as creative as you are. He should be able to understand the details of your wedding and suggest fresh ideas that fit your theme or style.

➤ Never be afraid to ask questions about what a certain flower or arrangement will look or smell like. It's okay not to be a floral expert.

➤ Add whatever creative touches take your fancy: With your designer's help you can decorate everything from the garden swing to the tips of your shoes with flowers.

➤ Don't forget the groom's feelings when choosing the flowers. He has likes and dislikes, too.

# Chapter 18

# Words to Marry By

## In This Chapter

➤ Finding the right officiant

➤ Deciding whether or not you want to write your own vows

➤ Reciting vows with grace and style

➤ Choosing readings

➤ Writing a wedding program

There's more to a ceremony than marching down an aisle (or a sandy beach or the bow of a boat, for that matter). You don't have to limit your creative ideas to the reception, only. There are so many ways you can personalize your ceremony to make a truly memorable and touching event for all parties involved. Everything from your wedding vows to the readings you select, to the person you ask to perform the ceremony, all can add to the unique quality of your day. In this chapter, I'll help you figure out how to make your ceremony an affair to remember.

## Finding the Right Officiant

Now, you may already have your pen and paper out, jotting down ideas for the perfect vows. After all, that's the most important part, right? Well, yes and no. Wedding vows are not recited in a vacuum. You say them before witnesses, and with the blessing of an officiant. The priest, judge, rabbi, or minister you choose to preside at your wedding should be able to help you find the right words to say and will lead you through the ceremony.

# The Best Man (or Woman) for the Job

You'll want to find an officiant who is not only comfortable with the creative ways you want things done, but supportive of you as well. If yours is a religiously mixed marriage, you may want to have two officiants—a priest and a rabbi, for example. In circumstances like this, you can't use just any priest or rabbi because not all of them will agree to or feel comfortable with a mixed marriage. You may have to marry in a more neutral setting, such as a Unitarian church, or in front of a justice of the peace or a judge.

One Catholic/Jewish couple I know found a cantor by calling an interfaith center and a liberal-thinking priest who agreed to perform their ceremony together. The ceremony was held in a nonreligious setting. The couple found ways to include elements from both religions: a huppah, a ketubah, a unity candle, readings from the Old Testament and readings from the New Testament. They wrote their own vows. During the ring exchange, the bride, who is Catholic, said some of her vows in Hebrew.

**Consultants Say**

Spend time with your officiant before the ceremony. Depending on your religion, you may be asked to participate in premarital counseling. The better you know your officiant, the more personal your ceremony will be. Since my mother's cousin was a priest, we asked him to perform our wedding ceremony. As a member of the immediate family, he knew us well, and it would have been hard to find anyone better!

Meet with the officiants of your choice well in advance of the wedding. Discuss your reasons for getting married in the manner you are suggesting. Ask for the officiant's advice and opinions. Does he or she think it's okay to forego the traditional vows used in that religion? Go over the details of the ceremony with your officiant. If you are planning to change the vows or write your own, make sure everyone is clear about what will be said. If you are marrying in a Christian service but still wish to incorporate some of the traditions of a Jewish ceremony, as the couple I just mentioned did, your officiant needs to know in advance and feel comfortable presiding over such a ceremony.

# Places, Please

For a mixed religion marriage, you will probably have to choose a nonreligious site. Even if the person of your choice in unable (or unwilling) to officially join you as husband and wife, you might still ask this priest, rabbi, or minister to come to the ceremony, to offer a blessing to you as a couple.

If your ceremony site is unusual, you may also face challenges. You'll have to look a little harder for the right person to officiate. Catholic priests, for example, won't perform a ceremony outside a church, let alone on a ski lift or roller coaster! Even if you're doing something as relatively simple as trying to get married on a boat, you'll need to take into account the needs of your officiant, who may not wish to spend four hours at sea. As you should with other aspects of the day, be ready to compromise. The officiant could probably marry you on board the boat while it's still docked, allowing him or her to disembark before you shove off.

No matter what your faith, have your religious leaders explain the rules and laws about marriage to you. If you are planning anything *different,* find out if it will be tolerated or sanctioned. Know the rules—and the consequences for breaking them—before you make any plans.

If you are choosing a church because of its beautiful setting, but you are not part of the congregation, talk to the minister or priest to make sure this individual will agree to marry someone from outside his congregation. Be forewarned that some may object to marrying you if they feel you are using the church for its architectural attributes, only.

## Putting Words in Your Mouth

Wedding vows are the promise that you make to one another before friends and family. Taking a vow is always serious and binding, but that doesn't mean your wedding vows can't also be sweet or even funny. Whether you step forward and repeat the same age-old vows that have been said for years, or write your own, this is the moment when you let your voice be heard, when you formally and publicly agree to become the spouse of another.

### *Going on the Record*

When you meet with your officiant, begin by asking about the wedding vows that couples typically recite. The officiant usually has at his or her fingertips a couple of different wordings that many other couples like yourselves have found appropriate. One bride told me she chose to use a poem her minister showed her. At her wedding, she borrowed lines from the poem and recited, "I love you not only for what you are, but for what I am when I am with you."

**Something True**

Imagine being able to have your best friend officiate at your wedding! In San Francisco you can give someone the power to officiate at a marriage for a day, or a "one time deputization" allowing the person to perform one marriage on a specific day. This way, a San Franciscan can be married by a significant person in his or her life, even though that person does not ordinarily have the power to marry anyone.

**Something True**

In the first century AD Christian and Jewish couples were wed by reciting just one short and simple line, "Be thou consecrated to me."

Depending on the religious faith in which you are marrying, however, there may be only one or two acceptable ways to make your vows. Read them over and ask yourselves if you feel comfortable with every aspect of the vows. If there are vows that relate to the religious faith in which you agree to raise your children, take time to discuss this, too. Even though children may be a ways off, you want to be able to recite vows that you honestly believe you can uphold in the years to come.

If you're thinking about making changes to the traditional vows, tell your minister or rabbi. Sometimes it may be as simple as leaving a line out, or changing a word here and there. If this is a religious service, make sure that your officiant doesn't have a problem with these changes. If you're thinking about writing your own vows, discuss this with your officiant as well. Does this create any problems for marrying within your religion? Is there anything in particular that the officiant feels must be included in the vows, such as a vow to raise children as members of your religion?

### Creative Corner

When a friend of mine married in a traditional Jewish ceremony, she and her husband-to-be recited the vows suggested by their rabbi. These were the words they spoke aloud in front of the whole congregation. When those vows were completed, however, the rabbi announced that the couple wished to make some private vows, as well, which they would whisper to one another. This was an intimate and touching moment in their ceremony, when they were able to make statements meant only for each other's ears. This allowed them great freedom to say something silly, sentimental, or even sexy without making a public spectacle of themselves. Private vows may work beautifully at your wedding, too, especially if you or your officiant feels strongly about the use of traditional religious vows.

### Consultants Say

Consultant Bev Dembo says that some of her brides have turned to children's books for inspiration when writing their vows, or when searching for appropriate readings. One particularly engaging book, *Oh the Places You'll Go* by Dr. Seuss (Random House, 1990) may fill you with inspiration or be used for a meaningful quote or two.

## In Your Own Words

These days it is not unusual for couples to make up their own vows. You may each decide to write your own words, in which case you may not be vowing to do the same things. Some couples get around this problem by writing separate vows but agreeing to end with the same line. You might write your vows together and decide that each of you will repeat the exact same lines. Or, you may decide to surprise each other at the ceremony with the lines each of you have written separately. When actor John Stamos married on September 19, 1998, he and his wife did just that. Interestingly, their vows turned out to be so similar it sounded as though they had collaborated. Among other things he said, "I promise I'll never ever let you cook," while she vowed, "I promise I'll never cook" (as quoted in *InStyle* magazine, Feb. 1999).

If you and your groom want to write your own vows or at the very least add something personal to them, sit down and talk over some ideas. Jot down phrases, sentiments, or stories that mean a lot to you, or seem to say how you feel. Spend some time reading about other religions. You may be surprised to find something that would be a perfect fit for you and for your vows, such as the Hindu mantra, "I am the word and you are the melody. I am the melody and you are the word." As you try to get some ideas for vows, think about how you met, how you became engaged, and why you want to marry each other. Do you want the vows to include promises of fidelity? A mention of your parents, in-laws, and siblings? A promise to children from a previous marriage? Later, talk with your officiant. The officiant may have some good ideas, based on other ceremonies he or she conducted in the past.

### Creative Corner

Adding an ethnic touch to your vows might be something you're interested in doing, but are unsure of how to go about incorporating such a thing. Use traditional songs, poetry, and prose for sources of inspiration. For example, if you want your ceremony to reflect your African American heritage, events consultant Lois Pearce suggests you check out, *African American Wedding Readings*, edited by Tamara Nikuradse (Dutton, 1998). The book includes poetry and love letters by African American writers as well as inspirational verses from the Bible and some African-inspired traditions.

To get those creative juices flowing, sit down with your partner and try to put some of your feelings into words. To break the ice, answer some romantic questions like:

1. What was the first thing you noticed about your partner?
2. Use three words to describe how he/she makes you feel?
3. What was the funniest thing that ever happened while you were dating?
4. In what ways have you changed since you met your partner?
5. How did you know you were in love?
6. I think you love me because of the way I _____.
7. When I see your face it makes me want to _____.
8. If you were a hit song your title would be _____.
9. The animal you most remind me of is a _____ because _____.
10. I love you as much as _____.

**213**

Even if you don't get any good vows out of this session, you'll have a lot of fun! It often works out better if you each take this little "quiz" separately and then compare answers.

### Creative Corner

Once you're sure of what vows you will say, hire an artist to hand write and illustrate a few lines of your vows. Frame it and hang it in your new home. You can also choose to reprint and frame the words from a reading, special prayer, or blessing that was given at your wedding. Of course, you don't have to actually frame and hang your vows to keep them near and dear to your heart. One groom I know wrote out his vows by hand and, he says, he has kept them in his briefcase ever since his wedding two years ago. He travels a lot for business and I guess he likes to know that they're there, even if he rarely takes them out to re-read them.

### Consultants Say

If you're going to all the trouble of writing your own vows, be sure they reflect your style. If sentimental mush is not who you are, don't feel obligated to suddenly launch into gushy, mushy vows. Neither do you have to become the next Tennyson or Keats. Your vows can be simple and straight from the heart.

Your wedding may have some very special differences that you wish to highlight in your vows. For example, if one or both of you has children from a previous marriage, you may decide to include promises to the children as well. One couple used the ring exchange as a special moment to include their children in the ceremony. The bride and groom exchanged rings with one another and then presented gifts to the children. The bride's son received an hourglass, with a promise that their love for him would be timeless. One of the groom's daughter's received a locket with the promise that she would always be held close to their hearts, and the other daughter was given a beautiful music box with the promise that their love for her would be as full of beauty and as timeless as a tune by Mozart. Other couples purchase family medallions, which are available through many bridal catalogues, as a symbol of their family unity.

## Creative Corner

At a medieval-theme wedding, you might want to mouth some fourteenth-century words (if you can pronounce them!). According to *Bride's Little Book of Vows and Rings* (Clarkson Potter, 1994), one fourteenth-century missal included the following vow: "Ich John, take the Jane to my wedded wife, to haven and to holden, for fayrere, for fouler, for bettur, for wors, for richer, for poorer."

# Reciting Your Vows with Style

The thought of standing up in front of a large group of people and using their own voices to say the words that will change their lives forever terrorizes some couples. If you're one of them, familiarize yourself with your vows to help you calm down. I memorized mine, and so did Peter. We still, however, had the priest read them and ask us to repeat them. I wanted to be comfortable enough with the words to be able to say a whole sentence at once, not just two or three words, but I didn't want to have the pressure of having to recite the vows with no safety net. By having the priest say them for us to repeat, we knew we couldn't mess up and yet we were comfortable enough with the vows not to trip over our words or get nervous.

"Public speaking can be a major stressor. For some people, the idea of getting up and being the main focus of attention with lots of onlookers as you try to exchange your vows is terrifying!" says Dr. Carl Pickhardt, Ph.D., psychologist, and lecturer on family-management issues in Austin, Texas. He says it's a mistake to ignore this feeling. "Talk about it. Say, 'I'm really nervous about this,'" he counsels.

Then you can start coming up with some strategies. You may decide, for example, to hold hands during the ceremony as a calming, stabilizing influence. Or, you might try to come up with a mantra that you can repeat to yourself as you go through the ceremony, such as "All is well." It can also help to shift the responsibility off yourself. You've worked hard; you've made tough decisions; you've gotten

## Consultants Say

If you are adamant about memorizing your vows rather than repeating them, write your lines on a very small note card. Wedding consultant Lois Pearce took the card and tucked it into her bouquet as a security blanket in case she froze and got stuck while reciting her vows. It helped her have some piece of mind. It might work as well for you too!

everything together from the bridesmaids' dresses, to the wedding programs, to choosing the readings. Now it's time to step back and let someone else take charge. "Remind yourself that it's the minister who's conducting the ceremony, not you. The officiant has the responsibility now, not you," says Dr. Pickhardt.

I also worried about whether or not people would be able to hear us. I have been to weddings where I never heard a thing the bride or the groom said. If possible, face the congregation when you say your vows, or at the very least turn sideways to the audience. If your backs are to the guests, they will never hear a word you say. In some congregations, the officiant might wear a microphone that will pick up the couple's words.

At the rehearsal, you will get a better idea of the way voices sound at your ceremony site. Are you marrying in a hushed chapel? A cavernous cathedral? An outdoor gazebo next to a noisily babbling brook? Each of these different sites will have different acoustics. Try sitting toward the back and see if you can hear the officiant or the maid of honor's reading.

If you're making a video of your ceremony, the groom may wish to wear a wireless mike so that the vows can be picked up clearly on the tape. Ask your videographer about this option.

**Consultants Say**

"Relax your expectations. The ceremony will go forward whether you stumble or not," says psychologist Dr. Carl Pickhardt.

## What's the Good Word: Readings

One of the nice things about readings is that you can choose people who mean a lot to you but who are not in your actual wedding party. At my wedding, the maid of honor and the best man did readings, but we also had Peter's father lead a prayer in Dutch. You can have readings done in English or even in another language to reflect your ethnic backgrounds and diversity.

If your ceremony is religious, read some different scriptures to find one that you would like to have read aloud at your wedding. Ask your minister or priest for some suggestions. A favorite prayer could be recited. A love poem may be perfect for a reading. A favorite song, such as a ballad from *West Side Story* or other popular musical, might be an appropriate affirmation of love at your wedding. (One couple used lines from *West Side Story* for their vows.)

**Consultants Say**

A rehearsal involving all the active participants in the ceremony is necessary if the wedding ceremony itself is to go off without a hitch.

Anyone who has been to a few weddings has undoubtedly heard the same readings over and over. Perhaps the most popular is the letter from Paul to the Corinthians (1 Corinthians: 13). This is indeed a beautiful passage and one you may decide to have read at your service. Rather than include it (and other popular readings) in this book, however, I've tried to collect some nontraditional readings from various sources, both religious and secular. Consider any of the following for readings (or even perhaps for use in vows):

> A loyal friend is a powerful defense:
> Whoever finds one has indeed found a treasure.
> A loyal friend is something beyond price,
> There is no measuring his worth.
> A loyal friend is the elixir of life,
> And those who fear the Lord will find one.
> Whoever fears the Lord makes true friends,
> For as a person is, so is his friend too.
> > —Ecclesiasticus 6:14–17.

> You ravish my heart,
> My sister, my promised bride.
> You ravish my heart
> With a single one of your glances,
> With a single link of your necklace.
> What spells lie in your love,
> My sister, my promised bride!
> How delicious is your love, more delicious than wine!
> How fragrant your perfumes,
> More fragrant than all spices!
> Your lips, my promised bride,
> Distil wild honey.
> Honey and milk
> Are under your tongue.
> > —Song of Songs 4:9–12.
> >
> > Excerpts from *The New Jerusalem Bible*
> > copyright©1985 by Darton, Longman & Todd, Ltd. and
> > Doubleday, a division of Random House, Inc. Reprinted by
> > Permission.

Feel free to borrow lines from poetry, plays, novels, even films. According to Lois Pearce, president of Beautiful Occasions and a wedding consultant in Hamden, Connecticut, (203-248-2661), couples find inspiration everywhere, including other cultures or religions. This Apache marriage blessing, for example, is quite beautiful:

> Now you will feel no rain for each of you will be shelter for the other. Now you will feel no cold for each of you will be warmth for the other. Now there is no more loneliness; now you are two persons but there is only one life before you. Go now together—and may your days together be good and long upon the earth.
> > —*Bride's Little Book of Vows and Rings*
> > (Reprinted, Clarkson Potter, 1994)

**217**

A quiet afternoon spent at the bookstore or library should yield many wonderful possibilities for readings.

# The Wedding Program

Printed programs provide a way of allowing the entire congregation to follow and understand your wedding ceremony. They are especially helpful and appreciated if you are planning a wedding that's straying from the traditional path, filled with lots of special touches that your guests might not otherwise fully understand. Guests appreciate having a program that tells them everything from who's in the wedding party to what songs will be sung. The order of the ceremony, prayers, readings, hymns and other musical interludes are all spelled out, making guests feel very much a part of the proceedings. At a creative wedding, the program can be particularly helpful to guests. You can use it to explain some of your unique touches, such as the significance of jumping the broom, sharing a cup of wine, or playing a certain song.

Programs can be a simple one pager, or whole little booklet, including such things as the words to the songs that will be sung or the translation of a foreign language reading or prayer. Within the program the bride and groom also have a chance to include some personal notes and thanks to those in attendance. For example, the program might read, "Today we come before our dearest friends and family to announce our love and commitment to one another. Thank you for being here with us."

Programs can also be used as a dedication or remembrance, if the couple wishes to acknowledge a deceased parent, grandparent, or other friend or relative. You might say, for example, "Our lives have been richly blessed by all of you and by the late _____." The program can also be the perfect place to acknowledge someone who is too ill or elderly to be able to attend.

You can make your wedding program unique by dressing it up with tassels or ribbons. The program could be cloth covered, appliqued with silk flowers, or have a velum cover.

Ink colors can coordinate with your wedding colors. The program may be printed on one sheet of paper, a folded card, an accordion-fold booklet, or a bound or stapled booklet. Names and wedding dates, and/or the title, "Our Wedding Program" is often printed on the front cover. Aside from being a practical way to guide your guests during the ceremony, a beautifully produced program also makes the perfect favor for guests to keep.

At the time you order your wedding invitations, look into the feasibility of having programs printed at a later date. Can the style of the program match your invitation? How much will it cost to print the programs? Since many aspects of a wedding ceremony may not be finalized until the last few months, ask how quickly a program can be printed for you. Some stationers need only about two weeks for this. More complicated programs may take much longer, however.

## The Least You Need to Know

➤ For a more intimate ceremony, choose an officiant who knows you well. Make sure the officiant is comfortable with the style, setting, and wording of your wedding.

➤ Discuss your vows with your officiant in advance.

➤ Sit down with your fiancé for a creative vow-writing session. Enjoy yourselves, as you find ways to verbally express your love for one another.

➤ Ask your officiant for suggestions for readings. If nonreligious readings are allowed, consider song lyrics, poetry, or passages from favorite books. Clear your choices with your officiant.

➤ Use your program to reinforce your wedding theme and to explain unusual aspects of your ceremony. It makes a beautiful keepsake.

# Look at the Birdie!

"You've seen one wedding album you've seen 'em all," you cynically sigh to yourself when you think about capturing your day on film. Not so. There's no reason for your photos to be stiff, posed pictures that don't seem to capture even an ounce of the fun you experienced. Or, maybe you like some of the traditional photos you've seen, but would like to throw a couple of black and white or action shots into the mix. There's a wealth of choices out there—all you need to know is you're not limited to one or the other. The images your chosen photographer produces will touch your lives for years to come. The few hours that you spend at your wedding will fly by but they become timeless when captured on film. In this chapter, I'll help guide you in making that all-important decision of how to capture your day with the best possible results. I'll also show you how you can have some fun with photos before, during, and after the wedding. They can be displayed at the wedding, given as favors, or used to tell a story.

## Pictures That Match Your Style

The first thing you need to think about is the style of pictures you want. Having in mind a basic idea of how you would like your album to look will help guide you when selecting your photographer. Do you want color? Black and white? Traditional? Photojournalistic style? Flip through some wedding books and magazines and mark the pictures that really stand out to you. Look at samples of different styles to determine what you want: Traditional? Stylized? Journalistic? Romantic?

Once you have a good idea of what you want, you can start the search for a wedding photographer. You should start looking 6 to 12 months ahead of your wedding day. Get recommendations from friends, especially if they were recently married them-selves. If you don't have any leads, contact the Professional Photographers of America (PPA) on the Internet at **www.ppa-word.org** for the names of five to six photogra-phers or videographers in your area. When you contact the photographers, make sure you specify the style you are hoping to create for your album.

### Consultants Say

Members of the Professional Photographers of America (PPA) display the symbol in their studios, or you can call 888-977-8679 to confirm a photographer's member-ship. This certification indicates that the photographer has met certain requirements and that he or she has the technical expertise to be in business. The PPA has over 14,000 members.

### Bridal Blunders

It's a mistake to hire a friend or relative to work your wedding. You're asking for trouble in the relationship, especially if it turns out that you're not 100 percent satisfied with the work. The problem is that your friend or relative is involved in the wedding and can not be objective—plus, he or she and is not a professional.

The biggest mistake I made at my own wedding was choosing the wrong photographer. Almost all the professionals we saw showed us books of overly posed and overly sentimental wedding photos that just weren't our style. We finally chose someone who said he could take the fun, natural shots we wanted. Instead, I got three candids. The rest of the photos were all posed. The fancy camera equipment he had bragged about proved too much for him; the photographer clearly didn't know how to use it. He may have even been using the wrong lens! The lighting was so bad that all the details of my dress are either washed out in a bright light or shrouded in darkness. It's a disaster that still makes me feel sad 17 years later, and one that I had no idea how to correct at the time.

Don't find yourself in the same situation. Make sure that the person behind the camera will take the kind of shots you want. The person I chose didn't have a history of the kind of shots I wanted but he said he could do it and I believed him. Don't make the same mistake. Interview several photographers before making your final decision. The following is a list of things to keep in mind when interviewing them:

➤ Make sure the person you choose understands what you want to see in your wedding pictures. Do you want a behind-the-scenes look at the wedding? Do you want the album to tell a story? Do you want to see lots of details (a close up of a bouquet, a pair of shoes, the expression on a flower girl's face)? Do you want formal portrai-ture? Do you want the wedding to be shot in color, black and white, or both? Whatever it is you want, make sure the photographer has a clear understanding and can provide this service.

➤ Make sure you *like* this person. You're going to be seeing a lot of him or her on your wedding day.

➤ Give the photographer some information about the style of your wedding. Is there a theme? Is it a formal or informal party? Are there any lighting issues he or she should be aware of? Will it be an evening wedding? An outdoor wedding in the bright sun?

➤ The photographer should, in turn, ask some questions to give him a better idea of what types of pictures you and your family want, such as: What kind of day are you planning? Who are your closest friends? When do you want your formal pictures taken? You want him to be able to tell a story that reflects who you are, and not just present you with a bunch of posed pictures.

➤ *Always* ask to see examples of the photographer's work. Do you like his or her style? Is this person's work representative of the images and style you have in mind?

➤ Make sure your photographer can come through for you in a pinch. Does this person have a backup plan in case he or she becomes ill? Will this person bring extra photographic equipment in case of mechanical problems?

➤ Read the contract carefully and make sure it includes the services you expect the photographer to provide. Go over all the fees, and determine what you get for that price. Will negatives be included in the price? (This arrangement is fairly rare.) How much will extra prints cost you? Will you have the option of buying the negatives after a certain amount of time has passed?

> **Consultants Say**
>
> "The most important thing to do when hiring a photographer is to look at a sample of all the photos taken at one wedding," says Andy Marcus, a New York City photographer. "When you see a full wedding, you get a real flavor of how that photographer tells a story." Almost anyone can get at least one or two good shots out of each wedding. However, if you see 30 pictures from the same wedding, you might find that half of them are too dark or are out of focus.

## Livening Up Traditional Wedding Photography

According to Stephen Morris, communications manager of Professional Photographers of America, there is a trend today toward black and white photography at weddings. "Many couples are opting for a photojournalism style, which is less posed. The photographer shoots the wedding as it happens," he says. Although the couple may still elect to have a number of posed pictures (the bride alone, the bride and groom together, and so on), the trend today is to have a wedding album that tells a story. "It's more like a photo essay of the day," explains Morris.

There might be pictures of the bride doing her hair, the dress on its hanger in the bride's bedroom, the flowers being delivered, a caterer setting the table, the family dog being shooed away from the canapés, a trumpet player tuning up, the groom arriving at the church. These are some of the little scenes that form the time line of your day. This style offers a casual, spontaneous record of your wedding. All those little moments, from the upturned face of the flower girl, to your embrace with a brother are captured and preserved for you.

You may decide that this photojournalism style is perfect for you. Be sure you and your photographer have the same thing in mind. Look at photos of other weddings the photographer has shot in the same style.

### Creative Corner

Peter and I married in the same church his parents had married in, and their wedding pictures were in black and white. We thought it would be fun to shoot a roll using the same black and white medium outside the front doors of the church, in the same spot where they had stood 23 years earlier. Our photographer brought along a second camera loaded with black and white film and shot a roll outside the church in the bright January midday sun. They're our favorite pictures for sentimental reasons. (They also happened to be the only pictures that he took that came out well, probably because they were taken in natural light.) You, too, may have a similar "historic" request. Let the photographer know!

Most couples who opt for the photojournalism style say that they also want posed pictures of the family. Even if you're not so sure now, "10 to 20 years down the road, you'll want the posed pictures," asserts photographer Andy Marcus. Gary Fong, a photographer in Los Angeles, recommends that you combine the storybook idea with traditional portraiture. You end up with two different albums, one that tells the day from start to finish, and one that has pictures of family and friends. Talk with your photographer about whether you will need two photographers to complete this job, or if you can get away with only one. If only one person is shooting the pictures, discuss in advance which shots should be black and white and which should be in color.

Some photographers like the bride and groom to give them lists of must-have photos. Maybe you've been glued to your best friend's side all week, as the two of you did everything together. At the actual wedding you may not spend much time talking with her, since you're busy talking with all the friends and relatives you never get to see. If the photographer hasn't specifically been told that you want photos with your friend, he or she may not realize you have a special relationship and will leave her out. Other photographers want to know only the big picture (mom and dad don't speak to each other, for example). "I find a list distracting. If I'm busy looking at lists, I'm not able to get the shots I want," says L.A. photographer Gary Fong, who can be reached on the Internet at **www.storybookweddings.com**.

## Snappy Albums

Wedding albums aren't the same static square-shaped books they once were. Images in the album might be square or rectangular, oval or even triangular. The photographer might include some special effects, such as cutouts or a popup design. This can be especially effective when trying to get the whole feel of a large space, like a cathedral. (As you open the page, the ceiling pops up into place, capturing the enormity of the site). Using digital imagery, the photographer can lay the pictures out to see how they flow before everyone makes a decision to order the prints.

If you are interested in special effects, choose a photographer who knows how to be creative with the latest technology. For example, a photo can be sepia-toned and made to look like an antique. Or regular film can be transferred to a CD and sent to a digital offset printer. The photographer is able to create some special effects this way, such as multiple images appearing on the same page.

The photographer can also include some soft-focus pictures, or silhouettes of the two of you against the sun. The album could also include a wonderful montage of photos on one page, giving it a scrapbook feeling.

**Consultants Say**

If something goes wrong, and you're unhappy with your wedding pictures, go back to your photographer. He'll want to try to make it right. A lot more can be done these days to fix photos digitally—red eyes, shadows, and poor lighting can all be improved upon, to an extent.

## Kodak Moments

Many couples not only *take* pictures at their weddings, they *display* them as well. For example, you may want to show off photographic images of your grandparents or great grandparents on their wedding days. Photos can be displayed or placed in an album to be perused at the reception.

Many couples are now also using old photos of themselves to tell a story. Guests can enjoy seeing photos of the couple as they were growing up or courting. Photos can be displayed in the lobby of the reception hall, on a card table, even in the bathrooms! If you prefer, stills can be transferred to a video. This can run in an endless loop at the reception (or at a rehearsal dinner) with some background music to enhance the effect. This often takes the place of the old-fashioned slide shows because the video is cleaner and more seamless.

Ask your photographer about some ways to use photos at the reception as entertainment. Consider, for example, setting up a special area where guests can have their own pictures taken and put on a souvenir mirror or pin. This is especially popular if you have lots of kids or teens at your wedding. Dress up items (such as hats and feather boas) can add to the fun. At a wedding with a historic theme, you can have Renaissance or colonial costumes available for guests to wear in the pictures.

Digital photography is opening up whole new arenas. You can do some really unique things with pictures at your wedding using this. Here's an example: The photographer takes a picture of the bride and groom. Then as each guest enters he takes a picture of them. Next, the two pictures are digitally combined making it appear as if the bride and groom had their picture taken separately with each couple. "You can set this up to be done at the wedding," says Marcus, adding that it makes a nice little gift for guests to take home.

**Consultants Say**

Consider having your pictures taken *before* the wedding ceremony begins. This means you'll have more time to enjoy your reception later. Too often the bride and groom and the wedding party disappear for an endless hour (or more!) of photos right when they should be greeting and talking with guests. If you can get over the fact that the groom will see you in your dress prior to the actual walk down the aisle, you can save a lot of time and get some beautiful pictures taken before make-up and flowers begin to wilt.

**Consultants Say**

If you would love to display some antique photos of your family or his, but they happen to be in poor condition, consider having them restored. Many photo shops and online services do photo enhancement restoration of old family photos.

## Photo Fun

A picture can be worth a thousand words...and there are so many ways to accommodate photography into your wedding:

➤ If you decide to put together a Web page to keep guests posted on an upcoming long-weekend wedding, for example, you could incorporate some fabulous digital photos—an amusing reenactment of the proposal with your groom on one knee before you, pictures of the chapel where you will marry, and more.

➤ Photos can be made into puppets for a silly scripted show at the rehearsal dinner. Get pictures of all the major players—moms, dad and siblings—well before the wedding, and take them to a photo store to transform them into hand puppets.

➤ Find one photo of you and one of your groom as babies. Display both of them in classic silver frames on an entry table, alongside a simple vase of roses.

➤ Take a black and white photo of you in your bridal gown and have an artist paint over it with watercolors. It makes a fabulous old-fashioned look. Blow it up to poster size and display it outside the reception hall.

➤ Run a slide show of family and friends during one of the prewedding parties. For more fun and a better effect, set it to music.

➤ At a wedding that takes place over a long weekend of surrounding events, make disposable cameras available at every party. Ask guests to take candid shots of each other and leave the cameras on the tables for you to gather and develop. A quick run to the photo store, and you have a fun album ready to be viewed at the reception.

➤ At a long-weekend wedding, take a quick snap of each guest as he or she arrives and post it on a big board in a central location.

➤ As a fun memento, have a wedding photo made into a puzzle. Give one to each attendant with a note saying something like, "It's not hard to figure out what made our whole day come together! Thanks for being a part of the big picture."

➤ A collage of photos of the bride and groom during their courtship period can be fun for guests to see at the reception and makes a great keepsake for the two of you later. Important memorabilia can be included as well—movie tickets, a matchbook cover, a restaurant menu.

➤ Ask guests to bring a favorite photo for inclusion in an album. The photo should be of themselves, themselves with the bride or groom, or a candid shot of the bride and/or groom alone. When guests arrive at the reception, they can place the photo in a specially decorated basket, or you can give each guest a blank page in a photo album, where they can insert the photo and write the couple a note. Alternatively, you could ask guests to send notes and photos in advance and put them together in a memory album that can be displayed at a reception table.

➤ Frame a favorite poem related to your lives, your love for one another, or your wedding. Decorate it with a vine of ivy, and display it on a gift table or near the guest book.

## Let's Go to the Videotape!

Many brides today are hiring a videographer as well as a photographer. You need to take as much care with this choice as you do with the photographer. (For more information on videotaping a wedding, see Chapter 7.) The PPA can give you names of people who have experience working at weddings. Here are some things to keep in mind when interviewing videographers:

➤ View their work. Demo tapes are usually available for comparison shopping. Make sure you like what you see.

➤ Ask about the site. It helps if your videographer has worked at your ceremony site before or is willing to come and see it before the big day.

➤ Ask about lighting. Ask if there are any issues with the lighting the videographer needs to know about. (Will there be both outdoor and indoor locations? If indoors, what kind of lighting is in the ceremony site, reception area, and so on.)

➤ Call for references *before* you hire anyone. References give you the good, the bad, and the ugly. Since most people want to say only positive things, I suggest asking a question like, "If there was one thing your videographer could have done better, what would it have been?" This allows the someone the freedom to say something that he or she might otherwise not have mentioned, such as the fact that the cameraman was dressed inappropriately, or the film editing took twice as long as expected.

➤ Get it in writing. Make sure your contract spells out all the details: location, date and time, fee, and the number of copies you're buying.

Finally, make sure you discuss the style of your day with the videographer and give some clues as to what kind of role you'd like this person to play. Do you want the videographer to interview guests? Do you want some of the wedding preparation on the video as well? Will he or she be adding any still photos from your lives? Is there a specific person (or even a pet) who absolutely must be captured on film?

No matter who you select, just make sure that this person can provide you with the photos and videography that best reflect your wedding's style. If you cover all of the areas mentioned in this chapter, you'll be sure to capture your memories in a way that you'll enjoy in years to come.

# Video Voodoo

Make some powerful magic with old home movies. Nothing warms the heart like an old family movie. Still photos can be incorporated into the video too—perhaps a few baby pictures of the bride's parents above the caption, "In the beginning there was Hope and Michael..." A good videographer should be able to help you splice old films together into a cohesive whole. The video can be shown at the rehearsal dinner and replayed in a side room at the reception where guests can stop in or not, as they choose.

You can also have fun with videos right on the spot. Set up the camera in a corner at the prewedding party or at the reception itself. Ask guests to be interviewed on camera. The videographer can be instructed to ask everybody the same question, such as "What are your wishes for the bride and groom?" or "What is it about Bill and Joan that makes you know they will live happily ever after?" To make the drama even more fun, you could ask guests to choose from a stack of cards containing questions or even directions, like "Do your best imitation of Bill" or "Give us your best rendition of Andy Williams's '(Where Do I Begin) Love Story' or Diana Ross's 'Endless Love.'"

## The Least You Need to Know

➤ Begin searching for a photographer and videographer 6 to 12 months in advance.

➤ Ask to see samples of the photographer's and videographer's work. Make sure his or her style matches your vision.

➤ Photojournalism tells the story of your day in candids. This style can be combined with an album of more traditional, posed pictures.

➤ Consider including some creative touches and special effects—unusual shapes, cutouts, pop-ups, multiple images—to set your album apart from the rest.

➤ Enhance your fun at the reception by displaying pictures, running a video that tells the stories of your lives, or creating instant photo souvenirs for your guests.

# Chapter 20

# Your Wedding...
# Your Way

---

## In This Chapter

➤ Hosting a fun rehearsal dinner

➤ Finding more creative ceremony ideas

➤ Putting the frosting on the cake

➤ Enhancing your reception

---

Maybe you're not looking for a particular theme. Maybe you're not going to get married over a long weekend or at a honeymoon site. But you *do* want a wedding with lots of creative touches. You envision a wedding that's different, imaginative, enchanting, and fun! The idea that you should do something just because everyone else does it that way leaves you yawning. You're willing to take some chances and incorporate elements that express who you are as individuals and as a couple.

If you've come to this chapter and skipped a few other chapters along the way because you didn't think they applied to you, go back. I really suggest that you read even those chapters that you think don't fit your wedding style, like the chapter on the country wedding or one that outlines a nautical theme. You may find something that works for you there anyway. Think of this as your wish book. It includes hundreds of fantasies for you—some of which you'll want to make a reality. In this chapter, I have included even more ideas. These unique touches will work at almost any wedding, and include new styles, trends, and plenty of creative tips for your party.

## The Rehearsal Dinner

Typically a special celebratory dinner follows your rehearsal the night before the wedding (although if you wish it can be held on a different day). Anyone may be invited—all out-of-town guests, just the immediate family and members of the wedding party with their spouses or dates, or a larger group made up of guest lists suggested by both the bride's and groom's families. This is a time to relax a little before the big event. It's also a time for your two families to mingle and get to know each other better. Choose a place where both families will feel comfortable, whether formal, informal, or somewhere in between. Rehearsal dinners can run the gamut from events that almost rival the wedding to a kick-off-your-shoes picnic or a pizza party, beach bash, or barbecue.

### Creative Corner

To help people get to know one another better, try some for these icebreakers:

➤ Ask someone at each table to make a toast or to "roast" the couple. Lots of funny memories, stories, and gentle teasing can get everyone laughing together, and will make all the participants feel as if they know each other better.

➤ Show slides or home videos (edit these into a cheerful montage of the couple growing up or courting).

➤ Ask trivia questions.

➤ Sing camp or college songs.

➤ Thank your attendants with a short rhyming poem and the presentation of gifts.

### Bridal Blunders

Although you may not be the official hosts of the party, you will certainly want to be included in the planning. Go over the guest list carefully with the hosts to make sure no one has slipped through the cracks. It's easy for someone to be forgotten if the hosts are not familiar with your friends.

The rehearsal dinner is often hosted by the groom's family but it may also be hosted by another relative or close friend. Talk with your hosts about the dinner arrangements—its location, style, and guest list.

The rehearsal dinner is a great time for everyone to have some fun and get to know one another before the pressures of the actual wedding day. The setting for the rehearsal dinner is often more relaxed and intimate than the wedding, and the bride and the groom can usually relax because they feel less responsible for the details of the party (unless, of course, they're hosting it themselves).

Some ideas for the rehearsal:

➤ A formal sit-down affair

➤ A party held at the site where you first met or had your first date (an ice-skating rink, restaurant, or coffee house)

➤ A burgers and dogs cookout or clambake on the beach

➤ A picnic in the park

➤ A sunset cruise

➤ A potluck dinner (complete with nicely prepared menu and recipe cards)

➤ An ethnic dinner (all Italian, Russian, Greek, for example)

➤ A sock hop

➤ A wine tasting in a wine cellar or vineyard

➤ A bowling party

➤ A pool party

➤ A simple dinner at a quaint country inn

➤ An evening of games (a trivia game about the couple, a scavenger hunt, charades, skits)

➤ An evening of magic (dinner combined with a magic show, palm reader, or astrologist)

➤ A dance party (disco, swing, or other)

➤ An ice-skating party

➤ A square dance

# Gift Giving

Before or after the rehearsal dinner, set aside some time to give each other a little token of your love. A wedding gift to your fiancé is traditional, but not necessary, especially if the two of you feel that gift giving would be more of a burden than a joy at this point in the wedding planning (and paying) process. Discuss gift giving in advance so it's not one-sided, making one of you feel bad. Of course, it doesn't need to be anything expensive, but it should be special. Consider:

➤ A photo album full of pictures of the two of you since you've known each other

➤ A book of poetry

➤ A poem penned by you, handwritten on beautiful paper

➤ A framed collection of date memorabilia (ticket stubs, matchbooks, napkins)

➤ A tape of all your favorite songs since you began dating

➤ A copy of a movie you both love (or saw together on your first date)

➤ Tickets to a special event (music, dance, theater, or sports) for an evening both of you will be able to enjoy as newlyweds

➤ Engraved cufflinks that he can wear at the wedding and cherish forever

➤ Scuba lessons in preparation for a delayed honeymoon

➤ Dancing lessons

➤ A silver keepsake (I gave my husband a silver Dutch marriage box I found in a museum shop. Although I imagine it probably should have contained my dowry, I instead tucked in a little love note.)

➤ A collectible (I collect miniature houses, so my husband gave me a little house that doubled as a piggy bank, since we were saving for our first home.)

➤ Jewelry (often expensive, but always appropriate, jewelry is something that will last throughout the years and can even be handed down to the next generation)

## Thanking the Attendants

Your bridesmaids and groomsmen should be thanked with special remembrances of their day with you. Here are some ideas:

➤ A necklace

➤ A bracelet

➤ An ankle bracelet (especially fun at a beach or honeymoon wedding)

➤ A picture frame (engraved if you wish)

➤ Crystal glasses (two wine, cognac, or martini glasses, for example)

➤ A drinking flask

➤ Beer mugs

➤ A clock

➤ A fancy pen

➤ A perfume flacon

➤ An evening bag

➤ A leather-bound calendar

➤ A jewelry box

➤ Glass or silver swizzle sticks

➤ A silver key chain

➤ A glass paper weight

➤ A ceramic collectible

## Ceremony Ideas

Ceremonies are imbued with lots of tradition and sometimes it may seem that there isn't much room left over for creativity. Not so! There are plenty of ways you can add unique expressions of love to your ceremony:

➤ Print copies of your wedding vows on beautiful parchment paper. Have everyone in the church or synagogues sign a printed copy of your wedding vows as they leave.

➤ Ask all the women attending to wear hats. It will change the whole look of your day and is especially appropriate for an outdoor summer ceremony.

➤ Opt for an all-white wedding from your attendants right down to your guests.

➤ Choose a natural site with meaning—a ski slope, a river bank, a valley.

➤ Throw a surprise wedding! Ask your unsuspecting guests to a dinner party. Dress: formal. When they arrive, they find it's not just a *party*, it's a *wedding*. Have the officiant on hand (no surprises there) to tie the knot in front of your amazed friends and relatives. He might begin the service by saying something amusing like, "I guess it's no surprise how Bob and Mary feel about each other." Another perfect place for a surprise is a costume party. The couple comes dressed as the bride and groom, and surprise! The man dressed as a minister really is one!

➤ Set your vows to music. If you're talented in this area, consider singing the words, rather than speaking them.

➤ Marry on stage in a local theatre. Vow to "maintain all the excitement of opening night over the coming years." Borrow lines from Shakespeare.

**Something True**

In a Quaker wedding service, the entire congregation signs the wedding license.

➤ Hand out wedding programs. This little extra can produce a lot of meaning and enjoyment. Include the order of the ceremony, an explanation of special touches, an open letter to parents or grandparents, meaningful quotes, wedding trivia, and more. The program can be as creative and unique as your wedding. If your service is new to many of the guests, it helps to have the ceremony explained in the program. Your program can also include any standard responses expected of the congregation. This way even guests not of your faith can feel comfortable participating. Programs can even be done on a home computer. They can be scrolled and tied with a ribbon or bound like a booklet.

➤ Have a Cinderella-style ceremony. Achieve a glass-slipper look by wearing clear shoes on your feet.

➤ Feel free to choose a "Best Woman" instead of a "Best Man" or a "Man of Honor" instead of a "Maid of Honor."

**Something True**

There are many theories about how we arrived at the expression to "tie the knot" for marriage. Knots have had significance throughout the centuries and in many and various cultures. Some historians even believe that primitive couples "married" by tying themselves together with reeds around their waists.

➤ Include a good luck symbol. So much of what goes on at a wedding is symbolic. Through the ages, cultures have included in the ceremony or reception tangible representations of good luck for the wedding couple. You can make up your own or borrow a few from past cultures. If you love to ride (or just believe in the luck a horseshoe can bring) have one hung over the reception door, or wear a tiny jewelry horseshoe somewhere on your person.

➤ If you're planning to tie the knot on a trip sans family, consider beaming your vows home via the Internet. The Cal-Neva Resort in Lake Tahoe will post your wedding on the Internet. All you need to do is to invite "guests" to log on at **www.calnevaresort.com.**

➤ Ask the florist to leave ribbons trailing from your bouquet. Tie a little love knot in each of the ribbons. Knots have long been considered to be symbols of good luck, loyalty, and constancy.

➤ Consider starting your wedding on the half hour. According to Chinese tradition, this will bring you good fortune, as you start your marriage on an "upswing" like the hands of the clock.

➤ Immediately after the ceremony, some couples schedule a few minutes of alone time during which they retreat to a private place. This allows them to congratulate each other in peace and quiet and enjoy a few moments of intimate solitude before rejoining their guests. This tradition comes from the Jewish *yichud* (seclusion), which calls for 10 to 15 minutes of private time for the newlyweds right after the ceremony.

## Creative Cakes

Gone are the days when wedding cakes all looked the same— plain white and boring, with a taste to match. Nowadays, we have cakes that know how to dress for a party!

Built to perfection, these cakes can really wow a crowd. Happily, they taste good too. Look at pictures of cakes in wedding magazines. If you're artistic and have a vision, sketch your own and show it to your baker. Maybe you have a picture of your parents' wedding cake and want it duplicated. Maybe you want the cake to tell a story or match the design on your dress. A really talented wedding-cake maker can be shown anything from a china pattern to a fabric swatch, and find a way to copy or complement that style.

**Something True**

The ancient Romans considered the cake to be a symbol of fertility. Baked with wheat or barley, it was often broken over the bride's head. Guests would run to pick up the crumbs.

Give the cake its own place to shine—a separate table where it can be admired by all. Decorate the table with flowers, greenery, or ribbons. Lay a beautifully decorated cake knife on the table next to the cake. You can choose a special knife that you will keep, or borrow one from you caterer and dress it with a ribbon in your wedding colors.

Tired of making wedding decisions? Every tier of your cake can be a different flavor—one chocolate, one vanilla, even one banana or carrot! Every tier can be a different color too, ranging from lavender to pale green and blue.

According to Gail Watson of Gail Watson Cakes, this is one place where you can have some fun and do something different. "The wedding cake is a decorative item. You should enjoy it," says Watson (you can reach her at 212-967-9167 or on the Internet at **www.gailwatsoncake.com**.) One bride, for example, asked to have a slice removed from the cake and replaced with a Rice Krispies treat as a funny surprise for the groom when the cake was cut. Another couple put a subway car on the top of the cake (that's where they met) and requested a cappuccino filling (Starbucks is where they went after they met). Cakes can really reflect who you are as a couple. Watson gives other examples: a cake decorated with pansies because "Pansy" was the groom's pet name for the bride; a cake decorated with violets because the groom gave her a bouquet of violets when they began dating.

Fresh flowers are always lovely but many couples are now opting for creative uses of gum paste instead. Some fabulous designs can be created, everything from 1960s pop-art flowers and peace symbols to Islamic-influenced designs. Cake toppers can be made of sugar and either eaten or saved. A petal-shaped cake can be decorated with gum paste butterflies and flowers for a formal garden party.

Use an old Victorian tradition and place favors or charms in the cake. Each favor is attached to a ribbon. Call up your bridesmaids and let each one pull a ribbon and get a tiny favor! The bridesmaid who finds a ring at the end of the ribbon is supposed to be the next one to marry.

For a variation on this theme: Consider baking a little surprise into the cake! Do it in a way that won't present a choking hazard. Be sure to warn guests in advance so they know what to expect.

A Victorian theme cake is usually lacy or flowery. "When a bride and groom say they're having a Victorian wedding, I always ask what they mean

**Consultants Say**

Order your wedding cake three to six months ahead of your wedding date. Start even earlier if your cake is going to be complicated. The most popular bakers fill up fast—and many get too busy to take on another job.

**Something True**

Queen Victoria's cake was believed to have weighed over 300 pounds. Princess Elizabeth and Prince Mountbatten of England beat that record in 1947 with a 500 pound confection. Now that takes the cake!

**Something True**

A box containing a piece of wedding cake from the marriage of the Duke and Duchess of York was auctioned off at Sotheby's for $29,000. Your wedding cake, of course, will be priceless!

**237**

before I plan the cake. What about the day is Victorian?" says Watson. The more information you can give you baker, the closer she'll be able to come to building your vision.

Toppers have come a long way from the plastic bride and groom perched on the top tier. Actually we've come so far around we're just about full circle. Retro figurines are popping back up. Couple figurines as cake toppers are making a comeback—either vintage toppers from the 1940s to 1960s or custom-made toppers designed to look like the actual bride and groom. Have some fun with the item that crowns your cake. It doesn't have to be expensive. Bride and groom cake toppers can even be made out of pipe cleaners (it worked at Cindy Crawford's wedding!). Or, borrow a Bermudian tradition and simply put an evergreen seedling on the top of your cake to represent growth.

Other new trends in wedding cakes include a display of tiered cupcakes in place of a whole cake. Each guest gets an individual cupcake rather than a slice of cake. "This can work well in the right venue. It's great for an informal summer garden party," says Gail Watson who does not recommend the cupcakes for more formal affairs.

**Something True**

At one time in England wedding cakes were piled one on top of another in a pile. The object of the game was for the couple to try to kiss over the top of this mountain without knocking it down. This evolved into today's tiered wedding cake.

Popular now is the pricey option of offering each guest his or her own mini three-tiered cake. They're not displayed prior to dessert; they're simply served to the guests at the usual cake-cutting time. "It's something unique. The separate cakes are like little gems," says Watson who points out that serving individual cakes avoids the cake cutting ceremony, which some couples don't like. The mini wedding cakes are perfect for smaller weddings or for the bride who's marrying for the second or third time and wants something a little more sophisticated and a little less traditional.

Include a groom's cake if you like. The groom's cake used to be a fruitcake, and pieces of it were sent home with the guests as favors. Today, the groom's cake can be any flavor or style. It often has a theme that reflects the groom's hobbies or interests. A cake can be shaped like a baseball or football, even a favorite food!

# More Creative Reception Ideas

Even if you stick with the tried and true at the ceremony, you may want to break out of the box at the reception. This is your party and you can be creative if you want to! You've already read about hundreds of reception ideas throughout the rest of the book. Here are a few more ideas you might want to explore:

➤ The circle is a meaningful symbol of love and life. Ancient Greeks and Romans believed that the circle symbolized eternity. Use this idea at your wedding reception by expanding on a circle theme. Play the song "Circle of Life" from *The Lion King*. Interlocking wreaths can be hung on the outside door to the reception hall. Place your centerpiece inside a circle of votive candles. Decorate your wedding program or menu with two interlocking circles.

➤ Have fun with your own names. One bride who was marrying into the "Fish" family used plenty of fish shapes at her wedding. For example, votives and serving plates were in the shape of fish. Bev Dembo was a consultant at the wedding of a bride and groom whose first names both began with an "M." What did they serve at the reception? Plenty of M&M's, of course!

### Creative Corner

What will the future hold? Invite guests to place their predictions in a mini time capsule. The tubes (size of a cigar) are placed on the guest tables (one per couple). Inside the guests find a pencil, label, and sheet of paper asking them to fill out questions tailor-made for the couple. Each table is given a timeframe for the predictions such as "10 years from now Mary and Joe will have ___children." "The president of the United States will be ___." "The average house will cost ___." When it is filled out it goes back into the tube and a label with the date sealed/by whom/and DO NOT OPEN UNTIL (10 years from wedding date) is put on. This is fun for guests to fill out during dinner and generates conversation. It is also fun for the couple to have 10 or 20 to open and read on each anniversary. You can order time capsules from John Quist, The 3rd Millennium, 408-927-9233.

➤ Throw a casino party, complete with black jack, roulette, and more. This is exactly what Terry McMillan, author of *How Stella Got her Groove Back,* did for her wedding reception in Danville, California.

➤ If you're inviting lots of kids to your wedding, consider hiring an on-site sitter or two to help keep them entertained (and out of the goldfish pond). A kids' corner can be created with a few board games and coloring books. One bride placed a huge white stuffed teddy bear in each child's seat at the reception—an instant cuddly playmate to greet all her little guests. Ask the caterer about a separate menu for kids (and be sure to discuss a reduced price as well).

### Something True

*Companion* comes from the Latin word meaning "a person with whom we share bread."

➤ Add a Lithuanian tradition—your parents serve you your first meal as a married couple. The meal must include wine for joy, salt for tears, and bread for work.

# Favor Ideas

Everyone likes to leave a wedding with a little memento of the big day. You can thank your guests for coming by presenting them with any one of the following small items:

➤ Tree seedlings

➤ Picture frames

➤ Tiny salt and pepper shakers (for the spice of life)

➤ A meaningful book

➤ A poem

➤ A candle

➤ Candlestick holders

➤ Candy (boxed and wrapped)

➤ Potpourri

➤ A donation to a favorite charity made in a guest's name

➤ Small watercolors

➤ Sachets

➤ Silver bells

➤ A handkerchief embroidered with your wedding date

You're really getting the hang of this now! From cakes to wedding favors, you're discovering ways to make unique touches beautiful, fun, and workable.

---

### The Least You Need to Know

➤ Use the rehearsal dinner as a time to allow the two families to get to know one another.

➤ Work with your host to make the rehearsal dinner reflect your style.

➤ Order your cake three to six months in advance. If you want something complicated or are planning on hiring a well-known baker, start looking even earlier.

➤ Let yourself be free to think of new and different ways to celebrate. Borrow an old tradition or start your own new one.

➤ Thank attendants and guests with a well-thought-out favor that matches your theme, style, or sense of humor.

➤ Surprise your guests with something unexpected or out of the ordinary!

---

# Chapter 21

# Grand Getaways

---

**In This Chapter**

➤ Knowing how long to stay

➤ Cutting the cake

➤ Finding alternatives to rice throwing

➤ Hosting a morning-after party

➤ Renting the right wheels

➤ Riding off into the sunset

---

It has been an absolutely perfect day. But all good things must come to an end. Although you are not going to be forced by a fairy godmother to leave the ball by the stroke of midnight, you should have some idea of when you're going to make your dramatic exit, and have planned how you're going to do it.

## The Party's Over

Knowing just *when* to get away is almost as important as deciding *how* you'll get away. Some couples just want to party the night away. You've worked hard to get this party off the ground and now you want to enjoy it to its fullest. Hearty partiers might even consider an all-night bash for the party that never ends! If you do choose to party until the wee hours, be aware that you'll probably outlast most of your guests. Traditionally, the bride and groom leave the party first. This allows the tired guests to feel that they can go home, too. Elaborate customs often help each wedding to wind down: the cutting of the cake, the throwing of the bouquet and garter, the getaway, the shower of rice, rose petals, or bubbles as the couple exits the church, or later, the party and begins their new life together.

If you choose to leave before your guests, you can do so while still wearing your wedding gown, or you can change into a going-away outfit. Choose something special that befits the occasion. Leave your wedding gown behind with instructions on where to take it to be dry-cleaned. A family member or friend can be put in charge of having it cleaned and preserved for you while you're away on your honeymoon. It's a good idea to get this done while you're away. If you wait until you get back, stains may have already set and be more difficult to remove.

When you leave before your guests, you have a few things going for you: You probably still look fresh and beautiful, you leave the party on a high note, and you feel like you left when you still wanted more (instead of the feeling that you stayed too long).

If you're worried that you won't get enough of friends and relatives after a mere three or four hours, plan to show up at brunch the next morning and visit again. Many couples wait for a day to leave on their honeymoons, anyway. This often gives them a chance to have a restful night at a lovely nearby inn, as opposed to grabbing a late-night flight or a few hours in an ugly airport hotel. This means you'll be around the day after your wedding for some more partying (but with fresh hair, fresh make-up, fresh clothes, and a fresh disposition). We'll talk more about the morning-after party in just a bit.

# The Cake Cutting

Toward the end of the reception, the bride and groom usually cut the cake or have it served. The cutting of the cake is traditionally the official signal to guests that the party is over and they are free to leave. Of course, you're delighted if they stay on to dance, talk, and be merry, but the cake cutting lets people know that things are starting to wind down. The cutting of the cake is usually announced by the band leader or by a reprise of the first dance number. Some couples still opt for traditional musical accompaniment of "The Farmer in the Dell" (The Bride Cuts the Cake) cake-cutting music, but its popularity is waning. If you want the cake cutting ceremony but without the corny music, ask the band to play an old favorite instead, such as "When I'm Sixty-Four" by the Beatles, or Simon and Garfunkel's "Feelin' Groovy," or the Motown classic "How Sweet It Is (to Be Loved by You)" made popular by Marvin Gaye.

**Something True**

Ancient Greeks began the tradition of serving wedding cake (a honey-drenched cake of sesame flour). In Russia, two loaves of bread are baked for the wedding. Called "Dora," one is eaten at the wedding and the other is saved. This custom is supposed to bring luck and prosperity to the couple.

The bride and groom may take this opportunity to have their picture taken with the cake. They then cut the cake and share the first piece, feeding bites to each other. Sharing the cake symbolizes your intention to share everything else in your marriage. Eating that first slice together is supposed to be bring good luck. Another old superstition is that if the guests make a wish while the bride and groom are cutting the cake, their wish will come true. Have the DJ or band leader remind guests of this old superstition if you like. However, you can also skip the cake-cutting ceremony and simply have the cake served up by waiters.

Many brides and grooms use a special cake-cutting knife that has some meaning to them and that can be saved. The knife may be an antique find, or have a handle shape that matches your theme (heart shaped or studded with seashells, for example).

## Bouquet and Garter Toss

Traditionally, the bride tosses her bouquet over her shoulder to the single women at the reception. Then the groom steps forward to remove the garter from the bride's leg. This is often done to the tune of stripper music. The garter is thrown to the single men in the party. The man who catches the garter is to dance with the woman who catches the bouquet. Often he also has some fun putting the garter on the leg of the woman who caught the bouquet. That's the way it goes…but it doesn't have to go that way at your wedding.

Some couples find that all that nonsense makes them uncomfortable and even downright embarrassed. Instead, you may wish to fill that blank with another ritual. An old Greek ritual involves a playful tug of war with a loaf of bread. The bride and groom each pull an end of the loaf and whoever gets the larger piece when it breaks will supposedly rule the roost. Or this may be the perfect time for entertainment by a children's choir or your alma mater's a cappella singing group. With toasts and good times, no one will notice if you skip the bouquet or garter toss.

The bride might choose to give her bouquet away to a close friend or sibling rather than toss it. At my wedding, we skipped the garter and bouquet toss and I gave my bouquet to my unmarried sister-in-law. If you do want to skip the garter toss but keep the bouquet toss, consider ordering a second smaller bouquet for tossing so you can keep your original bouquet for yourself. Have your florist make a "toss bouquet" for you.

**Consultants Say**

Keep the music going! If you want your party to continue after the cake cutting is over, make sure the band or DJ knows that you want them to begin playing dance tunes again immediately after the cake-cutting ceremony ends. If guests are met instead by silence, they will feel that the party is truly over and feel compelled to go home, even though the band was only taking a break.

**Bridal Blunders**

If you've taken the care to bring a special knife for your cake-cutting ceremony, make sure you have alerted someone in your wedding party to bring the knife home for you. Otherwise, it might be swept up with the caterer's equipment!

# It's a Toss Up!

Traditionally, guests threw rice or confetti at the couple as they made their exit. Rice was believed to be a symbol of fertility. Rice is falling out of favor, however, because guests can slip on it and it can be harmful to small birds. As an alternative, some couples give out birdseed to their guests and let them throw that. Unfortunately, birdseed can also be slippery so it may not be advisable or even allowed at your ceremony or reception site. Another environmentally friendly option is the throwing of flower petals. Choose fresh or dried flowers. Check with your florist for availability, quantity, and cost.

Be sure to check with your ceremony and reception sites to see if they have any rules about what can and can't be thrown. They often *do* have rules about this aspect of your day. Other traditional tosses from around the globe and over the years have included: wheat, bread crumbs, barley, almond blossoms, nuts, salt, candy, coins, sugared almonds, cotton seed, and dates.

If you don't want anything substantial thrown at you, bubbles are a great option. They're beautiful and they require no cleanup. If this is your choice, place little bottles of bubbles at each place setting or offer them as favors at the end of the party. Be sure to alert your photographer to when the soap bubbly will be flowing. That way he can be in the right place at the right time for a great photo.

At the end of the reception, you can also consider having guests release balloons or butterflies into the air. See the Appendix at the back of this book for places to call about butterflies.

# The Morning-After Party

A friend or relative may agree in advance to host a breakfast or brunch for you and your out-of-town guests on the morning after the wedding. This can be a nice way to say goodbye (again) to guests who have traveled long distances to be with you. In some cases, the wedding brunch or breakfast is open to all those who attended the wedding, whether from out of town or not (just as many rehearsal dinners have expanded to include more people). If this is the case, you can include an invitation to the morning-after party with your wedding invitations.

There's no need to go crazy with a formal breakfast. A buffet of breakfast items—baskets of bagels, muffins and croissants, along with jams, jellies, cream cheese, and fresh fruits, plus plenty of coffee and juices is all that is necessary. Quiet music may be played (live or not). Obviously, no planned seating is needed. Guests may come and go as they choose. Make the hours of the breakfast or brunch flexible (like an open house), to accommodate the various travel schedules of your many out-of-town guests.

If you had a tent set up for your wedding, it's probably no more expensive to leave it up through breakfast the next day. That way you can use this same site for a farewell breakfast buffet, and rest assured that you'll have plenty of tables and chairs. All you'll need are some fresh tablecloths and napkins (and someone to clean things up after the initial reception!).

# Making a Dramatic Exit

When the party's over, guests gather around to say farewell to the bride and groom. Prepare to leave in style by choosing the right transportation, one that matches your theme or just tickles your fancy. Consultant JoAnn Gregoli of Elegant Occasions in Denville, New Jersey (973-361-9200) says she has seen couples use trolleys, buses, carriages, double-decker buses, and even fire trucks to get from one place to another! You, too, can use your imagination to find the perfect way to travel from the ceremony to the reception or the reception to the honeymoon.

## *An Airy Exit*

Many couples love the idea of floating off into the sky in a hot-air balloon. Is this an option for you? Although a balloon getaway can add a nice touch to a summer wedding, hot-air balloon rides are dependent on the weather. If the winds are too strong, the balloon cannot go up. You may be able to change the time of your departure to coincide with the right winds, or you may have to forego the trip altogether if conditions are not right. Remember, too, that where you land can be unpredictable. As with marriage, the journey is different every time.

You can also leave the reception in a helicopter or private plane. Make sure, of course, that there's enough room for this kind of escape. Prepare guests in advance for the noise and the wind associated with such a takeoff.

Some brides and grooms hire sky writers to fly by and leave amusing or meaningful words behind in their wake. Some planes trail banners rather than use skywriting to get their messages across.

### Something True

The first hot-air balloon trips were made in France in the eighteenth century. It was customary for the balloonists to carry bottles of champagne with them, which they would present to the surprised farmers on whose fields they landed. Supposedly, the champagne, besides being a nice token of thanks, helped allay the fears of those who had never before seen a "man in a flying machine." Clearly, if the pilot had domestic French champagne with him, he wasn't an alien being from another planet!

## *Two If by Sea*

Hop in a boat and row or sail away. The boat can be festooned with flowers and ribbons, or hung with a "Just Married" sign. For a funny twist on the traditional, hang sandals and water shoes, rather than regular shoes, off the back of the boat.

Leave by barge, or paddle boat. Have guests stand along the river bank to wave you off with colorful handkerchiefs.

# The Love Bug

Cars make great get away vehicles. Vintage autos like Model-T Fords can be perfect for Victorian-theme weddings. A 1957 Chevy or other restored car from the fifties can make a cool fashion statement. (Don't forget the dark sunglasses as you make your get away!) A decorated VW bug can be the finishing touch to a sixties-style party. An elegant Rolls Royce makes the perfect statement for any occasion. Contact car rental companies and vintage auto clubs for information, availability, and prices.

### Something True

Shoes have always played an important symbolic role in history. The Hebrews used to seal a business deal by offering a sandal. Egyptian fathers would give the groom their daughters' sandals as a sign of their agreement to the wedding. Later, an Anglo Saxon custom included the groom tapping his bride on the head with a shoe to show his authority over her. People also used to throw shoes at newlyweds but today they're nice enough to tie them to the car's bumper instead!

Even if you leave in your own car, friends and relatives may decorate it for you. Traditionally, shoes and tin cans are tied to the bumper and the words "Just Married" are whitewashed onto the rear window or trunk.

Motorcycle enthusiasts can don leather jackets and take off on two wheels.

Once you know how you'll get around, consider some fun ways to transport guests. A fire engine or trolley car can transport guests from ceremony to reception site. In an urban setting, try a double-decker bus! Guests get the added pleasure of a mini tour of the city as they wend their way to your reception site.

## Horsing Around

What better way to end a country theme or beach wedding than by riding off into the sunset on two beautiful horses? Those who ride away will need to take this mode of transportation into consideration when planning their getaway outfits. Perhaps you and your groom could wear white riding breeches?

For those who love the idea of using horses but don't know how to ride, borrow a little fairy-tale magic from Cinderella and leave in a horse-drawn coach. For rustic charm, consider leaving via a hay wagon, sleigh, or tractor!

Although my husband and I married in the most urban site possible, on Fifth Avenue in New York City, we opted for the romance of leaving the church by horse and carriage. Prior to our wedding, we checked out the array of horses and carriages waiting to take tourists around the park, and chose our favorites. We spoke with the drivers and negotiated a deal with one to pick us up at the church and drive us downtown to our reception site. It worked out beautifully. After the reception, we left immediately for the airport, so a stretch limousine was much more practical. Ours had a horn that played "Here Comes The Bride" for a little added fun.

*Make your entrance or exit on horseback.*
©Phyllis Picardi/
International Stock

*What's more charming than a horse and carriage to sweep you away?*
©Monkmeyer/Goodwin

## The Least You Need to Know

➤ Decide in advance whether you plan to leave before your guests or with them, at the very end of the party.

➤ If you wish to skip the traditional cake cutting or bouquet and garter toss, it's perfectly acceptable to consider alternatives.

➤ Since reception sites often have rules about what can be thrown, be sure to supply your guests with the appropriate "arsenal." Have a friend hand out something for each guest to throw—rice, birdseed, dried flowers, flower petals, or bubbles.

➤ Make a dramatic exit using the transportation of your choice: plane, boat, tractor, vintage car, or horse and carriage.

➤ If you're not leaving town right away, you could spend a little extra time with friends and family at a farewell breakfast buffet the morning after your wedding.

# Part 5
# Survival Tactics

*There's nothing like a wedding to heighten your stress levels. Before you give up and decide to elope, read this section. Find out how to be in control without being bossy, how to explain your creative ideas to the traditionalists in your family, and how to happily blend two families' cultures.*

*There may be rocky shores ahead—problems with divorced parents, too much advice from a mother-in law, complaints from bridesmaids about their dresses—but you can successfully navigate these shoals by following some of the advice in Part 5.*

*Above all, relax and try to enjoy this very special time in your life. Realize that it's normal to be nervous and have the jitters. Accept the fact that no wedding can be perfect. Take time off from wedding planning to get back in touch with your fiancé and never lose sight of the reason behind all this fuss and hard work: your love for one another.*

# Chapter 22

# Who's in Charge Here?

> **In This Chapter**
>
> ➤ Blending two cultures
>
> ➤ Negotiating peace between two families
>
> ➤ Dealing with mothers
>
> ➤ Explaining creative ideas to traditionalists
>
> ➤ Preventing divorced parents from ruining your day
>
> ➤ Finding the right officiant

There's nothing like a wedding to bring out every family dynamic there is—the sibling rivalry between you and a baby sister, the strain between your divorced parents, the love/hate relationship between the groom and your mother.... Let's face it: The blending of two families is not always smooth. Cultural differences and unique family perspectives can make the simplest things turn out to be complicated. This can be especially true when you are planning a creative wedding, trying to incorporate some new or untested ideas instead of going by the book. How you handle the almost inevitable resistance says a lot about how smoothly the years ahead as wife, daughter, daughter-in-law, sister, and friend will turn out to be.

## Blending Two Cultures

"All relationships are multicultural," stresses Dr. Carl Pickhardt, psychologist and lecturer in Austin, Texas. He has a point. It's impossible to find two people with exactly the same backgrounds, and rare to find two distinct cultures that celebrate marriage—or anything else—in exactly the same way.

I'll give an example. Early in my married life I lived in Madrid for three years. There if your host invited you to a party that started at 8 p.m., the unwritten rule is, "Don't come before 9 or 10." To an American, to be an hour or two late for a dinner party seems unthinkably rude. In that culture, however, showing up *on time* is rude, since the host would not be ready for you. Fortunately, I had been warned about this in advance by American friends who had learned the hard way—showing up at dinner parties to find their host and hostess in their bathrobes and curlers! The point of this story is that you need to take the time to get to understand the culture you're linking up with. If you don't, you can easily make a misstep or make others uncomfortable without meaning to.

## Communication Is Key

When planning a wedding, it's important to be vigilant—to make sure that no one feels left out or misunderstood. Yes, this is your day and is about you, but it is also about family and the blending of families. The wedding lasts a day; your relationships with the people at the wedding will go on for years. You want to get started on the right foot. Sure, there will be times when you'll have to put that foot down. Other times, however, the best thing you can do is to give in or compromise.

The best place to start, of course, is by talking. At the very least you need to understand where the other party is coming from. Before making a creative addition to your wedding, ask your fiancé, "How do you think your parents would feel about this?" or "What does your sister want to do?"

"Parents should share their ideas and preconceptions with you as well," says Dr. Pickhardt. "The parent may have had a very clear picture of what your wedding would be like from the time you were little. Your mother may even have saved her dress for you in case you wanted to wear it." Such long-term expectations and dreams help explain why weddings often bring up strong feelings.

## Bend a Little: The Art of Compromise

Given how hard it can be to see things from another's perspective, you will do well to talk with people about their points of view if you find problems arising.

Say, for instance, your future mother-in-law thinks the heart-shaped invitation you've selected is tacky. First, before you make a stand, consider how important this issue is to you (and her). Get her to share her point of view. You might want to show her samples of heart-shaped invitations and explain how popular such creative shapes have become. Perhaps when she sees you're not such a maverick, she'll feel better about the idea.

Alternatively, you might decide to compromise and opt for a traditionally worded rectangular invitation on ecru paper, but with hearts cascading down the side. Or you and your fiancé might decide this is one battle you'd rather not fight at all. In that case, give in graciously. "We didn't think you were entirely comfortable with our idea for the heart-shaped invitations, and we weren't completely sold on it either. We gave some thought to your points and decided to go ahead with the more traditional look."

The more you know and understand where your loved ones are coming from, the more easily the planning stages should go. Making a nod to another way of doing things helps bridge the gap between families. By including another culture's music, food, or decorations, you have made a grand gesture that will translate into good relations later. "Being different can be a source of diversity or divisiveness, a barrier or a bridge," points out Dr. Pickhardt. It's your job to allow your two different families—in effect, your two different cultures—to coexist happily at your wedding, and to build that bridge so you can continue to coexist happily *after* the wedding, too.

## Who's in Charge Here?

Sometimes, unfortunately, a wedding can become a power struggle between parent and child or between two sets of in-laws. Discussions about the right music for the ceremony or the color of the bridesmaids' shoes can become heated. There's a lot more going on here, of course, than just choosing songs and shoes. People are trying to find a way to fit into this new blended family. They are exerting their own power to see, in part, where the bride's and groom's allegiances lie. Sometimes the parties involved are working out other subconscious issues, from sibling rivalry to a fear of losing you, to anger over an ex-husband's new wife.

Perhaps your parents have said, "Here's a budget. Run the wedding your way" and they mean it. That's great! Seize the day! But continue to check in with these "angels" to see if there isn't something you can do to make them even happier than they already are. My own mother paid for my wedding and never said a word about my plans except to compliment me. She gave advice when asked and came to New York to help me during that final crucial week when everything that was in place seemed to be suddenly falling apart.

### Consultants Say

Sad to say, your best efforts toward family harmony can sometimes be thwarted by ornery family members. Do your best, but don't blame yourself if some people seem determined to be out of sorts. Maybe that's just who they are.

### Something True

Take this pithy advice from Dale Carnegie and keep it under your hat: "The best argument is that which seems like an explanation," as quoted in *Peter's Quotations* (Bantam, 1977). So, don't argue—explain!

Her requests were few and far between (a very specific guest list being one of them) and so it was easy to comply. I take no credit for this. I simply lucked out with a mom who had no problem with my independence and no worries about how my marriage would affect our relationship. I did, however, find plenty of other family issues to worry about (pleasing the in-laws, and finding a way to include my father and his new wife so soon after a bitter divorce from my mother). So you see, every wedding comes with its own tensions.

Often, the person who pays the lion's share of the wedding bills feels that he or she has the biggest vote in how things get done. Even if that someone is you, it's important that you give everyone involved the feeling that they have a say. "You need to have a larger perspective," says Dr. Pickhardt. Many brides and grooms today are paying for their own weddings. Unfortunately, some of them think this gives them the same right overbearing parents once had—to tell everyone else what to do. "You have a choice—you can be centered on yourself, or sensitive to others," says Dr. Pickhardt.

The important thing at a wedding is that everyone playing a vital role feels represented. Let people on both sides of the family have their say on issues that are important to them. If you think it's nice to have grandparents walk down the aisle with you, but your grandparents think it's weird, what would be the point of making them uncomfortable? There are so many ways to show your creativity and originality at a wedding, that losing one element of your dream day should not be a disaster. Since you're a creative person, be flexible and come up with another idea. "We really want to find a way of recognizing you as our grandparents. Would it be okay if the flower girls presented you with flowers on their way up the aisle?" For every problem happily solved, your day will be that much more joyful.

Of course, there will be times when you'll need to say, "This is the way we're going to do this" and leave it at that. Perhaps someone in your family doesn't like the idea of personalized vows. If you're sure that this is the way the two of you want to express your love and commitment to each other, then by all means go ahead with your plans. If it becomes an issue, be respectful but firm. "I know this isn't what you would have chosen to do, but we feel very strongly about this. We hope you understand."

In the end, of course, no matter who pays the bills, you and your groom are the ones in charge of keeping the peace, and reducing the tension levels. Give everyone advance notice of anything unusual, pick your battles carefully, stand firm when necessary, compromise and bend where you can.

# Explaining Your Creative Ideas to Traditionalists

For those who expect a wedding to be run by the book, every little change can be a shock to their systems. From the "odd invitation" to the "wild color" of your dress, you may have to lead friends and family gently to your way of thinking. Having a book on the subject is very helpful, because family and friends can see that you're not the "only one" who tried something that strayed from the norm. If it worked well at another wedding, it might work for you, too. A bridal consultant can also be very good at calming frayed nerves and smoothing the way for a creative addition.

**Something True**

Take it from Ralph Waldo Emerson who said, "It is a luxury to be understood," as quoted in *Peter's Quotations* (Bantam, 1977).

Even the rich and famous struggle to please everyone at weddings. At Cindy Crawford's wedding, her Jewish groom wanted to be able to break a glass by stepping on it, as is traditional. Unfortunately, they also wanted to be married barefoot on the beach. A solution was found. Later, when the groom put on shoes for the reception, he was able to smash the glass—an untraditional time for a traditional event. If you find yourself in a similar circumstance, it may not hurt to say, "Look, these people did it this way…and it was great!"

The traditionalist may also be more accepting of the untraditional if you explain yourself. "It isn't that you have to defend your choices, but you do want to explain them. You don't want to take anyone by surprise at the wedding itself," says Dr. Pickhardt. It's enough to say: "I don't want anyone to give me away because I believe this is a commitment that two grown people are making. The idea behind being 'given' to someone makes me uncomfortable." Or "We think it would be really fun to have or wedding on an island because it will be like a family reunion, vacation, and wedding all rolled into one. We hope you can be there."

In the end, nobody is right or wrong. There are simply different traditions, values, and tastes. Your goal is to create a wedding that both sides feel comfortable celebrating. Above all, stay calm. In all likelihood, once the naysayers arrive at the wedding, even they will be happy. Just quietly stick to your guns until then.

## The War of the Mothers

Marriage is a rite of passage. If this is your first marriage, you are separating in a very visible way from your parents and declaring your independence. At the same time, you are becoming a daughter in another family. Now you have two mothers giving you advice and involving themselves in your decisions. Your mother may feel the need to hang on to you and exert a little power here and there to prove that she still rules your heart and feelings.

"For the parent, it can be difficult. The child now has significant connections and obligations to somebody else," points out Dr. Pickhardt. As soon as you become engaged, you'll find that you're trying to listen to your future mother-in-law, in addition to your own mother, and trying to be sensitive to the

**Consultants Say**

According to Renee Grannis, education director of the Association of Bridal Consultants in New Milford, Connecticut (860-355-0464), hiring a consultant can keep the peace. "Consultants have seen it all," she says. "The bride may only see something her way and the mom only sees it another way. The consultant can find ways to blend these two views and make it work." The consultant or other wedding professional can provide an outside voice of reason and help you to meld the unique with the traditional.

**Bridal Blunders**

You know the saying, "Divided we fall." So no matter what the issue, make sure you and your fiancé appear as a unified front. Neither of you should be seen as the bad guy or the difficult one.

way she, too, would like things done at your wedding. This may occasionally translate to your own mother as a rejection of her or her ways.

To keep both sides of the family happy, involve them both in your wedding decisions while at the same time making it clear that you are perfectly capable of solving problems yourself. Shop for your wedding dress with your mother, unless distance or other tensions prevent this from being a wise move. Ask your mother-in-law about her own wedding, with an eye to incorporating some of the things she did, or an ethnic touch from her background. Schedule a lunch where the three of you can go out and have some fun together. Skip the wedding talk, if at all possible, and just get to know each other better as people.

# Divorced Parents

So many people are divorced today, that extended and broken families no longer raise an eyebrow. Everyone involved in weddings—from ministers to photographers—is used to dealing with the intricacies of today's complicated family groups. Your wedding planning may have to take a number of people into account—parents, stepparents, stepbrothers, and stepsisters.

Only you and your groom will know what will work best in your family. A lot depends on whether divorced parents are amicably separated or not. If they are amicably separated, things usually go well. If they're not, your expectations should be lowered.

**Consultants Say**

Make sure the vendors such as your photographer, videographer, DJ, consultant, and banquet manager are aware of any potential issues involving divorced parents or other delicate family situations.

"Many are able to put aside their animosity for one day. Hopefully, they love their child more than they hate each other," says Dr. Pickhardt. Don't force a closeness that doesn't exist, however. Respect their separateness and keep them apart as much as possible.

Talk with your divorced parents separately about your plans for the wedding. If there is a lot of animosity between divorced parents, even simple things can be difficult. Where will they sit at the ceremony? (In cases of divorce, the mother sits in the first row and the father in the second, although this can be revised.) How will they be seated at the reception? (Typically, they are placed at different tables, each with their own group of friends and relatives.)

## *Dutch Treat?*

If you need financial support, give each of them a chance to offer it. Only one parent may end up paying, or they may agree to split it. Don't get into a competition between them about who's doing what or paying for what. If both parents are planning to help out, work out a plan of action. Will each give you a certain amount of money which you in turn would use to pay for everything? Or are they planning to pay as they go, with one picking up the florist's bill and another paying for the liquor? It can get confusing and lead to misunderstandings if there's a lot of piecemeal paying of bills. A better idea is to determine a budget and ask each to contribute his or her half (or other percentage, depending on how they wish to split it.) If it looks like you're going to need more money, you'll need to go back to both to find out if they can cover the increased costs.

## Role-ing in the Aisles

Once you have financial matters covered, you need to move on to the sometimes more difficult emotional issues. What will be each parent's role in the wedding? Will your father walk you up the aisle? Your stepfather? Both parents?

Even though this is your day, you're going to have to respect their feelings. If your parents refuse to sit in the same pew, for example, don't push it. If you don't want your father to walk you up the aisle and give you away because you feel closer to a brother, grandfather, or stepfather, tell your father you'll be walking with someone else, or try to find a way to include everyone. You could walk up the aisle with your father on one arm and your stepfather on the other, for example. You could walk up with mothers and fathers, as a group.

In some cases the father may not come to the wedding at all (perhaps he lives far away or the couple has agreed to celebrate with him separately). He might come to the ceremony but not attend the reception. I could list endless possibilities and variations on a theme, but the point is for your family to do what feels right for you and them. It may take a couple of "what if" brainstorming sessions to come up with the right solutions for everyone, but it can be done. Remember—if it works for your family, then it's the right thing to do.

It's important that all the details are worked out in advance, so that there are no sudden bursts of emotion or surprises at the ceremony or reception. For example, if you are having posed pictures, it's a good idea to give your photographer a list so he doesn't end up trying to corral two quarrelsome factions together in the same picture. Decide if you're doing a traditional first dance with your stepfather or father, or neither. Discuss the feasibility of a receiving line, and whether it would make you feel uncomfortable.

At my wedding, with only 80 guests, I was easily able to greet everyone individually and did not feel a receiving line was necessary. If you want a receiving line, decide in advance who will stand in it and how it should be organized. It's quite sufficient to simply include the mother of the bride, the mother of the groom, and the bride and groom. This lineup avoids a lot awkwardness for divorced and remarried parents. If you feel you must include

**Consultants Say**

If you're expecting a lot of tension due to divorced parents, you might choose to have an alcohol-free party, suggests psychologist Carl Pickhardt. "Alcohol can add fuel to a fire," he points out.

a stepmother or stepfather, it's usually advisable for the bride and groom to place themselves between the step parent and the biological parent of the same sex. You want the actual day to be as free of tension as possible (even if the months leading up to it took a lot out of you!). Be creative and sensitive when wording your invitations. For example, your mother's name might be on the wedding invitation and your father's on the reception invite, depending of course on who's hosting what.

In tense situations, it may be advisable to have a neutral third party, such as a bridal consultant, available to mediate. It can also be very helpful to talk with your minister, priest, or rabbi about the situation. He or she can offer support, comfort, and advice, and keep you focused on *your* marriage, not *their* divorce.

---

### The Least You Need to Know

➤ Yes, it's your wedding, but it's also a family affair and a blending of cultures— yours and his. Recognize this and learn early on the pleasure of letting others have their way from time to time.

➤ Whenever possible, compromise.

➤ Appear with your groom as a united force in your decisions. It's important that parents understand that *both* of you want a justice of the peace to perform the ceremony, for example.

➤ Work with divorced parents to make everyone as comfortable as possible. Don't expect that they will be able to act any differently than they usually do just because it's your wedding. If necessary, enlist the help of a neutral third part to help negotiate the peace.

➤ Go out of your way to make the two families feel loved, appreciated, and involved. Remember, you are not the only one under stress here.

---

# Wedding Jitters

I don't know of any brides who remain calm throughout the entire engagement period. Usually, the closer you get to the wedding date, the more butterflies there are flitting around in your stomach. You may be worried about everything from stumbling on the way up the aisle to the caterer over-cooking that great tuna steak entrée you picked out, to the notion that you like potato chips and your soon to be husband doesn't.

Then there are all the changes that you are facing: You may be changing your name, your address, your bank account, or your job right after the wedding. There are also other, more subtle changes that may be bothering you as much as the big ones. Will your relationship with your parents change? What about your single girlfriends? Your single guy friends? How will you adjust to being a twosome? Will you lose your sense of independence? Countless questions like these may be plaguing you, as you move ever close to saying "I do."

## Is It Normal to Be Nervous?

Wedding jitters are a normal and natural part of being a bride (or groom, for that matter). Everyone worries about almost every aspect of the wedding and marriage that lies ahead. The pressures and planning of the wedding day, as well as the knowledge that your relationship is about to change dramatically, can unnerve the most stable person.

You may be worried about losing your privacy or independence after you marry. This is a normal concern. "To gain a commitment, you lose a certain kind of freedom that you had before. Now you begin to make decisions for two, not just for one," says Dr. Pickhardt.

Talk to your fiancé about these fears. He may be worried about many of the same things. Communication between the two of you is so important. Without it, you both remain ignorant of each other's feelings and concerns. Discuss specifics. Bring up scenarios. Ask, for example: "Will it bother you if I meet my friends for a girls-only night every once in a while?" Learn to respect each other's privacy. He may already know, for example, that nobody is allowed to watch you do your morning sit-ups. You may have already discovered that bath time is his own private time for meditation.

### Consultants Say

"Planning a wedding is usually an extremely stressful experience due to high expectations, possible conflicts, and decisions about how to handle them," says Dr. Carl Pickhardt, psychologist and lecturer in Austin, Texas. "You're stepping off into unknown territory, and taking a major transitional step and that's scary." If you have questions about love and marriage, contact Dr. Pickhardt at his Web site at **www.austin360/lovelink.com**.

Another issue that's of the utmost importance to discuss *before* you get married is finances. Sure, you've had the wedding budget to plan out together, but day-to-day fiscal responsibilities are a whole other animal. If you're just moving in together after the marriage or have maintained separate finances up until this point, ask yourselves the following questions:

➤ How will you combine your two incomes?

➤ Will you maintain separate accounts?

➤ What kind of debts do you each hold (credit card, student loan, for example.)?

➤ Will you put aside money each month for savings? How much?

➤ What kind of budget will be mutually agreeable to you both?

If you have already been living together, a lot of these issues may have been ironed out a while ago. You may already have set up your finances to be workable for the two of you. Take it a step further now:

➤ How, and on what, do you each spend money?

➤ What will be your main expenses after the wedding is over? The rent? The mortgage?

➤ Are you saving for a new house? A new car?

Keep a record of your spending for a few weeks, then sit down and discuss how you're doing. Make the financial

### Something True

No need to worry about budgeting if you married one of the richest men in the U.S., Bill Gates. His assets total over $18,500,000,000. Though he was a bachelor for much of his career, he finally tied the knot in 1994. He probably snores and leaves the cap off the toothpaste, anyway.

plans necessary to make your dreams a reality. Marriage is all about understanding another person's needs and making compromises so the two of you can live together happily. Melding your financial philosophies ahead of time will help you ease back into the daily grind when the honeymoon's over.

By talking out various areas of concern, you should feel a little more sure of your next steps. You may not be able to get answers to every question ("If there's only one scoop of ice cream left in the carton, would he eat it or leave it for you?") before the wedding. But at least you'll know that the lines of communication are open and that you're ready to face the future together (and cross that empty ice cream carton when you come to it).

# Different Isn't Wrong

There's a lot of pressure on you to make everything look great and run smoothly and to be sure that you have made all the right decisions. Luckily, this book is not about "perfect" weddings. You have wisely chosen to read about creative weddings, instead. Perhaps you already realize that no wedding can be perfect. All weddings can be creative, however.

The little things that go wrong on your wedding day all become part of the wonderful memories. Some will even be funny! At my wedding, my bridesmaid forgot her shoes. We were all at the church already and by that point, I don't think I would have cared if she walked up the aisle barefoot. Luckily, however, a helpful friend made a mad dash back to the apartment and retrieved her shoes just in time.

By choosing to have a creative wedding instead of a perfect wedding, you have both reduced your worries and added to them. You're not doing everything by the book, so you don't have to worry about breaking a rule or "messing up." On the other hand, you're writing your own rules. There's really nothing with which to compare because this day will—hopefully—reflect who you are. Your wedding may be a little different from everyone else's (and sometimes being different is scary) but that's what's going to make your day so special. Just because your wedding is not going to be exactly the same as your older sister's doesn't diminish it in any way.

You've made some unique additions to your day that you love—having the ceremony on a beach, the long rectangular invitations, the recessional choice of "Feelin' Groovy." Hopefully, you have done your best to incorporate everyone's wishes regarding your wedding. Close relatives should be allowed to add their two cents about everything from the guest list to what kind of food you're serving. "Differences can be seen as a barrier or a bridge, depending on how they're handled. People support only what they help create. You want

**Something True**

Winston Churchill has been quoted as saying, "My most brilliant achievement was...to persuade my wife to marry me."

everyone important to you to make some creative contributions to your day, so together everyone will support your day," says Dr. Pickhardt.

With that said, understand that not every guest will approve of each creative addition you've made. While you certainly don't want to intentionally insult anyone, you can't have your hands tied by guests who may not like the same things you like. This is your wedding, not theirs.

If you have your heart set on having your dog be the ring bearer, for example, you may have to be strong enough to go ahead with that plan above the objections of an aunt or in-law. When compromise and change work, go for it. But if there's something that's really important to you, don't sacrifice your wishes to someone else's taste. You will never be able to make everyone happy. The important thing is that you give those close to you advance notice of your plans. Don't surprise mom and dad with vows set to drum music at the ceremony or a Cajun band at the reception. "Tell them what you're planning and make an explanation about why you want it that way," says Dr. Pickhardt. Say something like, "I know this is different from what you were imagining. We wanted to let you know about this ahead of time. We're willing to listen if you have something to say about it."

**Something True**

You think *you* have a lot to do and worry about! In Puritan Massachusetts, a girl had to be proficient at candle making, soap making, weaving, beer brewing, broom making, and fabric dyeing all before she would be allowed to wed. She also had to be able to make an antidote for poison. Now that's a bride who's prepared for married life!

Although some of your new and different additions to your day may give you a little extra cause for worry, they can make for some really rewarding moments. In the end there's nothing more gratifying than hearing guests say, "I'd never seen it done that way before. It was so moving!" or "What a novel idea. It was beautiful!" The creative additions you have made are going to give your day personal meaning and make it memorable.

## Too Many Cooks Spoil the Bridal Broth

It's as though you are wearing a sign around your neck that says, "Tell me what to do." The minute close relatives and friends hear you're having a wedding, they start giving advice. They know exactly how big the wedding should be, where it should be held, and what should be served. The problem is that you just can't listen to everyone. Your mother-in-law is whispering one thing in one ear, while your own mother is filling the other ear with something entirely different.

Sometimes you want the advice and have sought it out. More often than not, however, the advice and opinions are unsolicited. Needless to say, you want to be gracious and listen to a close relative's feelings on a certain matter. But when it comes right down to it, you and your fiancé are the ones who have to make the final decisions. Listen to all sides, read books and articles on the topic, talk with your bridal consultant or minister, and then make your decision. "You can't please everyone. Sometimes you simply have accept and respect their discomfort with some aspect of your wedding and do it anyway," says Dr. Pickhardt.

At my wedding, for example, the bridesmaids dresses were hated by…guess who? My sister, the maid of honor! Since I had chosen a white velvet dress for myself, I knew I wanted velvet dresses for my bridesmaids, too. There weren't many to choose from. Both my bridesmaids lived too far away to be of any help, so I sought the advice of a friend and coworker. She came with me, tried on a red velvet gown I had discovered, and advised me to go for it. She was the same size as my sister and sister-in-law and the dress fit her fine. She and I both believed the dress to be totally unobjectionable. It was simple, elegant, and it fit my wintry theme.

Unfortunately, my sister hated the dress. The color, the style, the fabric, everything. Had my sister been with me that day, she would have chosen a different dress…and one that my other bridesmaid would probably have disliked. I tell this story only to point out the fact that every person's advice is going to be different. You can't always win…even if you have only two bridesmaids to please, as I did! You have to make the best decision that you can and ask everyone else to go along with it. Obviously, my sister wore the dress and we all survived. I've been married 17 years and my sister still occasionally mentions the "hideous dress she was forced to wear" but we both laugh about it now.

## Creative Help from Professionals

When you add inventive touches, you may feel like you're in over your head. Will it really look okay, sound okay, work out the way you planned? A wedding consultant, expert caterer, or good banquet manager can help make the innovative aspects of your wedding more inviting. These professionals can offer sound advice and give direction. Although some of the ideas you are suggesting are new to you, as professionals they may have seen other couples do the same thing before. Even if you're trying to do something they've never done before, they can probably figure out a way to accomplish the task with grace and style. With a little professional assistance, you should be able to handle almost any wish tastefully.

You can use the banquet manager or consultant who is associated with your reception site, or you can hire an outside consultant. To find a caterer with the ability to help plan and run a wedding, contact Leading Caterers of America on the Internet at **www.leadingcaterers.com** or call 800-743-6660. Better yet, rely on good word of mouth. Ask other recent brides who they used as a caterer. To find a wedding coordinator, ask friends and relatives for recommendations. If no one you know has used a consultant, contact the Association of Bridal Consultants at 860-355-0464 for the name of someone in your area. Wedding professionals can give plenty of reassurance and advice. When it comes to creative ideas, they have the resources to track down what you need, and the know-how to implement it with style.

# Winding Down Before You Gear Up for the Big Day

When the stress and tension of your approaching wedding really starts getting to you, it's time to step back and find some innovative ways to relax. Making time for relaxation will help you maintain healthy relationships with everyone from your groom to your future mother-in-law. You won't be in any shape to negotiate rationally or provide loving support if you're stressed to the max. When you take care of yourself it shows. You don't want to end up looking haggard and harried on the big day itself.

**Something True**

According to a study done by Stanford University School of Medicine and published in *Annals of Behavioral Medicine* (Vol. 20, No. 20), participants reported a decrease in physical activity right before a wedding. Interestingly, once wedding bells had rung, the participants returned to (or began) exercise routines with gusto. Researchers noted a dramatic rise in physical activity in the first few years of marriage.

It's important that you continue with your usual exercise regimen, even as things become hectic. If your groom is looking for a good wedding gift for you, suggest a package plan with a personal trainer. This may be one gift you want to give yourself if no one else does it for you! Not only can working out keep you in shape for the one day when you really want to look great, but it can help reduce stress levels.

A little pampering can't hurt, either. A day spent at a spa, complete with massage, facial, and pedicure, for example, can be almost as good as a vacation!

Some other tension reducers that will keep you calm as the wedding day approaches:

➤ When things get really tense, step outside and get a breath of fresh air. Breathe deeply. Exhale slowly.

➤ Are you sitting there with your shoulders hunched up to your ears? Tense one set of muscles at a time. Then relax them. As you work through each body part—neck, face, arms, legs, and so on—note the difference between the muscle tension and feelings of relaxation. You may not have been aware of how tense you really were.

➤ Stop rushing. Get up 15 minutes earlier in the morning, so you don't start your day feeling hassled and hurried. Take the time to actually have a quick breakfast before heading out. Set out for appointments 10 minutes earlier than you usually do. You'll arrive in better spirits.

➤ Take one step at a time. Don't try to do everything at once. Concentrate on projects in the order of their importance and necessary lead times. You don't need to worry about invitations and favors 10 months out, for example.

➤ Get wedding plans done in a timely fashion. If you leave everything, from picking your photographer to deciding where to rent a limo, until the last minute, you'll feel really stressed.

➤ Get a calendar and get organized. When planning for a wedding, it's like having multiple jobs. To keep everything straight and prevent missed appointments and over bookings, keep track of all your "to do's" and dates on one calendar. You'll stop having that panicky "I think I'm supposed to be somewhere" feeling and you'll get more done.

➤ Lower your standards a little. Perfection is not only impossible, but trying for it is extremely stressful. If you've listened to two bands and feel happy with one of them, stop the search. There's no need to track down three more bands just for comparison, because you're worried that there's something even better out there somewhere.

➤ Concentrate on the good stuff. You're getting married to the man you love! You're celebrating that love with family and friends. Does it really matter that the church won't allow any secular music during the ceremony?

➤ Go to bed! Nothing will wear you out faster or make you look worse than lack of sleep. Staying up late at night balancing your wedding budget or worrying about how your mother will react to your latest wedding decision will not help resolve matters. Attack these issues during the day when you have more energy. Everything always looks better in the light of the day.

➤ Take time off with your groom. Unplug the phone and stay home. Do not discuss the wedding. Give yourselves a needed break from the planning and the working and the worrying.

➤ Keep a journal of the prewedding months. Write about your frustrations, your concerns, your pet peeves. The nice thing about journals is, they don't judge and they don't talk back!

➤ Visualize the wedding day exactly as you would like it to be. Take the fear out of some aspect of your day (the walk up the aisle?) by imagining it going perfectly. Think positively and positive things are likely to happen!

➤ Get organized! If your wedding papers are all over the place, you'll be in a state of constant anxiety. Keep all receipts and bills together in a file folder or three-ring binder. Use notebooks to take notes as you search for a reception site or band. A sense of peace comes from knowing that you can put your hands on every aspect of your wedding day.

➤ Confide in a friend. It helps if you can blow off a little steam by talking to someone you trust (someone who is not involved in the wedding planning).

➤ Delegate. You can't personally oversee every single aspect of this wedding yourself. Hire a consultant. Let your sister or a friend help!

➤ Let it roll off. Emotions can run high and family members may not always be on their best behavior. Learn to forgive and forget. Give those around you the benefit of the doubt. They probably mean well and are trying their best.

## The Least You Need to Know

➤ It's normal to be nervous before you get married.

➤ Creative touches show your individuality. They can also throw you into un-charted waters. Remind yourselves that being different isn't the same as being wrong.

➤ Take advice from those you trust, but don't try to listen to everyone. Too much advice is not only confusing, it's discouraging.

➤ Turn to a wedding professional to help guide you through the wedding-planning process. The ideas that you think are novel and off beat are probably familiar to them. This means that they'll have the resources and the know-how to carry it off with style.

➤ Find ways to kick back and relax, or you'll be a bundle of nerves by the time you say "I do."

# Resources

## Bridal Attire

**Exclusives for the Bride**
Chicago, Illinois
Contact: Cetta Fessett, Manager
Phone: 312-664-8870

## Butterflies for Sale

**Carolina Biological Supply Co.**
Phone: 800-227-1150

**Magical Beginnings Butterfly Farms**
Phone: 888-639-9995

## Cakes

**Gail Watson Custom Cakes**
New York, New York
Contact: Gail Watson
Phone: 212-967-9167
Web site: **www.gailwatsoncake.com**

## Caterers

**Leading Caterers of America**
Miami, Florida
Contact: Bill Hansen
Phone: 800-743-6660
Web site: **www.Leadingcaterers.com**

## Floral Design

**Belle Fleur**
New York, New York
Contact: Meredith Waga Perez
Phone: 212-254-8703

**Preston Bailey Design**
New York, New York
Contact: Preston Bailey
Phone: 212-691-6777

## Historical Weddings

**Renaissance Entertainment Corporation (REC)**
Phone: 909-880-6211 x203

**Medieval Times**
Phone: Buena Park, California, 800-899-6600
    Kissimmee, Florida, 800-229-8300
    Schaumburg, Illinois, 800-544-2001
    Dallas, Texas, 800-229-9900
    Lyndhurst, New Jersey, 800-828-2945
    Myrtle Beach, South Carolina,
        800-436-4386
    Ontario, Canada, 800-563-1190

**New York Renaissance Festival**
Phone: 212-645-1630

**Renaissance Magazine**
Phone: 508-325-0411
For period costumes:
**www.footlite.com**
**www.magiccostumes.com.**
**www.ffcostumes.com**

## Organizations

**Amazon DryGoods**
Phone: 800-798-7979

**Association of Bridal Consultants**
New Milford, Connecticut
Phone: 860-355-0464

**June Wedding Inc.**
Las Vegas, Nevada
Phone: 702-474-9558
www.junewedding.com

**Professional Photographers of America**
Atlanta, Georgia
Phone: 888-97-STORY

## Photography/Videography

**Gary Fong, Photographer**
Los Angeles, California
Phone: 310-649-5858
Web site: **www.storybookweddings.com**

**Holland Video Productions**
Atlanta, Georgia
Contact: Lance Holland
Phone: 404-527-3600

**Fred Marcus Photography**
New York, New York
Contact: Andy Marcus
Phone: 212-873-5588

## Relationships Counselor

**Dr. Carl Pickhardt**
Austin, Texas
Phone: 512-452-4543
Web site: **www.austin360.com/living/
lovelink/letters/**

## Travel Agents

**Shenandoah Travel**
Davie, Florida
Contact: Audrey Goldstein
Phone: 954-424-8715

**Vacation Home Rentals Worldwide**
Contact: Doris Gedon, Reservations Manager
Phone: 800-633-3284

## Underwater Weddings

**Amoray Dive Center**
Key Largo, Florida
Phone: 305-451-3595

**Lady Cyana Divers**
Islamadora, Florida
Contact: Gloria Teague
Phone: 800-221-8717
Web site: **www.ladycyana.com**

## Visitor Information for Popular Honeymoon Wedding Destinations

**Disney World**, 800-370-6009
**Hawaii Tourist Network**,
800-599-9902
**Las Vegas Visitors Information**,
702-892-7575
**Poconos**, 800-762-6667
**Caribbean**, 800-356-9999

## Wedding Consultants

**Affairs to Remember**
New York, New York
Contact: Brenda Rezak
Phone: 212-986-3966
E-mail: **NYevents@aol.com**

**Beautiful Occasions**
Hamden, Connecticut
Contact: Lois Pearce
Phone: 203-248-2661
Web site: **www.weddingdetails.com/
beautiful**

**Dembo Productions**
Northbrook, Illinois
Contact: Bev Dembo
Phone: 847-835-5000

**Elegant Occasions**
New York, New York and Denville, New Jersey
Contact: JoAnn or Frank Gregoli
Phone: 973-361-9200 or 212-704-0048

**L'Affaire du Temps**
Milpitas, California
Contact: Patricia Bruneau
Phone: 408-946-7758
Web site: **www.laffairedutemps.com**

**Princeton Wedding Consultants**
Princeton, New Jersey
Contact: Charrisse Min Alliegro
Phone: 609-683-4467

**Weddings with Elan**
Nashville, Tennessee
Contact: Elaine Parker
Phone: 615-292-7433

### Web Sites to Browse

To find what I'm looking for on the Web, I use my favorite search engines, **www.altavista.com**, **www.askjeeves.com**, and **www.webcrawler.com**, but there are many others you can use. A search engine will help you find just about everything you want to know about weddings, traditions, food, and anything else you can think of. The following is a list of Web sites to get you started:

**www.brides.com**
From the folks at *Bride's Magazine.*

**www.bridalink.com**
An Internet "superstore" for wedding accessories and favors.

**www.theweddingpages.com**
Find out about bridal shows, how to find consultants and vendors in your area, plus use the wedding information center to find answers to frequently asked question and articles from *Today's Bride.*

**www.ModernBride.com**
From the magazine by the same name, dresses, wedding planning advice, and even a chat room.

**www.weddingchannel.com**
Bridal fashions, wedding planning, online shopping, sweepstakes, lists of local vendors, and more.

**www.usabride.com**
Wedding planning, wedding store including favors and gifts, free newsletter.

**www.weddings-online.com**
Described as "the Internet's information resource since 1994," lists vendors across the country.

**www.theknot.com**
Planning tools, ideas and advice, wedding-gift registry, etiquette, fashion, chat room, and message board.

**www.weddingcircle.com**
Products and services listings, feature articles on everything from cake to wedding speeches, customs, and traditions, lists of honeymoon and wedding Web sites.

**www.tncweddings.com**
From *Town and County* magazine, planning, advice, horoscopes, and resources.

**www.weddingbells.com**
A wedding Webzine, free stuff, fashion, ideas, etiquette, travel, fun polls you can be a part of and see results of at the same time.

**www.barnesandnoble.com**
The world's largest online bookseller. Search for your book by title or subject.

**www.honeymoonmagazine.com**

**www.weather.com**
Top weather stories, pollen readings for over 100 cities.

**www.mapquest.com**
Get and print maps worldwide, plus travel guides and driving directions.

**www.leadingcaterers.com**
Find a caterer, read up on catering trends, wedding ideas, best wine buys.

**www.wednet.com**
Bills itself as "the Internet's premier wedding planning site."

## *Further Reading*

*African American Wedding Readings* edited by Tamara Nikuradse (Dutton, 1998).

*Bridal Flowers* by Maria McBride Mellinger (Bulfinch, 1992).

*Brides Little Books of Vows and Rings* (Clarkson Potter, 1994).

*The Bride* by Barbara Tober (Abrams, 1984).

*A Bride's Book of Wedding Traditions* by Arlene Hamilton Smith (Hearst Books, 1995).

*Bride's Little Book of Customs and Keepsakes* by the editors of *Bride's* magazine (Clarkson Potter, 1994).

*The Complete Idiot's Guide to the Perfect Wedding* by Teddy Lenderman (Alpha Books, 1997).

*For as Long as We Both Shall Live* by Roger Fritts (Avon Books, 1993).

*Happy Is the Bride the Sun Shines On* by Leslie Jones (Contemporary Books, 1995).

*How to Have a Big Wedding on a Small Budget* by Diane Warner (Better Way Books, 1997).

*Jumping the Broom: The African American Wedding Planner* by Harriet Cole (Henry Holt, 1995).

*Life in a Medieval Castle* by Joseph and Frances Gies (Perennial, 1974).

*Off The Beaten Aisle: America's Quirky Spots to Tie the Knot* by Lisa Primerano (Carol Publishing, 1998).

*Something Old, Something New* by Vera Lee (Casablanca Press, 1994, 1998).

*Storybook Weddings: A Guide to Fun and Romantic Theme Weddings* by Robin Kring (Meadowbrook Press, 1999).

*The Wedding Sourcebook* by Madeline Barillo (Lowell House, 1996).

*With These Words: Contemporary Wedding Vows for Today's Couples* By Barbara Eklof (Adams Publishing, 1989).

# Index

# G

**283**